THE HAWAIIAN JOURNAL OF HISTORY

Devoted to the History of Hawai'i, Polynesia, and the Pacific Area
Volume 39 • 2005

ARTICLES

BOOK REVIEWS

BIBLIOGRAPHY

Abbreviations

ABCFM	American Board of Commissioners for Foreign Missions
AH	State Archives of Hawai'i
BH	Board of Health, AH
BHL	Board of Health Letters, AH
BHM	Board of Health Minutes, AH
BPBM	Bernice Pauahi Bishop Museum
BPRO	British Public Record Office
CCM	Cabinet Council Minutes, AH
DB	*Daily Bulletin*
DPI	Department of Public Instruction, AH
EB	*Evening Bulletin*
F	*The Friend*
FO & Ex	Foreign Office and Executive File, AH
FOLB	Foreign Office Letter Book, AH
HA	*Honolulu Advertiser*
HAA	*Hawaiian Almanac and Annual;* also called Thrum's *Annual*
HBC	Hawai'i State Bureau of Conveyances
HG	*Hawaiian Gazette*
HHS	Hawaiian Historical Society
HJH	*Hawaiian Journal of History*
HMCS	Hawaiian Mission Children's Society
HSB	*Honolulu Star-Bulletin*
ID	Interior Department, AH
IDLB	Interior Department Letter Book, AH
IDLF	Interior Department Land File, AH
IDM	Interior Department Miscellaneous, AH
MH	*Missionary Herald*
P	*Polynesian*
PCA	*Pacific Commercial Advertiser*
PCR	Privy Council Records, AH
PP	*Paradise of the Pacific*
RHAS	Royal Hawaiian Agricultural Society
SIG	*Sandwich Islands Gazette*
SIN	*Sandwich Islands News*
SSB & A	*Sunday Star-Bulletin and Advertiser*

JOSEPH THEROUX

Genius Displayed: Jules Tavernier

ON DECEMBER 23, 1884, Jules Tavernier stepped onto the wharf in Honolulu. The *Pacific Commercial Advertiser* reported on Christmas Eve:

> Amongst the passengers by the Alameda was Mons. Jules Tavernier, the celebrated French painter, whose works have attracted so much attention in Europe and America. Mons. Tavernier visits these islands for "studies," and hopes to visit the other islands of the group during his stay.[1]

Tavernier would make his name in the Islands for his oil and pastel landscapes of the volcano, yet the same issue of the *Advertiser* announced that the *Wasp* in San Francisco was already publishing "a grand and realistic picture of the burning lake at Kilauea . . . done in fourteen colors." He had done his first view of the volcano never having seen it.[2]

EARLY LIFE

All biographical notes on his early life rely on a statement[3] issued by Tavernier himself in 1887 and reproduced in his obituary: that he was born in Paris in April 1844, raised in Paris and London, and educated from 1861 till 1864 at the studio of Felix-Joseph Barrias of the Ecole

Joseph Theroux is principal of Keaukaha Elementary School on the Big Island.

The Hawaiian Journal of History, vol. 39 (2005)

des Beaux Arts. He joined the Companie des Marche as a field artist in the Franco-Prussian War. On the day the armistice was signed, February 3, 1871, he returned to England and was employed for a time for the *London Graphic,* working with one Allen Mesom as his engraver.[4]

His American years are more reliably documented. In 1872 he immigrated to New York with Mesom and worked for *Leslie's Illustrated Paper, Harper's Weekly,* and others papers. He was sent out West, accompanied by the artist Paul Frenzeny, working for *Harper's* for a year, beginning in the summer of 1873. Their travels took them through Texas, Kansas, Nebraska, Wyoming Colorado, Utah, and finally, California, sketching the plains and Indians, buffalo and trains. Both sketched, but Tavernier was the color specialist. Their *Harper's* illustrations frequently filled an entire page, for which they were paid $75.00, and sometimes were spread out gloriously over two pages, which paid double. In 1874, they published many studies, including Tavernier's *Sioux Sun Dance,* and the following year his *Shooting Antelopes from a Railroad Tram in Colorado.* The artists would draw their sketches on wood using a mirror (they sometimes reversed the Ns in their names), before sending them to the engraver.[5]

He made his way to San Francisco, and there had a shouting match with Frenzeny, apparently over money. It ended their partnership.[6] Jules Tavernier found himself proposing to a girl he met there named Lizzie Fulton. They were married on February 24, 1877.[7] The marriage wouldn't last ten years.

In San Francisco, he also met the painter Joseph Dwight Strong and they soon were sharing a studio at 728 Montgomery Street. Strong, the son of a New England missionary of the same name who had preached at Honolulu's Fort Street Church in the 1850s, had recently returned from several years of art study in Munich. Strong was courting a local girl named Isobel "Belle" Osbourne, whose mother, Fanny, meanwhile, was being wooed by an unknown Scottish writer named Robert Louis Stevenson.

Belle said that Jules "was shorter than his wife, and wore the moustache and imperial made fashionable by Napoleon the Third, [and] always spoke with an accent though he had been many years in America."[8] Lizzie, she said, was "tall, dark with an aquiline nose and fine eyes, [and] wore her curly hair cropped short in a fashion very unusual then but most becoming."⁹

Perhaps to disguise the disparity in their height, Jules composed a dual portrait *In Wildwood Glen* with Lizzie perched in a tree holding a Japanese parasol, while the adoring artist gazed up at her, his easel and paintbox on the ground.

Belle went on, "Though Jules was a most amiable person, and Lizzie good nature itself, the two of them had a continual quarrel that would burst out unexpectedly in the most surprising way." When she "would remind him of their debts, Jules would explode into fury and the battle raged."¹⁰

Volatile, explosive, and "peppery," were some of the words used to describe Tavernier. Once, a disagreement with a patron over a com-

FIG. 1. The only known photograph of Jules Tavernier, right, at the Old Jail at Monterey, California, ca. 1881. Jules Simoneau, left, owned a restaurant (located in the old jail) and helped many struggling artists and writers. From Anne B. Fisher. *No More a Stranger: Monterey and Robert Louis Stevenson,* Stanford University Press, 1946. p. 227.

missioned work culminated with Tavernier pulling a knife and slashing his own work.[11] He later maintained that he only "kicked his foot through it." The patron, though, referred to him as "that crazy Frenchman."[12]

In San Francisco Jules and Joe organized the first Author's Carnival, to raise money for local charities. They were also among the prime movers behind the Bohemian Club, which hosted, among others, Oscar Wilde, during his cross-country speaking tour.

To Hawai'i

In October 1882, the Strongs, along with their son Austin, moved to Hawai'i. Joe had a commission to paint landscapes for another JDS, the shipping magnate John D. Spreckels, son of the Sugar King Claus Spreckels. For a year the Strongs wrote to the Taverniers, urging them to come to the Islands.

In 1883 Tavernier was making some money with his oils of Western life, even with a couple of impressions of the volcano based on photographs.[13] But his income couldn't keep up with his bills. He was always using commissions to buy whiskey or items like dueling pistols or peacocks for studio props.[14] In early November he wrote to the Strongs that he was planning a visit.[15]

Tavernier left San Francisco on December 15, boarding the *Alameda* at three in the afternoon. He left his wife Lizzie there, escaping creditors as well as a rocky marriage. The voyage to Honolulu took nearly eight days. He came to Hawai'i with a well-established reputation, having exhibited his work at the National Academy of New York, as well as in New Orleans and Sacramento. His work was in collections worldwide, yet it would be his Hawai'i work that would make his reputation. The Strongs greeted Tavernier at the wharf.

Tavernier and Strong

Joe and Jules had a remarkable friendship. They were the classic "boon companions." Though nine years older than Joe, and with a greater reputation and much-published body of work to his name, Jules shared Joe's love of art, of course, but more than that, they enjoyed setting off with easels and working outside all day, feeling the freedom that dark European studios had not afforded them. After a day of intense sketching and painting, they would then spend the evening drinking and carousing, as both were prodigious imbibers. In addition to sharing a studio, they held joint exhibitions and boosted each other's work. But while Jules was sometimes an angry drunk, they never argued but once. Both grew big beards and painted and sang. They worked together as closely as Tavernier had done with Frenzeny and Mesom, but on their own canvases.

On his second day in Hawai'i, Christmas Eve, Jules decided he needed to add to his paintbox.[16] Joe took him to the best art supply house in the Kingdom, King Brothers, on Hotel Street, which carried a wide range of artist materials, as well as providing framing, packing and shipping services. They also acted as agents for artists and exhibited their work in a well-lit gallery.[17] Jules picked out four red sable brushes, eight bristle brushes, as well as seven tubes of assorted oil colors. He returned the day after Christmas and bought French charcoal sticks and a box of watercolors. Before the month was out he was back for canvas and stretchers and several tubes of white oil paint.[18]

He and Joe decided to form The Palette Club to attract the interest of the public in their work.[19] To reporters they pontificated on the philosophy of the French Impressionists and disparaged the traditions of the Munich Academy. They stressed light and color, rather than the "indoor landscapes" of studio work, and historical paintings based on photographic-like work in the classical traditions. And though both had been schooled in this tradition, their Hawai'i work was much more like the French Impressionists than their European instructors like Piloty and Wagner. They spoke, instead of Duveneck and Dielman (other American artists who had studied in Europe) and encouraged buyers to visit their Nu'uanu studio. They made extra money, giving instruction in painting techniques to "several ladies."[20]

Tavernier at first shared the studio with Joe at Nu'uanu and then at the Government House (now Ali'iōlani Hale) garret. He later rented a studio in a building in the McInerny Block, over Walter C. Peacock's liquor store, on Merchant Street. (Still later, he moved into rooms at 110 King Street, above the Spreckels Bank.) He became friendly with Peacock, who would display his paintings in his window. Another artist friend arrived, Felix Ollert, who had also worked for *Harper's* in

New York. Ollert was an accomplished engraver as well as a concert pianist who performed occasionally at the Honolulu Opera House.[21]

Tavernier easily convinced Joe to visit the Big Island. There was so much to see and paint—volcanoes, pastures and ranches, tropical forests, snow-capped mountains, lava fields, banana and sugar plantations, rivers and waterfalls, the place Mark Twain had said you could "nibble a snowball . . . and see . . . tufted coco palms."[22] Twain had complained that Cook had dismally named the place the Sandwich Islands when he should have called them the Rainbow Islands.

So, soon after New Year's Day 1885, they booked tickets for the island of Hawai'i. They left on January 6 on the inter-island steamer *Kinau*.[23] They stopped first at the Kona side, where they sketched the impressive *heiau* at Kawaihae.[24] They traveled around Hilo where they painted Rainbow Falls and the Wailuku River. Then they made for the volcano called Kīlauea, whose sulphurous smell, Twain had reported, was "not unpleasant to a sinner."[25] They were followed around by a young man who watched them paint. His name was D. Howard Hitchcock, soon to make his name as one of Hawai'i's leading artists. "When I met him in Hilo with Joe Strong . . . it was the first time I had seen a real artist . . . . Like a parasite I followed Tavernier and Strong to Kilauea to watch them at their painting."[26]

When they returned to Honolulu they set to work at the Nu'uanu studio for the rest of the month and throughout February. They went to Chinatown and the immigration depot to sketch workers as they disembarked. They sketched *sumo* matches at the depot, black and white studies for planned oils and to sell to *Harper's*. At night they painted Diamond Head and fishermen by torchlight. At the end of March they had a joint exhibition.[27]

In early March, King David Kalākaua summoned Strong to the palace. Along with various government ministers, including Walter Murray Gibson, and R.G. Irwin, the King explained that he wanted a painting for the Emperor of Japan, showing industrious Japanese plantation workers. An impressive painting would also help recruit laborers in Japan. The commission resulted in one of Strong's most accomplished and well-known works, *Japanese Laborers at Sprecklesville Plantation*.

The *Advertiser* reported on March 4 that "the artists Tavernier and Strong took their departure yesterday by the *Kinau* for a flying visit to Maui."[28] They went to the plantation at Spreckelsville, near Wailuku, and did sketches. They also visited and painted the volcano at Haleakalā.[29] They returned five days later on Saturday, March 7, on the *Likelike*.[30]

On March 10 they visited King Brothers again and Jules bought a new easel and a maul stick (or *mahl*, the bridge that steadies the artist's hand). Over the next couple of weeks, he replenished his supply of paint tubes, canvas and stretchers, varnish, turpentine and siccative courtray (a chemical that reduces the drying time of oils).[31] He was also looking for a color to approximate the fiery lava. He settled on rose madder, that orangy red color that resembles blood. Over the next couple of years he would buy an array of the usual primary colors, with a few special colors like vermillion or Van Dyke brown added, but rose madder was the special color he selected most often. He eventually bought a dozen tubes of it. Sometimes he was able to pay cash for his materials, but many of his purchases were on credit.[32]

In July Tavernier exhibited some new volcano pictures at his studio: *View of the New Lake of Fire by Moonlight* and *Bird's-eye View of the Crater*. The newspaper reporter stated that "[t]he effects of coloring and light and shade are simply wonderful." But there was some rift between the two artists; that month Tavernier left the shared studio and "moved to a room over Irwin & Co.'s bank."[33]

IN HILO

In September 1885, Jules Tavernier apparently suffered an asthma attack. He left for the Big Island a week later, saying he wanted to go for his health and to continue painting the volcano. It's difficult to imagine that breathing the sulphurous fumes would help his respiratory condition. In fact Tavernier was again escaping his creditors. He would be gone several months, painting and running up more bills. He rented a studio near Hilo's bay front, above Jimmie Hill's store. He became friendly with Charles Arnold, the chief road supervisor for the island of Hawaiʻi,[34] who had a house on Pleasant Street (now Ululani Street)[35] just back of downtown, overlooking the Wailuku River.[36] In October he was making sketches for a book about the Islands to be written by Horace Wright, a *Harper's* reporter. It was to be called *The Rainbow Land, An Artist's Rambles Through the Hawaiian Islands*.[37] The project, however, came to nothing.

In early November, Jules' wife, Lizzie Tavernier, and her sister arrived in Honolulu from San Francisco, and on November 8 they departed for Hilo. Tavernier had rented a house on the Volcano Road, between Hilo and Volcano Village. There he did a series of paintings that Whistler would have approved of, volcanic explosions against a night sky, lava flowing like a river, the seething cauldron of the crater lake. It was among the finest work he had ever done. But his home life and drinking were still chaotic. The marital disputes were becoming more violent. Once, visiting Arnold in Hilo, there was an uproar in the parlor. Belle Strong wrote in a private letter, "There they had a terrific quarrel, and . . . Charlie Arnold rushed in and wrestled a knife out of Jules' hand in time to save Mrs. T." She added, "JT owes everybody in Hawaii and Hilo . . ."[38] The story never made it into Belle's memoir. Soon after, Lizzie Tavernier left the islands, returning with her sister to San Francisco.[39] The marriage was over.

That same November Tavernier had two volcano studies exhibited at King Brothers gallery. "The larger one is a horizontal composition, showing the general view of Kilauea, weird and wonderful in the moonlight; the other is a view of Halemaumau at night, equally vivid and clever . . . ."[40]

Joe Strong had placed an ad in the Honolulu City Directory. That December Tavernier followed suit and placed a newspaper ad that ran for a few weeks:

FIG. 2. Announcement for Tavernier's studio, *Pacific Commercial Advertiser*, December 1, 1885.

Near Christmas 1885, a year after his arrival, and soon after Lizzie's departure, he complained of asthma and a new problem: "acute rheumatism in the right arm." The pain was so great that he found painting "very painful and at times impossible." In addition, the Hilo weather was getting to him. It was "simply atrocious," he said, "wet, windy and icy cold." But he was determined to continue painting when he felt better.[42]

One clear winter morning in 1886, finding Mauna Kea covered in snow, Tavermer climbed down the embankment of the Wailuku River directly opposite Charlie Arnold's house, and sat on a rock beneath what is now the Wainaku Street bridge. He sketched the rocks in the river, the hillside on the left, the rock shelf that jutted into the river from the right. The composition included small figures, but mainly draws your eye up to a glorious depiction of the "white mountain" in the distance. He did the final version in pastels. Critic David Forbes described the "dramatic beauty of this tropical mountain landscape" and its "sheer mastery of composition and his handling of the pastels.[43] Art historian H. M. Luquiens called it, "the best of his landscapes I have seen," and thought it better than his volcano landscapes, but was under the impression that it was an oil.[44] It is now part of the collection of the Honolulu Academy of Arts.

THE CREDITORS' AUCTION

In mid-February 1886, Tavernier asked King Brothers to ship over some furniture, including an easel, a set of table and chairs, and other items.[45] To pay some of his bills with King, he exchanged several volcano paintings. He figured they were square.

In March 1886, Tavernier's San Francisco creditors—and perhaps Lizzie—were auctioning off his studio and its contents. "The entire inventory," he read in the *Advertiser*, "of sketches, . . . utensils, curios, bric-a-brac and art rubbish . . . was sold . . . [A] small study of Indian heads . . . started at 25 cents [and finally went for] $27 . . . ." That was the highest amount paid. "A portfolio of sketches [brought] $9. The sale aggregated over $1000. The prices generally were considered by artists ridiculously low."[46]

THE CYCLORAMA

Since his first visit to the volcano, Tavernier envisioned a grand cyclorama depicting the erupting crater, which would make him some real money. People would pay admission and stand in the center of it and view 360 degrees of volcanic landscape. He began his project in mid-summer 1886 in Hilo. He erected a massive canvas, fully eleven feet high and ninety feet long. Working on the floor of a warehouse, he sketched out the features of the landscape, the volcano and Mauna Kea and Mauna Loa. It took in "all points of the compass." He worked on it intermittently, "and seemed indifferent to the hour of day or night." He calculated that it cost him $2,000.00 in canvas and paint. The last few weeks he worked solely on getting the colors right, barely adjusting the outlines of the figures. He completed it in mid-October 1886 and it was put on exhibition at the only large circular venue Hilo could offer, the Beckwith Skating Rink building.[47] It was called "wonderful, beautiful [and] grand . . . Hawaii's Wonder,"[48] exhibited in Maui and Honolulu,[49] and then sent on to San Francisco. He had a four-page broadside printed up, which included a biographical sketch, advertisements, and laudatory quotes.[50] There were plans to exhibit it there, as well as in Chicago, Philadelphia, Boston, and London, but a contract was never struck, and Tavernier was afraid that—even though it had been photographed and copyrighted in Washington, DC—the image would be reproduced by others. He also said that he could do another, even better. But he never attempted one of the dimensions of *The Great Panorama of Kilauea*. After sitting in the nation's capitol, it was claimed by a creditor and stowed "in a garret in the State of Maine." It has never been recovered.[51]

In 1887, he was completing one of his largest volcano studies—apart from the Panorama—nine-foot by five-foot behemoth depicting Halemaʻumaʻu by moonlight. He was working on another showing the crater, "just before sunset." The *Advertiser* reported in September, that his work, "will doubtless be the means of drawing an ever-increasing stream of tourists."[52] One view of Kīlauea was titled *The Last Glow* and described by the *Advertiser* as "a perfect poem on canvas," in which the volcano fires are abating in the evening.[53] He also did quiet landscapes of the Wailuku River and Hilo Bay,[54] as well as street scenes of downtown Hilo. Samuel Parker and other notables of Honolulu society purchased his volcano studies.[55] He also worked in pastel. One such fiery volcano pastel is on permanent display at the Volcano House at Kīlauea.

In addition to his oils, Tavernier used a variety of media, including watercolors, charcoal, crayon pastilles, pastels and India ink. He also worked on a variety of surfaces, trying for different effects. In addition to the usual canvas—both on boards and stretched—he used different textures of paper (academy and tinted), cardboard, strawboard and wood. On one occasion, he had King Brothers prepare some *koa* panels for him to paint on.[56]

THE KING BROTHERS LAWSUIT

In September, 1887, King Brothers sent him a bill for $275.95, totals for art supplies and services over the previous three years. Tavernier ignored it. He recalled paying $60.00 in cash in his first year. Later, he gave them three volcano paintings, two worth $75.00 and a larger one worth $175.00. He had also given them a six-dollar frame for the attorney (later judge) James Monsarrat. What more did they want? He had forgotten that his total bill with them had been exactly $666.95.

A five-page lawsuit was filed in the Supreme Court. It was accompanied by an accounts list of seven pages. His lawyer, Francis M. Hatch, replied to the court, stating his client "denies the truth of all the allegations." The case was to be heard in the January 1888 session.

Supreme Court Justice Lawrence McCully scrawled a note on the suit, "Let process of Attachment issue as prayed for on filing an approval bond in the sum of three hundred dollars." (That is, the sum sued for plus court costs.)

At noon on October 4, the court marshal John Kaulukou went to Tavernier's Honolulu studio with a "garnishee summons" and "attach[ed] the property of said defendant and also 3 oil painting [sic] of the volcano views from the said Garnishee . . ." Included in the lawsuit was another man, "the said Garnishee." King Brothers asserted that Tavernier's "goods and effects . . . are concealed in the hands of L. J. Levey, so that they cannot be found to be attached or levied . . ."⁵⁷ Levey was a local auctioneer and appraiser.

When confronted with the summons and the detailed accounts King Brothers had submitted, Tavernier was forced to admit their accuracy. He agreed to have the pictures sold. Where had the $300.00 come from? In mid-October the *Pacific Commercial Advertiser* carried a small item in the "Local and General" column, "Mr. Louis J. Levey sells a number of pictures by Tavernier today."⁵⁸ It raised enough to satisfy the plaintiffs and on November 3rd Tavernier and King Brothers signed a document that discontinued the suit.⁵⁹

Tavernier and Hitchcock

In March 1888, he was completing another "three Volcano pictures," as well as "a view of the Pali." Another, "a view of Kilauea in full blast . . . one of Mr. Tavernier's best, and will [be] present[ed] to the Emperor of Japan." He had recently sold "a general view of the Volcano showing Mauna Kea in the background," as well as "seven sketches of views between Hilo and Volcano to a tourist . . . which should help to advertise the Islands."⁶⁰

He traveled between Hilo and Honolulu throughout that year, teaching and drinking and producing beautiful work. He sometimes visited young Howard Hitchcock's studio and on occasion would allow the young painter to complete his sketches. Once, Hitchcock did a complete copy of *Sunset at Kilauea,* signing it "Jules Tavernier by HH." He was surprised when Tavernier "became furious and went off in a rage."⁶¹

Last Months

On January 24, 1889, Robert Louis Stevenson arrived in Honolulu. He was no longer the obscure scribbler they had known in Oakland, but the world famous author of *Treasure Island* and *Dr. Jekyll and Mr. Hyde.* And though he dressed like a bohemian, with red sashes and flowing curls, he had earned enough money to be conservative in his views on public decorum and public drinking. He wanted the Strongs to behave. He also wanted them to stop associating with the drunkard Jules Tavernier.

Louis and Fanny had taken a dislike to the Frenchman, and Belle began snubbing him, too. "When I passed him on the street I looked the other way." When they met one day in a Honolulu drug store, Jules pleaded with her to talk to him. "He was lonely and desperately unhappy . . . [w]ith tears shining in his eyes he begged me to say we would be friends again." But she turned away and used words she would ever after regret: "I am Lizzie's friend."[62]

In April 1889, Colonel Z.S. Spaulding, a Kauaʻi sugar planter, bought a good-sized Tavernier (20 inches × 36 inches) volcano in oils and planned to hang it at the Paris Exhibition. At the same time the artist was doing some black and white studies of the volcano for publication in *Le Monde* to coincide with the Great Exhibition.[63]

Still struggling to pay off debts, Tavernier would sometimes duplicate earlier successes if a buyer was at hand, even if it meant reproducing much earlier work. The last painting he was known to have worked on was such a piece. He began it during his last visit to Hilo and completed it at his Honolulu studio above Walter Peacock's store. It was called *Sunset in Wyoming* and depicted "groups of Indians with their campfires and wigwams."[64]

In May, 1889, when Robert Louis Stevenson applied for a permit to visit the leprosarium on Molokaʻi, Joe brought his father-in-law to see Dr. Nathaniel B. Emerson (1839–1915), then President of the Board of Health. Emerson had seen Joe's work and in 1887 had commissioned a portrait of himself. Joe had done a fine likeness in oil, though perhaps there had been delays. In any event, while he may have been happy with the likeness, he did not think much of the painter. He wrote in his diary that evening: "Stevenson to have his letter. Came to the office today with Joe Strong, who was as usual— DRUNK . . ."[65]

No historian has pointed out why Joe had been drinking that particular day.

It was May 18th. That same morning his friend Jules Tavernier had been found dead in his room on King Street. He was 44 years old. Belle Strong later reported in her memoir that Tavernier had been "shot through the heart"[66] and over the years readers assumed that he had been murdered or had committed suicide. After all, no autopsy had been conducted. But the truth was more commonplace, at least according to doctors who were quoted in the papers.

Dr. George Trousseau, a prominent Honolulu physician and surgeon, declared that no autopsy was necessary, adding that the cause of death had been "excessive use of alcoholic drinks." Joe Strong would serve as a pallbearer that afternoon at St. Andrew's Church, along with their friends Peacock, Wright, and Ollert.[67]

As an indigent, and without family, Tavernier's remains were placed off to the side at Oʻahu Cemetery on Nuʻuanu Avenue, in a plot designated for seamen and other transients who died far from home. The area of the cemetery is known as the Strangers' Lots.[68]

The Stevensons departed Hawaii a few weeks later, taking Joe and leaving Belle and son Austin. Joe would never set foot on the Islands again, but they would all settle for a time in Samoa, where Stevenson would be buried.

The following year, the Bohemian Club of San Francisco shipped over a nine-foot granite obelisk. It arrived December 3, 1890, aboard the *Consuelo*,[69] the same ship that had brought the Strongs to Hawaii in 1882. It was placed over Tavernier's grave, against the cemetery wall, just off the main street and gate. Wreaths and bouquets arrived from friends and admirers when a graveside service was held on the 21st.[70] The stone is inscribed:

IN MEMORY OF
JULES TAVERNIER
ARTIST
BY THE MEMBERS OF
THE BOHEMIAN CLUB

There is no biography of Tavernier, and basic facts of his life are difficult to come by, and many are misleading. The first study of any sort was a paper delivered in 1940 by H. M. Luquiens, the head of the University of Hawaii's art department, to the Social Science Association of Honolulu.[71] Yet most of it was based on that broadside Tavernier had printed in 1887, as well as anecdotes from Belle Strong's colorful but unreliable memoir. A 1996 article in *Honolulu* magazine drew on these and introduced new misconceptions.[72] Eugen Neuhaus, an artist and critic, in his *History and Ideals of American Art,* calls Tavernier merely a "western painter," ignoring his Hawaiian work.[73]

David Forbes called him simply "the best painter of the period in Hawai'i," the portrayer of "spectacular images" and the artist whose "personal interpretations of the volcano became firmly implanted in the minds of his audience who found it difficult to think of volcano paintings without having one of his dramatic night scenes come to mind."[74]

FIG. 3. Sketch of Jules Tavernier from the *San Francisco Sunday Call,* April 6, 1911.

The *Advertiser* gave a more generous summation when it predicted a month after his death:

> There is no doubt that the pictures of the late Jules Tavernier will increase in value, as his works represent a school of art that is not of a common kind; and the subjects are always interesting and valuable in proportion to the genius displayed."[75]

NOTES

[1] *PCA* 24 Dec. 1884.

[2] *PCA* 11 Nov. 1884.

[3] Autobiographical sketch, part of the broadside "Tavernier's Volcano Panorama. Honolulu, H.I. Jan. 1887," AH.

[4] "Jules Tavernier–Sudden Death of the Celebrated Artist and Painter," *PCA* 20 May, 1889.

[5] Rober Taft, "Pictorial record of the Old West 1. Frenzeny and Tavernier," *Kansas State Historical Society* (14 Feb. 1946) 1–35. This otherwise reliable article states that Joseph Strong was "a brother-in-law of Robert Louis Stevenson" (p. 30). Of course, while he was technically Stevenson's "step-son-in-law," RLS often called him his "son-in-law."

[6] Hjalmarson, Birgitta, *Artful Players, Artistic Life in Early San Francisco* (Los Angeles: Balcony Press, [1999]) 52.

[7] *San Francisco Call*, 25 Feb. 1877, p. 7, c. 8.

[8] Field, Isobel, *This Life I've Loved* (New York: Longsmans, Green and Co., 1937) 126.

[9] Field, *This Life* 126

[10] Field, *This Life* 140

[11] Hjalmarson, *Artful Players* 49.

[12] *PCA* 20 May 1889.

[13] *PCA* 11 Nov. 1884.

[14] Field, *This Life* 141.

[15] *PCA* 11 Nov. 1884.

[16] This paintbox actually turned up, along with two sketches, in Hitchcock's Honolulu studio in 1939. Its present whereabouts is unknown. *HA* 16 Aug. 1939.

[17] *PCA* 22 Oct. 1885.

[18] King Bros. vs. Jules Tavernier, Law Division, Case #2547, First Circuit Court Records, AH.

[19] *PCA* 6 Jan. 1885.

[20] *PCA* 20 May 1889.

[21] *PCA* 20 Apr. 1889.

[22] A. Grove Day, *Mark Twain's Letters from Hawaii* (Honolulu: U of Hawaii P, 1975) 201.

[23] *PCA* 7 Jan. 1885.

[24] *PCA* 7 Apr. 1885.

[25] Day, *Mark Twain's Letters,* 297.

[26] *HA* 16 Aug. 1939.

[27] *PCA* 2 Apr. 1885.

[28] *PCA* 4 Mar. 1885.

[29] *PCA* 26 Aug. 1885.

[30] *PCA* 9 Mar. 1885.

[31] King vs. JT.

[32] King vs. JT

[33] *PCA* 25 July 1885.

[34] *PCA* 3 Nov. 1885, and obituary *PCA* 25 Sept. 1890.

[35] Pleasant Street. In 1909, most Hilo street names were changed to Hawaiian names. Information courtesy of the staff of the Lyman House Museum, Hilo, Hawai'i. One of the few exceptions is Furneaux Lane, named for the Hilo-based painter Charles Furneaux, originally from Melrose, MA. An apartment house now stands at the site of Arnold's house.

[36] *PCA* 12 Oct. 1885.

[37] *HG* 25 Aug. 1885.

[38] Letters from Joseph Dwight Strong and Isobel Strong to Charles Warren Stoddard; from the Charles Warren Stoddard Collection, reference HM 37959-3165, originals at the Huntington Library, San Marino, CA; Isobel Strong to Stoddard, 4 Feb. 1886.

[39] Charles Warren Stoddard Collection, Huntington Library.

[40] *PCA* 4 Nov. 1885.

[41] *PCA* 1 Dec. 1885.

[42] *PCA* 22 Dec. 1885.

[43] Forbes, David, *Encounters with Paradise: Views of Hawaii and its People, 1778–1941* (Honolulu: Honolulu Academy of Arts, 1992) 195.

[44] H. M. Luquiens, "Jules Tavernier," *Honolulu Academy of Arts Annual Bulletin* 2 (1940), 29.

[45] King vs. JT

[46] *PCA* 23 Mar. 1886.

[47] *PCA* 25 Oct. 1886.

[48] *PCA* "Hawaii's Wonder—Jules Tavernier's Great Panorama of Kilauea," 21 June 1889.

[49] *PCA* 22 June 1887.

[50] "Tavernier's Volcano Panorama. Honolulu, H.I. Jan. 1887, W. H. Stone, Manager." Broadside, AH.

[51] *PCA* 21 June 1889.

[52] *PCA* 23 Sept. 1887.

[53] *PCA* 25 June 1886.

[54] *PCA* 30 Mar. 1886.

[55] *PCA* 3 Nov. 1885.

[56] King vs. JT.

[57] King vs. JT.

[58] *PCA* 18 Oct. 1887.

[59] King vs. JT.

[60] *PCA* 5 Mar. 1888.

[61] Forbes, 183.

[62] Field, *This Life,* 248.

[63] *PCA* 13 Apr. 1889.

[64] *PCA* 14 June 1889.

[65] Kent, Harold W., *Dr. Hyde and Mr. Stevenson* (Rutland and Tokyo: Tuttle and Co., 1973) 256.

[66] Field, *This Life,* 248.

[67] *PCA* 20 May 1889.

[68] "Jules Tavernier" reference card and "Strangers Lots Map" p. 156, Records File, Oahu Cemetery Office, Honolulu.

[69] *PCA* 4 Dec. 1890; "Monument to Famed Island Painter Stands in Nuuanu After 50 Years," *HA,* 13 Dec. 1940. When Nu'uanu Avenue was straightened in 1917, the outer wall of the cemetery was moved in, along with several graves. Tavernier's grave was one of those moved. This seems to be the reason his grave stone abuts the wall. See *PCA* 2 Dec. 1917.

[70] *PCA* 20 Dec. 1890.

[71] Luquiens, 25–31; Huc Mazelet Luquiens was an artist as well as the head of the art department at the University of Hawai'i in the 1930s and 40s; obituary, *HA* 11 May 1961.

[72] Steven Mair, "Jules Tavernier: Hawai'i's First Real Painter," *Honolulu Magazine* 93 (Nov. 1996) 81–84. Errors include, but are not limited to, people's names (he calls Isobel Strong Field "Isobel Fields Strong" and H. Howard Hitchcock "Howard Hitchcock"); he thought that the Taverniers came to Hawaii together; they did not; that Lizzie Tavernier lived for some time in Honolulu and was, with her husband "an integral part of high society." As bohemians they were not in "high society." The article repeats the story—that originated with Neuhaus—that people with unpaid debts were not allowed to leave the Islands, and thus Tavernier was unable to depart with his wife. No evidence is given for either assertion. In fact, the King Brothers lawsuit suggests that he had made good on much of his debt. Maier, like Luquiens, generally tends to exaggerate Furneaux's influence, and diminish Strong's.

[73] [Karl] Eugen Neuhaus, *History and Ideals of American Art* (Stanford California: Stanford UP, 1931); cited in Luquiens, 26.

[74] Forbes, *Encounters in Paradise,* 178.

[75] *PCA* "Tavernier Pictures," 14 June 1889.

FRED GREGURAS

Spanish-American War Sites in Honolulu

THIS BRIEF HISTORY of Spanish-American War sites in the Honolulu area was prompted in large part by my purchase on eBay of photos of two military hospitals established in Honolulu in 1898: Independence Hospital and Buena Vista Hospital. My curiosity as to what
happened to these hospitals led to more research and, finally, a site
exploration visit to Honolulu in June, 2004. The purpose of the site
exploration was to try to locate military sites of the 1898 period, particularly the hospitals, and to compare the past with the present. The
original hospital photos are now in the collection of the U.S. Army
Museum of Hawai'i at Fort DeRussy in Honolulu. My hope is that this
paper will also encourage others with information to provide input
so that more is known about this time in Honolulu.

THE SPANISH-AMERICAN WAR

First, some background on the Spanish-American War of 1898. William McKinley was president of the United States, and the precipi-
tating event was the explosion of the battleship *USS Maine* in the harbor at Havana, Cuba on February 15, 1898. War was declared on
Spain on April 25, 1898, and the United States moved to do battle
in several Spanish possessions. Regular and volunteer soldiers were

*Fred Greguras is an attorney with the Silicon Valley, California law firm of Fenwick & West
LLP where he has practiced for almost 25 years. His history interests include the Spanish
American War and Nebraska where he grew up. His military service includes being a pla-
toon commander with a Marine Corps rifle company in Vietnam.*

The Hawaiian Journal of History, vol. 39 (2005)

transported to staging and embarkation camps at San Francisco and on the East Coast. The U.S. naval victory at Manila Bay in the Philippines occurred on May 1. The first Philippine expedition left San Francisco on May 25. The Cuba invasion force won victories on July 1 at El Caney and San Juan Hill. The Spanish fleet was destroyed on July 3 as it attempted to flee from Santiago, Cuba. The peace protocol ending the war was signed on August 12, and the formal peace treaty, the Treaty of Paris, was signed on December 10, 1898. Even after the fighting in Cuba ended, fierce fighting in the Philippines continued through the insurrection period.[1] Ironically, more American soldiers died of disease than in actual combat during 1898 due to typhoid fever and malaria.[2]

Meanwhile, Hawai'i, particularly Honolulu, had gained strategic importance because of its geographical position relative to the U.S.'s new Pacific possessions, Guam and the Philippines. In the culmination of years of maneuvering by American residents, Hawai'i was formally annexed to the U.S. in a ceremony at 'Iolani Palace on August 12, 1898.[3]

Honolulu served as a stopover point for the expeditionary forces sailing to the Philippines. There was no assigned garrison here until the 1st New York Volunteer Infantry regiment ("1st N.Y.") arrived in Honolulu on various ships between August 15 and September 3, 1898.[4] The regimental commander, Colonel Thomas Barber, had arrived earlier on August 6 to select a camp site. The 3rd Battalion, 2nd U.S. Volunteer Engineers ("2nd Engineers") began arriving in Honolulu on August 14, 1898.[5] The engineers were sent to build a military post and to survey strategic locations such as Pearl Harbor.

The 1st N.Y. returned to San Francisco beginning in late November, 1898 with the last units departing on December 10, 1898.[6] The 2nd Engineers was stationed in Honolulu from August 14, 1898 until April 20, 1899.[7]

THE RACETRACK CAMP

A temporary camp was established on August 15, 1898 by the 1st N.Y. on the "infield" of the racetrack at Kapi'olani Park.[8] This was a one-mile racetrack with a large open infield. The first detachment of the 2nd Engineers arrived on August 14 and began laying out the camp.

The main body of the 2nd Engineers arrived in Honolulu on August 17.[9] The two commands were camped alongside each other, as though they were one large regiment. The racetrack camp of the 1st N.Y. and 2nd Engineers was not named.

Camp McKinley

On August 27, 1898, Companies F, G and H of the 1st N.Y. arrived and camped on the Irwin tract of property at the foot of Diamond Head, just east of and visible from the racetrack camp (the "Irwin Tract").[10] This was the beginning of the move from the racetrack camp. On August 30, 1898, Companies C. E, I, K, L, M and a detachment of Company D moved to the Irwin Tract. The Irwin Tract camp was named "Camp McKinley," in honor of the president, about August 22, 1898.[11] On September 3, the remainder of the regiment arrived and also camped at Camp McKinley. The 2nd Engineers also moved to Camp McKinley and camped alongside the 1st N.Y.

According to an official New York state publication:

> The camp site was chosen by a Board convened for the purpose, consisting of officers of the 1st Regiment, New York Volunteers, and of the 2nd Regiment, Volunteer Engineers, and approved by Colonel Barber. It was near the only ocean-bathing beach on the Island and the reported site of a proposed Sanitarium selected by the resident physicians in the immediate vicinity of the best residential quarter of the Island. In addition it had shade in the park, a drill and parade ground on the racecourse, city water, and was accessible.[12]

The troops used the bathing facilities at the Sans Souci Resort which was located on the beach at the southeast corner of the park. Newspaper articles indicated they were unhappy with the facilities.[13] This beach is still known as Sans Souci Beach.

Kapiʻolani Park's racetrack closed in 1926, but approximately half the infield area of the racetrack remains an open area.[14] The "Waikīkī Shell," an outdoor performance amphitheater, is in the north part of the racetrack infield. Monsarrat Avenue cuts through the north end of the racetrack site. The tennis courts on the west side of the park are about where the racetrack grandstand was located. The grandstand can be seen in a number of 1898 photos, and Diamond

Head is the most prominent landmark in many of these same photos. This landmark makes it possible to locate today approximately where such photos were taken. Residences have been built throughout the Irwin Tract, but enough trees remain so the views from the park and above from Diamond Head are similar to the 1898 views. The Sanborn Fire Insurance maps, produced to show most urban areas in the U.S., can be used to determine the stage of development in this location. The Irwin Tract area is not detailed in the 1914 edition, which means there were not many buildings in the area at the time.[15] The 1927 Sanborn map shows street detail in the Irwin Tract area, but a 1926 aerial photo shows only a few buildings there.

CAMP OTIS

Camp Otis was a short-lived camp of Philippine expeditionary troops who arrived on the troop ship *Arizona* on August 27, 1898 and were left in Honolulu when the ship went on to Manila.[16] The soldiers camped inside the racetrack at Kapi'olani Park.[17] The camp was later moved east within the racetrack to a point "nearly opposite Camp McKinley."[18]

Camp Otis consisted of detachments of the 3rd U.S. Artillery, the 10th Pennsylvania Volunteer Infantry, the 18th U.S. Infantry and detachments of recruits for the 1st Colorado Volunteer Infantry, 1st Nebraska Volunteer Infantry ("1st Neb.") and other units already in Manila.[19] Camp Otis was abandoned about November 7, 1898 when the *Arizona* returned and the troops departed for Manila.[20]

The camp was named after Major General Elwell S. Otis, U.S. Volunteers, the commanding officer in the Philippines in 1898–99.[21] He followed General Merritt in commanding the Eighth Corps and was the commanding general of the Department of the Pacific with headquarters in Manila as of January 7, 1899. He was second in command to General Merritt when the Philippine expeditionary force and Eighth Corps were established.

When the 1st Neb. recruits arrived in Honolulu on board the *Arizona,* a newspaper reported: "The First New Yorkers are camped among the trees outside the east track. Their camp is known as Camp McKinley, while the camp of the troops from the Arizona is called Camp Otis, in honor of Major General Otis."[22]

The Military District of Hawaii and Camp Otis were established in September, 1898. Official orders of the time stated:

> Hdqrs. Dept. of California, Sept. 4, 1898. For better administration and subject to the approval of the Secretary of War, the territory lately constituting the Hawaiian Republic is hereby constituted a Military District, to be known as the District of Hawaii, under command of Brig. Gen., Chas. King, U.S.V., with Headquarters at Honolulu. The officers in charge of supply depots in that city will, in addition, act as Chiefs of the Staff Departments they represent.
>
> The troops present in the District will be consolidated into two camps, one to be called Camp McKinley, consisting of the 1st New York Volunteers and Battalion of U.S. Volunteer Engineers as now, under command of Col. T.H. Barber, 1st New York Vols.; and another to be called Camp Otis, comprising all expeditionary troops temporarily in the District, and commanded by the senior officer of those forces present.[23]

The Military District of Hawaii and Camp Otis lasted only until early November, 1898:

> Upon the arrival of the U.S. transport Arizona at Honolulu, H.I., the District of Hawaii will be discontinued, the Commanding Officer thereof turning over all records, etc., pertaining to that district to Col. Thomas H. Barber, 1st New York Vols., commanding Camp McKinley. Brig. Gen. Charles King, U.S.V., will then embark on the Arizona for Manila, P.I. with all officers and enlisted men designated in S.O. 111 and 118, c.s., D. Cal., and temporarily delayed in Honolulu; and including all others of the Expeditionary forces fit for duty and left at that station by transports other than the transport Tacoma. Upon arrival at Manila, Brig. Gen. King will report to the Commanding General, Department of the Pacific.[24]

Convalescent Camp

In late November, General Merriam reported on the health problems of the troops in Honolulu:

> From San Francisco Maj. Gen. Merriam telegraphs: "Reports from Honolulu to Nov. 14. Arizona sailed for Manila with Gen. J. King's

detachment, Nov. 10, leaving about 160 men in the hospital. Statement of sick in general hospital as follows: Typhoid cases, 1st New York Regiment, 63, and expeditionary troops, 48; total typhoid, 111; malarial fever and others, including convalescents, 1st New York Regiment, 99, and expeditionary troops, 102; total, 201. Total patients, 312." Gen. Merriam gives it as his opinion that the city of Honolulu is thoroughly infected with typhoid fever. He thinks that in a measure this is possibly due to the men that were sent from here with the disease, who were taken off the transports at Honolulu and put in hospitals there. Gen. King's departure abandons Camp Otis, and Gen. Merriam says it will not be again occupied by troops. Camp McKinley has also been moved to new ground, and every possible sanitary precaution taken to insure the good health of the men.[25]

The 1st N.Y. was moved to a camp site away from Camp McKinley because of malaria and typhoid fever. Dysentery was also a problem. Company E of the 1st N.Y. moved to Wai'alae on October 22 on the north side of Diamond Head, about seven miles from Honolulu and three miles from Camp McKinley.[26] Company H was moved October 27 and Companies A, B, C, D, F, G, I and L about November 4. The camp was on the Paul Isenberg estate on the beach at Wai'alae.[27] This camp became the regimental camp, at least temporarily.

A letter from a member of Company I of the 1st N.Y. while at this camp states: "The tents are pitched on the sandy beach at Waialie (sic) . . ." The discovery of "scores" of human skeletons on this camp site caused the "tall tale" that the camp was located where Kamehameha initially landed on O'ahu and defeated the islanders.[28]

This "health resort" camp was called Camp Kaalawai. One of the newspaper articles refers to Camp Kaalawai as being "around Diamond Head" in Wai'alae, Kā'alaāwai Beach is on the southeast side of Diamond Head, south of Wai'alae.[29] There are numerous references to the camp being on the beach at Wai'alae, so it is not clear why it was named after a completely different place.

German-born Paul Isenberg was an important businessman and major landowner on O'ahu at the time.[30] One account indicates his land stretched from Kapahulu Avenue to Kāhala Beach on the east shore of O'ahu.[31] While an 1897 map of Honolulu does not extend to the Wai'alae coast, a 1920 map shows the Isenberg shore property was where the present day Wai'alae Beach Park and Wai'alae Country Club are located. Keala'olu Avenue, which runs from Kalaniana'ole Highway to Kāhala Avenue, was named Isenberg Road in 1920 and the Isenberg property was north of where Keala'olu intersects with Kāhala. Wai'alae Beach Park or the Country Club was very likely the site of Camp Kaalawai.

SECOND CAMP McKINLEY

The 2nd Engineers built barracks and other buildings for the new Camp McKinley just north of Kapi'olani Park. The south edge of the camp was only about a quarter of a mile from the park. The engineers moved to be near the construction site in early November, 1898.[32]

In early December, 1898, the first Camp McKinley was abandoned and the camp moved to the new barracks on Kapahulu Road.[33] The barracks were occupied by the 2nd Engineers on November 27, 1898 although work on the camp buildings continued until March, 1899. This new Camp McKinley remained in existence until Fort Shafter was opened in late June, 1907. The garrison was either artillery or coast artillery troops during this period.[34] The camp was located just south of Kapahulu, between Lēahi and Kana'ina avenues.[35]

There was a "false start" on the second Camp McKinley. Construction on two temporary barracks had actually begun east of Kapahulu Road. These were subsequently torn down and the materials moved to the new site. A map shows the location of the "false start" location along Kapahulu but without any cross street identified.[36] It was probably near Kapahulu and Pākī Avenue in order to minimize the intrusion on the park.

The area of the second Camp McKinley is not detailed in the 1914 Sanborn Insurance map but is in the 1927 edition. The camp headquarters building appears in the 1927 map but no other buildings appear to have survived to that date.

The site of the second Camp McKinley is now covered by businesses along Kapahulu Avenue and residences in the other areas of the site. During a site tour in June, 2004 led by Judith Bowman, Curator of the Army Museum of Hawaii, we followed the camp map around and across the perimeter of the camp to look for possible remains. A boundary marker/fence post and parts of a fence base and pillars made of volcanic rock along Kanaʻina Avenue may date back to the camp.

HOSPITALS

Local hospitals were used for the sick soldiers until Independence Park Hospital was established on August 15, 1898.[37] The Red Cross also established a hospital for soldiers in the Child Garden Building on Beretania Street in June, 1898.[38] The Independence Park Hospital was located in a dance pavilion at Independence Park, southeast of the corner of Sheridan and King Streets.[39]

The Independence Park Hospital was closed in January, 1899.[40] A November 1, 1898 letter from a member of Company I of the 1st N.Y. reports that General King had visited the military hospital at Independence Park and officially condemned the place as a hospital site because of the heat and humidity.[41]

FIG. 1. Independence Park Hospital, Honolulu, late 1898, looking southeast. U.S. Army Museum of Hawaiʻi.

The Independence Park pavilion appears on the 1897 map of Honolulu but not on the 1901 map. The building was likely burned after being occupied by typhoid patients in order to reduce any possible contagion. The site today is covered with business establishments along busy King Street, with no indication a park was ever there.

In October, 1898, concern over conditions at Independence Park Hospital and the large number of sick soldiers required that additional hospital space be obtained.[42] The overflow required the use of local hospitals and a hospital camp on the Dow lot on the south slope of Punchbowl.[43] The Nuuanu Valley Military Hospital, at a spot known as Buena Vista, was established in early November, 1898.[44] The hospital was also known as Buena Vista Hospital. It was located at the former John Paty home, known as Buena Vista house, which was on the east side of Nu'uanu Avenue at Wyllie Street. The Paty house was immediately south of Rosebank, the home of F. A. Schaefer.[45] Cottages and other buildings on the Paty property were also

FIG. 2. Buena Vista Hospital, Honolulu, late 1898, looking north. U.S. Army Museum of Hawai'i.

used for the hospital. In addition, frame buildings for hospital wards were constructed.

Buena Vista had become available from a developer who purchased the Paty property. John Paty had died in 1897. According to an advertisement that ran several times in the *Pacific Commercial Advertiser* in early August, 1898, the new owner was dividing the property into eight lots for development.[46]

F.A. Schaefer purchased the "Buena Vista Hospital" premises of over five acres from Charles S. Desky in early 1900.[47] The property was leased to the government until July, 1900.[48] As indicated, Schaefer also owned Rosebank, the property immediately north of the hospital. Schaefer completely rebuilt his home Rosebank into a grand mansion in 1900.[49] The addition of the Buena Vista property to the south later gave him a better view of the ocean once the hospital buildings were gone. The hospital was still being used in late 1904 although it was then called the U.S. Army Hospital.[50] It was likely used until the Fort Shafter Hospital was opened in July, 1907.

The hospital site area is not detailed in the 1914 Sanborn Insurance map but is detailed in the 1927 map. The 1927 map indicates that a different house was on the Paty property site. This house is also in a 1952 aerial photo. The new house was southwest of the Buena Vista house site. Buena Vista Hospital, like Independence Park Hospital, was likely burned or otherwise destroyed rather than reused.

The site of the John Paty home, the primary building when Buena Vista Hospital was established, is now covered by the Nuʻuanu-Pali Highway interchange, just north of the Community Church of Honolulu at 2345 Nuʻuanu Avenue. This interchange was built in the late 1950s or early 1960s.[51] A cottage on the east side of the church reportedly dates back to one of the prior houses on the site. It may have been a servants' quarters. Palm trees still stand where the entrance road into Buena Vista was located. The palms and entrance road are visible in one of the 1898 hospital photos.

CAMP CEMETERY

According to newspaper articles, many of the soldiers who died in Honolulu were buried at the Nuʻuanu Cemetery, now known as the Oʻahu Cemetery, at 2162 Nuʻuanu Avenue.[52] This is just south of the Buena Vista Hospital site described above. At least one soldier was buried in the King Street Catholic Cemetery at 839 South King Street.[53] News accounts don't mention any cremations, although this would have been a way to try to avoid further sickness. These Honolulu burials are a mystery. Existing cemetery records do not reflect the initial burials, let alone disinterment for shipment of remains back to the U.S. mainland.[54]

CAMP LANGFITT

This camp was established at Pearl City by Company I of the 2nd Engineers during its survey of Pearl Harbor and was occupied from September 27 to October 19, 1898.[55] It was named after Major William Campbell Langfitt, commanding officer of the battalion of the 2nd Engineers. The camp was at Remond Grove, an early picnic and recreation area.[56] The troops camped inside the large dance pavil-

FIG. 3. Buena Vista Hospital, Honolulu, late 1898, looking east. U.S. Army Museum of Hawai'i.

ion.[57] Remond Grove was south of Kamehameha Highway, east of Lehua Avenue and primarily north of the H-1 freeway in the vicinity of Sunset Memorial Cemetery.[58]

CAMP GULSTAN

This was the name given to the Waikīkī chapel named in honor of Catholic Bishop Francis R. Gulstan:

> About 300 members of the N.Y. Regiment attend divine service at the Chapel at Waikiki every Sunday. This chapel was build through the efforts of the Catholic ladies of Honolulu. They call the place Camp Gulstan after Bishop Gulstan. It is a pretty structure, built of cocoanut leaves, like the native 'lanai.' Palms and cut flowers adorn the altar. Several tables are fitted up with writing materials. A tank of ice water and an abundance of literature make it a comfortable place of rest for the weary soldier.
>
> Mass is celebrated each Sunday at 8:30 a.m. by Rev. Father Valentine. A choir composed of soldiers enliven the services. Those wishing to go Sunday can meet at guard house at 8 o'clock. All are welcome.[59]

CAMP SAGUE

On November 8, 1898, Companies K and M along with a small group of men from Company I of the 1st N.Y. sailed from Honolulu to Hilo on the island of Hawaiʻi, and from there marched to the Kīlauea volcano.[60] The troops landed at Waiākea in Hilo and stayed in a large warehouse for one night before going to the volcano. The detachment returned to Honolulu on November 27.[61]

A November 24, 1898 letter from a member of Company I of the 1st N.Y. indicates the camp was near the crater of the volcano, about two miles from the Volcano House "in a large [koa] grove with lots of dead wood on the ground."[62] The camp was named after Major John Sague of the 1st N.Y. who was in command of the detachment. The troops were in this camp for only three days.

*   *   *

While there are few, if any, man-made remains at any of the Honolulu sites, the open space at Kapiʻolani Park with Diamond Head in the background and the remains of the palm drive at Buena Vista provide a basis for visualizing several key military places in Honolulu during the Spanish American War. If you survive the climb, with a little imagination, you can still see the tents and cooking fires of Camp Otis and the first Camp McKinley from the top of Diamond Head.

NOTES

1 This timeline is based on the chronology in Stan Cohen, *Images of the Spanish-American War* (Missoula, Montana: Pictorial Histories Publishing Co., Inc., 1997) v.

2 Battle deaths were 332; other deaths in service were 2,957 according to Patrick Sherry, "Casualties During the Spanish American War," www.spanamwar.com/casualties.htm. The Department of Veterans Affairs web site, www.va.gov, indicates there were 385 battle deaths and 2,061 other deaths. Other sources may have slightly different numbers but the ratio of death from diseases to combat deaths is very high.

3 State Historian, *The History of the Empire State Regiment in the War with Spain* (Albany: Published under the direction of the State Historian, 1903) 23.

4 State Historian, *Empire* 21–23.

5 William Venable, *The Second Regiment of United States Volunteer Engineers* (Cincinnati: McDonald & Co., 1899) 104.

6 State Historian, *Empire* 24.

7 Venable, *Second Engineers* 104–106.

8 State Historian, *Empire* 21.

9 Venable, *Second Engineers* 104.

10 State Historian, *Empire* 22.

11 State Historian, *Empire* 22.

12 State Historian, *Empire* 22–23

13 *The Weekly News Muster,* October 15, 1898: 5; October 29, 1898: 4. This was the weekly newspaper published by the 1st N.Y. while in Honolulu (hereinafter *News Muster*). It was published from September 24, 1898 to November 26, 1898, a total of ten issues.

14 Robert Weyeneth, *Kapiʻolani Park: A History* (Honolulu: Kapiʻolani Park Preservation Society, 2002). This is a good source on the history of the park but is not accurate with respect to how long a military camp was located within the park.

15 Map Collection, Hamilton Library, University of Hawaii Mānoa (hereinafter UH Map Collection).

16 *Omaha Evening Bee,* September 26, 1898; General Order 16, Department of California, September 22, 1898.

17 There are two photos of Camp Otis on pages 47 and 54 in: *Picturesque Cuba, Puerto Rico, Hawaii, Philippines* (Springfield, Ohio: Mast, Crowell and Kirk-

patrick, 1899 (Farm and Fireside Library No. 168)). Page 47 shows Camp Otis inside the racetrack. The photo on page 54 is captioned "Camp McKinley and Camp Otis, . . . Camp McKinley in the foreground among the trees and Camp Otis in the open ground beyond." This photo shows Camp McKinley in the Irwin Tract and Camp Otis inside the racetrack.

18 *HG,* November 1, 1898: 3.

19 *Omaha Evening Bee,* September 26, 1898; Camp Otis section in "Post Office in Paradise," www.hawaiianstamps.com/garrison.html

20 The November 7, 1898 *Hawaiian Star* reported the abandonment of Camp Otis and the boarding of the transport *Arizona.*

21 See page 100 of Cohen, *Images of the Spanish American War* for a brief biography of Otis.

22 *Omaha Evening Bee,* September 26, 1898.

23 General Order 16, Department of California, September 22, 1898.

24 Special Order 150, Department of California, October 6, 1898.

25 *Army and Navy Journal,* November 26, 1898: 298.

26 State Historian, *Empire* 23.

27 *News Muster,* October 29, 1898: 5; November 12, 1898: 3.

28 Scrapbook of newspaper clippings and other items of Company I of the 1st New York in the author's collection (hereinafter *Scrapbook*). The newspaper clippings are from the Middletown, New York newspaper (probably the *Daily Argus*) and are letters from one or more soldiers in Company I. Dates provided are the date of the letter in each article. November 8, 1898 letter.

29 *HG,* October 28, 1898: 1 and November 8, 1898: 2.

30 Brief biography in Chris Cook, "Germans in Hawaii," www.islander-magazine.com/germans.html.

31 June Watanabe, *"Better Days,"* HSB, April 23, 1996 www.starbulletin.com

32 *Hawaiian Star,* November 8, 1898.

33 *HG,* December 2, 1898: 7.

34 Roster of Troops booklets for the Department of California and Pacific Division, Army War College Library, Carlisle, Pennsylvania.

35 Map of post in Venable, *Second Engineers* following page 110.

36 *News Muster,* October 15, 1898: 7.

37 *PCA,* August 16, 1898; *HG,* August 2, 1898: 5.

38 *HG,* June 26,1898: 3.

39 See Tripler Hospital web site, www.tamc.amedd.army.mil/information/overview.htm. Independence Park and the pavilion are on the 1897 map of Honolulu, UH Map Collection.

40 According to the *HG,* January 10, 1899: 2, the Independence Park Hospital was "practically abandoned."

41 *Scrapbook,* November 1, 1898 letter.

42 *Hawaiian Star,* November 2, 1898: 1.

43 *Hawaiian Star,* November 2, 1898: 1; *PCA,* August 16, 1898; *HG,* August 2, 1898: 5.

44 *Hawaiian Star,* November 19, 1898: 1.
45 The history of Rosebank is in Else Waldron, *Honolulu 100 Years Ago* (Honolulu: Fisher Printing Company, 1967), beginning on page 59.
46 For example, see the *PCA,* August 6, 1898.
47 *HG,* November 22, 1900: 5.
48 *HG,* November 22, 1900: 5.
49 Waldron, *Honolulu 100 Years Ago:* 63.
50 *HG,* November 22, 1904: 7.
51 Various road maps of Honolulu before and after the interchange appears on the maps.
52 *News Muster, HG* and other newspapers.
53 Thomas Hannan was buried in the Catholic Cemetery as reported in the *News Muster,* October 29, 1898: 6.
54 Research by Nanette Napoleon, Honolulu, cemetery research specialist
55 Venable, *Second Engineers* 109.
56 *HG,* September 30, 1898: 6.
57 *News Muster,* October 29, 1898: 8.
58 1895 Map of Pearl City, UH Map Collection
59 *News Muster,* October 1, 1898: 10.
60 State Historian, *Empire* 23.
61 State Historian, *Empire* 23.
62 *Scrapbook,* November 24, 1898 letter.

JEFFREY K. LYONS

The Pacific Cable, Hawai'i, and Global Communication

PRIOR TO THE COMPLETION of the British and American Pacific cables in 1902 and 1903, the Atlantic submarine telegraph cable was completed in July of 1866 connecting the European continent to North America.[1] The significance of the Atlantic cable was that Europe and North America were suddenly linked in both time and space. Communication, which previously traveled only as quickly as the fastest ocean-going vessels of the time, was remarkably reduced to mere seconds—since telegraphic communication travels at the speed of light.[2] In contrast, on the other side of the globe at the dawn of the 20th century, the Pacific Ocean remained a vast barrier to inter-continental communication. News between the Americas and the continents of Asia and Australia, and the countries of Japan and the Philippines, continued to move only as quickly as the swiftest ships of the day.

At the beginning of the 20th century, two nations were poised to accept the challenge to traverse the Pacific Ocean with undersea communication cables, which would permit telegraphic messages to be transmitted across thousands of miles within seconds. England and its ally, Canada, sought to lay submarine telegraph cables to Australia and New Zealand, which had commonly shared political ties.

Jeffrey Kaumuali'i Lyons is part-Hawaiian and a graduate of the University of Hawai'i at Mānoa. He is currently teaching at Hawai'i Pacific University in the College of Communication. Mr. Lyons is currently studying for his Ph.D. in Communication at Regent University, Virginia, where he also earned a master's degree in communication.

The Hawaiian Journal of History, vol. 39 (2005)

England's younger offspring, the United States, sought to establish communication to Hawai'i, the Philippines, and its trading partners Japan and China.

The advent of the submarine Pacific telegraph cable (hereafter simply referred to as the Pacific cable) is the story of a shift in dominance between two global news agencies—from the British agency Reuters to the American agency the United Press. At the same time, the United States was expanding its political influence in the Pacific basin, through its annexation of Hawai'i in 1900 and its governance of the Philippines beginning in 1898 (a result of the Spanish-American War). This essay is a description of the history behind the American Pacific cable, and the circumstances that led to its completion in July of 1903.

As a starting point, I will examine the Atlantic cable, the forerunner of the Pacific cable. It is important to understand how the technological achievement of the Atlantic cable influenced the eventual completion of the Pacific cable. Next, we will turn to the global telegraphic communication race between England and the United States —with particular attention on the British news agency Reuters and its American competitor the Associated Press. For the United States in particular, Hawai'i became a strategic stepping stone towards the realization of its political expansion in the Pacific basin. I will show a timeline of events, which preceded the completion of the Pacific cable. I will also discuss Cable Day in Hawai'i, the day which officially marked the opening of the Hawaiian leg of the Pacific cable. Finally, I will address the implications of history, culture, and technology and how the synthesis of these elements continues to impact worldwide communication.

THE TRANS-ATLANTIC CABLE

The Atlantic cable was the world's first trans-continental telegraph cable to link North America and Europe. American entrepreneur Cyrus W. Field, who made his earlier fortune in manufacturing paper, formed The Atlantic Telegraph Company, in 1856, for the purpose of laying a cable between England and the United States.[3] Field was able to convince both the United States and Great Britain of the success of the project and to secure financing. After numerous unsuccessful attempts, in July of 1866, the Atlantic cable was finally completed, successfully connecting the two continents via undersea telegraphic communication.[4]

Commenting on the significance of the trans-Atlantic cable and the genesis of worldwide telegraphic communication, Arthur C. Clarke in his book, *Voice Across the Sea* writes:

> Our civilization could not exist without efficient communications; we find it impossible to imagine a time when it took a month to get a message across the Atlantic and another month (if the winds were favorable) to receive a reply. . . . Not until the scientists of the early nineteenth century started to investigate the curious properties of electricity was a servant discovered which within little more than two lifetimes would change the face of the world and sweep away the ancient barriers of time and distance.[5]

The cable ship, the *Great Eastern,* which had laid the Atlantic cable, continued to lay two more trans-Atlantic cables between 1866 and 1869. The *Great Eastern* as a vessel was an astonishing accomplishment. According to the British Broadcasting Corporation, the *Great Eastern* "was 680 feet, with a breadth of 120 feet over the paddle wheels."[6] In addition, the ship was five times larger than any other ship of her time. She had an odd dual configuration which included a conventional propeller along with giant paddle wheels on each side. This greatly aided in her maneuverability, allowing her to rotate at a fixed position by reversing one of the paddle wheels.[7] Modern cable ships also use multiple propulsion systems, with rotating fore and aft propellers. The end result is the same: It allows for extremely accurate maneuverability at sea, which is critical in maintaining the correct tension while both laying and repairing submarine communication cables.

Continued progress was made as numerous cables were laid across the Atlantic including a cable from Brazil to Europe in 1874.[8] Cyrus Field's persistence and determination had set in motion a communication revolution, which continues today as the Internet now links the continents through undersea fiber optic cables and satellite technology. Field, at the age of 47, reflected on the achievement in a speech that he gave to the New York Chamber of Commerce on November 15, 1866. In that speech, Field cited the socio-cultural ties between

America and England, which were further bonded through instant telegraphic communication:

> America with all her greatness has come out of the loins of England, and though there have sometimes been family quarrels, still in our hearts there is a yearning for our old home, the land of our fathers; and he is an enemy of his country and of the human race, who would stir up strife between two nations that are one in race, in language and in religion.[9]

In 1870, only four years after his successful completion of the Atlantic cable, Cyrus W. Field petitioned the United States Congress to lay a telegraph cable across the Pacific Ocean. The story was covered in the Hawaiian Islands newspaper, *The Pacific Commercial Advertiser (PCA)*. Field proposed a route which went from the west coast of the United States to Hawai'i and on to Japan and China.[10] Cyrus Field was a true visionary and entrepreneur who had proven himself as a leader by completing the Atlantic cable project. Field's comments of 1870 helped to mark the destiny of the Hawaiian Islands. The course was set for a second communication revolution to breach the shoreline of Hawai'i, even though it took 33 years for the vision to be transformed into reality.

The first communication revolution in Hawai'i began in 1820, when Protestant missionaries converted the Hawaiian language to a written form and taught the people to read. In 1870, when Field made his comments about the Pacific cable, the Kingdom of Hawai'i was one of the most literate nations on earth with a 90 percent literacy rate. There was also a thriving indigenous Hawaiian press in place which reached its maximum influence in the 1890's. Hawaiian nationalist newsmen Robert Wilcox and John Bush were in favor of the Pacific cable because they saw the benefits of expanded newsgathering, and more efficient business communication with the outside world. Henry Whitney, editor of the *Hawaiian Gazette* wrote, "A cable connecting us with the outside world will make a complete revolution of the business methods in this community."[11] What was occurring in Hawai'i at the end of the 19th century was a reflection of the larger trend of American expansion that was simultaneously taking place throughout the Pacific basin.

THE GLOBAL TELEGRAPHIC COMMUNICATION RACE

After the success of the initial trans-Atlantic cable and numerous others that began to tie Europe with the Americas, steady progress began to span the globe linking other continents by common nationalistic ties.[12] In the midst of this worldwide communication revolution, Great Britain desired to link itself with its former English colonies and allies around the globe. The independent child of England, the United States, also desired to link itself with foreign nations; such communication would greatly aid continued American economic prosperity. The global telegraphic communication race was on, and the lens of history now shifted to the Pacific Ocean, where tiny islands, some of them uninhabited, suddenly became highly coveted real estate. Hawai'i was now thrust into the center of a global communications race, and under the spotlight of world events.

In 1875, King David Kalākaua negotiated the Reciprocity Treaty between the Kingdom of Hawai'i and the United States. Kalākaua's efforts allowed for unrestricted trade without tariff barriers between the two nations.[13] The greatest export from Hawai'i at the time was sugar, and so the treaty had an immediate impact upon the economic success of the powerful Hawaiian sugar plantations, which mostly were owned by American businessmen living in Hawai'i. It is important to note the long-term effect of the political and economic ties between Hawai'i and the United States which resulted from the Reciprocity Treaty. At the turn of the century, 25 years after the signing of the treaty, the United States, at a clear advantage over Britain, requested the landing of a submarine telegraph cable in Hawai'i.

REUTERS VS. ASSOCIATED PRESS

At the beginning of the 20th century, Hawai'i was regarded as a strategic landing point for telegraphic communication between the Western United States and Asia. Because of this, Hawai'i became the focus of attention of American business people on the West Coast and politicians in Washington, D.C. Prior to the coming of the Pacific cable to Hawai'i, England dominated worldwide telegraphic communication, along with the dissemination of world news. London,

England, was the socio-political center of world news. The British news agency Reuters reigned supreme as the primary vehicle which both gathered and disseminated world events—to the family of nations.

The challenger to Reuters for worldwide news coverage was the American news agency, the Associated Press. The Associated Press already had numerous international news bureaus including correspondents who were located in Japan, the Philippines, and portions of China. Unfortunately, news had to be relayed across European telegraphic connections which passed through Europe and then on to New York. The result was that Reuters, through its headquarters in London, always had the upper hand in scooping any news from Asia. This was due to the fact that Reuters had field reporters in the same locations as the Americans (Associated Press), and all news wire stories from Asia passed through London first, before being relayed to New York. The only chance that the Associated Press had to challenge Reuters's news supremacy in Asia and the Pacific was to secure an alternative route, whereby news could be transmitted directly to New York, bypassing London entirely.

The British were not interested in having their dominance of world news and global communication challenged by the Americans through the completion of an American Pacific telegraph cable. Aware of the intent of the Americans, the British tried unsuccessfully to secure permission to land a cable in Hawai'i. The British were interested in using Hawai'i as a relay point for a British-owned Pacific cable. At the end of the 19th century, the Hawaiian Kingdom was not open to the idea of a British Pacific cable terminating in Hawai'i,[14] since the sovereign nation of Hawai'i did not want to jeopardize the standing Reciprocity Treaty that it had with the United States.[15]

THE BRITISH AND THE AMERICAN PACIFIC CABLE ROUTES

Thus the British were shut out of Hawai'i as a stepping stone for a Pacific cable. The Hawaiian sugar industry experienced over a quarter of a century of prosperity as a direct result of the Reciprocity Treaty. Both Hawai'i's private and public sectors were beneficiaries of the treaty. As a result, the British had to secure a different route across the Pacific Ocean. Ultimately, the British decided to proceed in the following manner:

> . . . from Vancouver to Fanning Island, thence to Suva, in the Fijis, thence to Norfolk Island, and from there it will bifurcate [split into two directions, see Fig. 1] to Southport, Queensland, and to Doubtless Bay, New Zealand."[16]

In contrast, the Americans chose a route which began in San Francisco, proceeded to Hawai'i, continued to the Midway atoll, through Guam, and terminated in the city of Manila, in the Philippines. The total distance was 6,817 nautical miles.[17] The tiny atoll of Midway was uninhabited except for occasional squatters and had little significance until the arrival of the Commercial Pacific Company in 1902. According to F. C. Hadden, an entomologist who studied Midway Island in the 1930's and 40's, "In order to maintain and operate a submarine cable across the Pacific it was necessary to establish a relay station at Midway."[18] In 1902, the Commercial Pacific Cable Com-

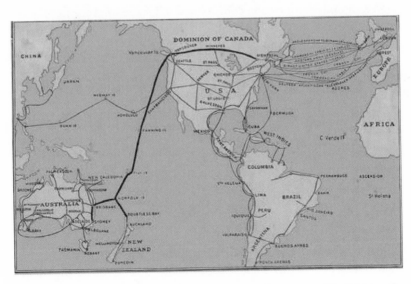

FIG. 1. Map showing the Pacific Cable route and connections, 1903. The British cable is the dark line; the American cable the lighter line in the Pacific Ocean.[19]

pany landed on Midway Island and began to construct facilities. Although the purpose of this essay is not to examine the history of Midway, it is a fascinating aside. As a direct result of the landing of the communication cable on Midway in 1903, the island was transformed from an uninhabited forgotten sandy island, to a cable station complete with thousands of tons of imported soil, imported trees, and living quarters for telegraph operators.

The Completion of the British and American Pacific Cables

As it turned out, the British were able to complete their Pacific cable about seven months prior to the American Pacific cable. The British completed their Pacific cable on December 8, 1902, opening up traffic to the public.[20] An article in the *The Brisbane Courier* reported that the British cable "was open to business yesterday morning when a certain number of messages were ready for dispatch. The business has been carried on satisfactorily and without a hitch."[21]

In December of 1902, after the British had completed their Pacific cable, the American Pacific cable began to lay the final segment from the Philippines to Hawai'i. The American Pacific cable was finally completed in Hawai'i on July 4, 1903, when the cable coming from the Philippines through Midway Atoll was connected to the segment in Hawai'i, which extended to San Francisco. The next day, the *Los Angeles Times* both hailed the event and noticed that its accomplishment was not being sufficiently acknowledged in the continental United States: "No excitement marked the opening of the great wire that is acknowledged to be the grandest triumph in mechanical skill since the completion of the trans-continental railway."[22] While there may not have been a tremendous amount of excitement in Los Angeles in July of 1903, the people of Hawai'i enthusiastically celebrated Cable Day in Hawai'i, earlier that same year, in January, when Hawai'i was connected to San Francisco.

Even though the British completed their Pacific cable about six months prior to the Americans, the ultimate significance of the American cable was that the British monopoly on worldwide news gathering had been broken. This is a crucial point since, according to Canadian sociologist, Robert Pike, and Canadian journalism professor,

Dwayne Winseck, "British companies dominated, maintaining almost complete control over the manufacture and laying of cables and owning two-thirds of the world's cables by 1900."[23] These key undersea cable routes were all controlled by the British company, Cable and Wireless.[24] Prior to the completion of the American Pacific cable, news,

> . . . had to travel across the Atlantic to the Far East via Cape Town and the Indian Ocean, or via London to Russia, then across the Russian landline to Vladivostock, then by submarine cable to Japan and the Philippines"[25]

The completion of the American Pacific cable was profound in that it forever changed the worldwide dominance of British news gathering and reporting.

THE AMERICAN PACIFIC CABLE: A SHIFT IN WORLDWIDE NEWSGATHERING

In a revealing article written in September of 1904, in *The New York Times,* the press commented on the shifting locus of world news gathering, from England to the United States, as a direct result of the American Pacific cable:

> . . . since the laying of the Pacific cable, a great change has been observable in the news distribution of the world. New York is rapidly becoming, and in many ways has already become, the world's news center.[26]

The article goes on to describe how prior to the Pacific cable the primary source of world news was the British news agency Reuters:

> In former times—in fact, in times so recent that the word 'former' hardly seems the proper word to use—news from the Far East was sent from Asia to Europe by Reuter's Agency. Reuter supplied it to the Associated Press, which cabled it across the water for American use. Now all that is reversed. The Eastern news is sent across the Pacific to the Associated Press, which furnishes it to Reuter's over the Atlantic cable for European use. The centre of Far Eastern news, for the supply of the world, has shifted from London to New York.[27]

Under the prior system, which was used by the British news agency
Reuters, there were a total of 12 relay stations across Asia. This slowed
down the transmission of the news, since each message had to be read
and then retransmitted. With the advent of the new system provided
by the American Pacific cable, news could reach London more
quickly than it could under the old system. In an earlier article that
ran in March of 1904, *The Los Angeles Times,* stated similar sentiments
about the diminishing dominance of the British press agency Reuters,
in comparison with its American competitor, the Associated Press:

> Under the old system the British capital practically became the clear-
> inghouse for news from the extreme East. The British papers and
> those in other European capitals, as well, not only had time to receive
> extensive news dispatches and get them into print where only the
> briefest account of some Far Eastern event appeared in the American
> papers . . . This has all been reversed by the Pacific cable, which ends
> in Manila, where the Associated Press has a well organized and fully-
> equipped bureau.[28]

The Pacific Cable Reaches Hawai'i—A Timeline

Two pivotal events occurred in Hawai'i which paved the way for the
American Pacific cable to come to the Islands. First, the transfer of
Hawaiian sovereignty to the United States took place in August of
1898, under President McKinley. And second, the passage of the
Organic Act, by the United States Congress on April 30, 1900, made
Hawai'i a territory of the United States.[29] In 1898, the United States
won the Spanish-American War and gained control of the Philippines. Congress was therefore interested in establishing a direct communication link to the Philippines. In April of 1900, an article
appeared in the *PCA* stating that the United States Congress would
finance a Pacific cable between San Francisco and Honolulu,
Hawai'i.[30] Even though the Organic Act did not actually go into effect
until June 14, 1900, Congress suddenly seemed quite willing to fund
the Pacific cable project. For both American citizens and Hawai'i's
merchants there was great interest in being connected to San Francisco and the continental U.S.

It is interesting to note that in 1870, the first article in the *PCA* regarding the Pacific cable appeared on page two of the paper. It was not until April of 1900, thirty years later, that the topic was presented on the first page of the same newspaper. That article covered congressional financing for the Pacific cable project.[31] Communication scholars refer to this as agenda setting, when a story is moved up in both frequency and prominence as it is presented to the public.[32]

The title of an April of 1900 article in the *PCA* was, "Hawaii to Get a Cable—Three Million Dollars Appropriated."[33] The article stated that the United States Congress had passed an appropriation bill to provide funding for the Pacific cable. Perhaps the editor of the *PCA* felt that the positive editorials regarding the Pacific Cable that had been written over a 30 year time span were about to become a reality, and thus decided to place the article on the front page. Secondly, the coming of the cable meant more timely and accurate domestic and world news coverage in the *PCA*. Certainly the editor and publisher would have been aware of the fact that the success of the Pacific cable project could have a direct positive economic impact upon the newspaper and Hawai'i's merchants.

What follows is a brief timeline of the Pacific cable. It is important to keep the following points in mind when reading it. First, the idea of a Pacific cable was proposed to the United States Congress as early as 1870 by Cyrus Field and others. Second, lawmakers in Washington never considered Hawai'i as the ultimate destination of the Pacific cable. Hawai'i was in fact a stepping stone across the Pacific, strategically necessary in order to circumnavigate the world with a submarine telegraph cable. This same opinion was mirrored by the editor of the *PCA*, in 1878. Third, there was a need for local telegraphic communication between the islands of Hawai'i. Communication between the islands was established through undersea telegraph cables completed in August 1889, four years before the arrival of the Pacific cable from San Francisco.[34]

Pacific Cable Time Line

May 1870   A petition is made to the U.S. Congress by Cyrus W. Field to lay 8,500 nautical miles of undersea cable in the Pacific Ocean.[35, 36]

Sep. 1889   The Pacific Cable company is formed, with the objective of laying a cable to Hawai'i, and continuing on to Manila.[37]

Apr. 1900   The U.S. Senate appropriates $3 million for the construction of a Pacific cable from San Francisco to Honolulu.[38]

Sep. 1901   The *New York Times* reports the incorporation of the Commercial Pacific Company, in Albany, New York. The Pacific cable will establish a new link to both China and Japan, by way of existing cables in the Philippines. The new cable route to China should reduce cable rates 30 to 60 percent.[39]

June 1902   The Pacific cable lands in Waikīkī, at Sans Souci Beach. The site was chosen due to an opening in the offshore reef.[40]

Jan 2, 1903   January 2, 1903 is proclaimed Cable Day in Hawai'i in celebration of the completion of the Pacific cable.[41] Greetings are sent to President Roosevelt from Henry E. Cooper, the secretary of Hawai'i. The merchants of San Francisco send greetings to Hawai'i merchants.[42]

Jan. 3, 1903 The first news dispatches are sent over the Pacific cable, to Hawai'i by the Associated Press. One story reports that Marconi successfully completed the first radio transmission from the United States (Massachusetts) to Italy.[43]

July 5, 1903 On July 5, 1903, one day after the Manila cable was spliced into the Pacific cable in Hawai'i, a message sent from New York takes nine minutes to go around the world. President Roosevelt sends his greetings to the people of the Philippines.[44]

After the completion of the Pacific cable, the frequency of articles relating to the cable began to diminish. The continuing impact of the Pacific cable was seen on the front page of Hawaiian newspapers, such as the *PCA* and *Hawaiian Star,* as current news (less than 24 hours old) from Europe, the Americas, Asia, and other parts of the world was reported in detail.[45] The people of Hawai'i, who were accustomed to reading world news that was two to three weeks old, suddenly became as informed about world events, as the citizens of Los Angeles and New York.

The significance of the advent of the Pacific cable to the people of

Hawai'i was astounding. Hawai'i is the most isolated group of islands on the face of the earth. Located in the center of the Pacific Ocean, the Hawaiian archipelago is more than 2000 miles from any major land mass, by any compass point. It was not until January 18, 1778 that the Western world became aware of the Hawaiian Islands, when the British explorer Captain James Cooke sighted the islands of O'ahu and Kaua'i.[46] Prior to the arrival of Cooke, news between Hawai'i and the rest of Polynesia traveled in long ocean passages by Polynesian voyaging canoes. Only 125 years after Cook's arrival in Hawai'i, the speed in which news would travel to and from Hawai'i to the rest of the world would be transformed from months to a few seconds.

CABLE DAY IN HAWAI'I

Cable Day was celebrated with much anticipation and enthusiasm on January 2, 1903, on the grounds of the executive building in Honolulu, with a celebration ball in the evening. The event was so significant that many of the merchants of Honolulu were expected to close their places of business after midday in order to join in the celebration, which was scheduled for two o'clock in the afternoon. One of the anticipated events was the receipt of a message from the President of the United States, which would be signaled by a 100-gun salute. Music by the Royal Hawaiian band was provided between numerous speeches throughout the afternoon. Henry Berger, the bandmaster composed the "The Pacific Cable March" and dedicated its performance to John Mackay, the president of the Commercial Pacific Company, which completed the Pacific cable project.[47] After sunset, there was a fireworks display from downtown Honolulu, which continued for an hour and a half.

The headlines in the *PCA* on Cable Day read: "Cable Day Will Be Celebrated with a Mass Meeting and Ball - Holiday Maybe declared in All Lines of Business and the Merry-Making continued during the Remainder of the Week."[48] Sadly, John Mackay, the founder of the Commercial Pacific Company, passed away before the Pacific cable was completed. His son Clarence, who was also involved in the project, was sent the following message by Henry E. Cooper, the Secretary of Hawai'i:

> Mr. Clarence H. Mackay, President Commercial Pacific Cable Company, N.Y. We send this token of our high appreciation of the completion of the great enterprise undertaken by your company on laying a telegraph cable from the Coast of California to these Islands. Mingled with our joy is a feeling of deep regret that John W. Mackay did not live to see the completion of his project and we assure you that his name will ever be cherished in fond remembrance by our people.[49]

The final chapter in the story of the completion of the Pacific cable occurred later in 1903. On the afternoon of July 4, 1903, at 5:08 PM, Honolulu was connected to the Pacific cable from Midway Island, which extended east to the Philippines and China. On that day, the Pacific cable commenced full operation between Asia and Washington, D.C. A greeting was sent from the President of the United States to the American Governor, William Howard Taft in the Philippines: "I open the American Pacific Cable with greetings to you and the people of the Philippines. [signed] Theodore Roosevelt."[50] William Taft served as the governor of the Philippines until late in 1903 when he returned to Washington, D.C. Taft was elected president of the United States in 1908.[51] Clarke noted that one newspaper editor hailed the Pacific cable as the "Girdle Round the Earth."[52] On July 5, 1903, the *PCA* ran a number of front page articles covering the extension of the Pacific Cable from Hawai'i to the Philippines:

> At just eight minutes past five o'clock last evening communication was opened with Midway Island from the Honolulu end of the cable and the last link in the great American cable was complete. Half an hour afterwards the cable was flashing back and forth messages between Oyster Bay and Manila, via San Francisco, Honolulu. Midway and Guam, and *President Roosevelt's desire to use the cable on the Forth of July had been gratified* [original emphasis].[53]

Perhaps it was destiny; perhaps it was one of those moments in history when technology, politics, and culture all seem to converge. It was President Roosevelt's desire to open the Pacific cable on the 4th of July—and undoubtedly Roosevelt was aware of the great symbolism that it represented. America had gained its political independence from England many years prior, but with the completion of the Pacific cable, America became independent from England once again—this time in news gathering, journalistic thought, and the framing of world events. When a nation controls its news sources, and in turn is able to disseminate that news to the rest of the world, it assumes a new position of both prominence and responsibility, in comparison with other nations that are primarily consumers of news and information.

CONCLUSION

The history of the Pacific cable is significant in that it entails multiple sub-plots. The balance between two world press organizations, the extension of political and economic trade zones between nations, the annexation of Hawai'i, which provided and continues to provide, strategic communication and military positioning for the United States in the Pacific basin, are all topics for future research. In this essay, I have recounted the story from the American perspective with a particular emphasis upon Hawai'i. The story could have been told from the British perspective as well. The technological achievement of the British cable was no less significant than that of its American counterpart. I have focused on the American perspective however, which casts light on the shift of world communication flow as it moved from the once dominant British news agency Reuters to its American competitor, the Associated Press.

There are a variety of areas for further research. Additional research could be done from a sociological and communication perspective, considering how the effects of the rapid change of technology impacted Native Hawaiians. The impact upon the Hawai'i mercantile industry as a direct result of the Pacific cable could also be investigated. Finally, the Commercial Pacific Company could be further researched, including its impact upon the islands of Midway, Guam, and the Philippines.

In 1903, the strategically situated islands of Hawai'i were thrust into the middle of a global socio-political communication transformation. The Pacific cable represents the shattering of age-old space and time barriers. The cable that girdled the earth launched a communication revolution that continues to this day, in various manifestations of undersea fiber optic cables, communication satellites, and broadcast technology. It is interesting to point out that at this writing there is a permanent undersea cable repair vessel stationed in Honolulu Harbor owned by the Tyco Corporation. The ship is on call year-round to repair telecommunications cables anywhere in the Pacific Ocean.

Human history seems to demonstrate that certain cultures strive for technological dominance in order to extend their influence around the world. Most modern communication technologies find their roots in telegraphy. Prior to the 20th century, wars had been fought for geographical sovereignty. The example of the Pacific cable demonstrates that the future may continue to be a battleground for technological communication supremacy and access to information. These are bloodless battles, as seen in the example of the Pacific cable. Yet, similar battles persist to this day in the field of communication. Multi-national corporations compete daily on a global scale for dominance in the areas of satellite distribution of news and information, undersea fiber optic cable access and bandwidth, land-based telecommunications networks, and cellular transmission frequencies.[54]

Notes

[1] "Cyrus West Field." *Microsoft Encarta Reference Library* 2002. CD-ROM. Redmond: Microsoft (2001).

[2] Joseph R. Dominick, *The Dynamics of Mass Communication—Media in the Digital Age,* 7th ed. (Boston: McGraw Hill, 2002) 65.

[3] Arthur C. Clarke, *Voice Across The Sea,* revised ed. (New York: Harper & Row, Publishers, Inc., 1974) 36, 80.

[4] Clarke, *Voice Across The Sea* 99.

[5] Clarke, *Voice Across The Sea* 13.

[6] Simon Winchcombe, "The 'Great Eastern'," *bbc.co.uk,* Dec. 28, 2004. <http:// www.bbc.co.uk/history/society_culture/industrialisation/seven_wonders_ gallery_04.shtml>

[7] Clarke, *Voice Across The Sea* 78–79.

[8] Clarke, *Voice Across The Sea* 192.

[9] Clarke, *Voice Across The Sea* 99.

[10] "Pacific Telegraph," *PCA,* May 14, 1870:2.

[11] Chapin, Helen G. *Shaping History—The Role of Newspapers in Hawai'i* (Honolulu: U of Hawaii P, 1996) 103–104, 117.

[12] "History of the Atlantic Cable & Submarine Telegraphy," *FTL Design,* August 20, 2004 <http://atlantic-cable.com/Cables/CableTimeLine/index1850 .htm>

[13] Ralph S. Kuykendall and A. Grove Day. *Hawaii: A History From Polynesian King-dom to American State,* revised ed. (Englewood Cliffs: Prentice-Hall, 1976) 161.

[14] Phillip E. Koerper, "Cable Imbroglio in the Pacific: Great Britain, the United States and Hawaii," *HJH,* 9 (1975) 114.

[15] Hugh Craig, "Hawaiian Cable," *Overland Monthly,* XXV (1895) 654.

[16] "Opening of the Pacific Cable," *The Brisbane Courier,* Dec. 9, 1902:4.

[17] "Plans of the Cable Company," *PCA,* Jul. 1, 1902:10.

[18] F.C. Hadden, *The Hawaiian Planters' Record,* XLV, no. 3 (1941) 6.

[19] "Pacific Cable," *Cable and Wireless A History,* Dec. 28, 2004. <http://www.cwhistory.com/history/html/Pacific1.html>.

[20] "Pacific Cable," *Cable and Wireless A History,* Dec. 28, 2004 <http://www.cwhistory.com/history/html/Pacific1.html>

[21] "Opening of the Pacific Cable," *The Brisbane Courier,* Dec. 9, 1902:4.

[22] "Distance Annihilated—Mackay's Dream Realized," *The Los Angeles Times,* Jul. 5, 1903:1.

[23] Robert Pike and Dwayne Winseck, "The Politics of Global Media Reform, 1907–23," *Media Culture & Society,* 26, no. 5, (2004) 3–4.

[24] "Cable and Wireless and the British Empire," *Cable and Wireless A History,* Aug. 20, 2004 <http://www.cwhistory.com/history/html/CWEmpire.html>

[25] "Commercial Pacific Cable Company" *The Free Dictionary,* Aug. 20, 2004 <http://encyclopedia.thefreedictionary.com/Commercial+Pacific+Cable+Company>

[26] "New York is Now the News Centre of the World," *The New York Times,* Sept. 25, 1904:33.

[27] *The New York Times,* Sept. 25, 1904:33.

[28] "The Pacific Cable a Godsend," *The Los Angeles Times,* Mar. 6, 1904: E11.

[29] Kuykendall and Day, *Hawaii a History* 194.

[30] "Hawaii to Get a Cable—Three Million Dollars Appropriated." *PCA,* Apr. 24, 1900:1.

[31] *PCA,* Apr. 24, 1900.

[32] Dominick, *The Dynamics of Mass Communication* 492.

[33] *PCA,* Apr. 24, 1900.

[34] "News Summary," *PCA,* Aug. 24, 1889:2.

[35] This writer would like to acknowledge columnist Bob Krauss of *The Honolulu Advertiser,* who graciously allowed me to use his personal index in order to research articles in the *PCA* and *Hawaiian Star* related to the Pacific cable.

[36] "Pacific Telegraph," *PCA,* May 14, 1870:2.

[37] "The Pacific Cable Company," *PCA,* Sep. 4, 1889:2.

[38] *PCA,* Apr. 24, 1900.

[39] "A Submarine Cable to the Philippines," *The New York Times,* Sep. 24, 1901:7.

[40] "Cable to Land at Sans Souci," *PCA,* Jun. 26, 1902:1.

[41] "Cable Day will be Celebrated with a Mass Meeting and Ball," *PCA,* Jan. 2, 1903:1.

[42] "Hawaii Exchanges Greetings With The World Over the Pacific Cable," *Hawaiian Star,* Jan. 2, 1903:1.

43 "First Cable News Report to Hawaii," *Hawaiian Star*, Jan. 3, 1903:1.

44 "The President Sends the First Cable Message," *PCA*, Jul. 5, 1903:1.

45 Chapin, *Shaping History* 117.

46 Kuykendall and Day, *Hawai'i a History* 14.

47 "Berger Gives his Cable March," *PCA*, Dec. 31, 1902:1.

48 *PCA*, Jan. 2, 1903.

49 *PCA*, Jan. 2, 1903.

50 *PCA*, July 5, 1903.

51 "William Howard Taft," *Microsoft Encarta Reference Library 2002*. CD-ROM. Redmond: Microsoft (2001).

52 Clarke, *Voice Across The Sea* 102.

53 "Pacific Cable completed to the Far East—Last Link in the All-American Line Completed at Honolulu Yesterday," *PCA*, 5 Jul. 1903:1.

54 Erik P. Bucy, *Living in the Information Age: A New Media Reader*. 2nd ed. (Belmont: Wadsworth Thomson Learning, 2005) 94–95.

BRIAN IRELAND

Remembering and Forgetting at The Waikīkī
War Memorial Park and Natatorium

ON THE WESTERN SLOPE of Diamond Head, commanding a majestic view west towards Waikīkī, Honolulu, and further towards Pearl Harbor, there once stood a Native Hawaiian structure known as Papaʻenaʻena Heiau. Clearly visible from nearby Waikīkī village, the *heiau* or place of worship, measured 130 feet in length and 70 feet in width. It consisted of a *mana* (supernatural or divine power) house approximately 50 feet long; an oven house *(hale umu);* a drum house; a *waiea* or spiritual house; an *anuʻu* or tower; a *lele* (altar) and twelve large images. The *heiau* was bordered by a rectangular wooden fence approximately six to eight feet tall with an eight-foot wide base, which narrowed to three feet at its apex. On the western side of the *heiau* there were three small terraces, on the highest one of which were planted five *kou* trees at regular distances from each other. The *heiau* was the center point of an area of land considered sacred or spiritual to Native Hawaiians, which may have stretched across what is now Kapiʻolani Park as far as to the Kupalaha *heiau* situated near the present-day intersection of Kalākaua and Monsarrat Avenues.

It is likely that the *heiau* was built in 1783 by Kahekili, the *mōʻī* or ruler of Maui, as part of a victory celebration following Kahekili's conquest of Oʻahu. After King Kamehameha's victory at the Battle of

Brian Ireland was born in Belfast, Northern Ireland, and attended the University of Ulster where he earned a BA in Humanities and an MA in American Studies. He lived in Hawaiʻi for five years while he was enrolled in the doctoral program in American Studies at the University of Hawaiʻi. He graduated in December 2004 and currently lives in England.

The Hawaiian Journal of History, vol. 39 (2005)

the Pali in 1895, Kamehameha ordered the sacrifice of the defeated *aliʻi* (chiefs) of Oʻahu at Papaʻenaʻena Heiau. The *heiau* was probably used for sacrificial or sacred purposes for 35 years. However, following the death of Kamehameha and the subsequent diminishment in status and practice of Hawaiian religious beliefs, the *heiau* was leveled along with many of the other traditional religious *heiau* and monuments. Its ruins lay relatively undisturbed until the 1850s when the stones that comprised the *heiau* were carted off to build roads in Waikīkī and walls at Queen Emma's estate.[1]

In sharp contrast to Papaʻenaʻena Heiau, and nine other sacred structures that once stood in and around Kapiʻolani Park, there now stands an incongruous *beaux-arts*-style, neoclassical memorial, another *place de memoire,* called The Waikīkī War Memorial Park and Natatorium, which opened in 1927. Although it has fallen into disrepair, in its prime the memorial was an impressive structure. The swimming pool was over 100 meters long, twice the size of an Olympic pool, the *mauka* (mountain-facing) wall was composed of an arch at least 25 feet high, flanked by two 12-foot arches each topped with four large eagle sculptures. Approximately 9,800 of Hawaiʻi's citizens served in the U.S. armed forces after America's entry into World War I in 1917 and the names of 101 of those who died are inscribed on a plaque attached to the "Honolulu Stone" situated *mauka* of the Natatorium and unveiled in 1931.[2]

There is, however, some considerable doubt as to the veracity of those casualty figures. According to statistician Robert Schmitt, of the 9,800 Hawaiʻi residents who served in World War I,

> 102 died—14 overseas during the war, 61 in Hawaiʻi or North America or after the armistice, and 27 in unknown circumstances. Twenty-two of the 102 recorded deaths occurred among Island residents serving with the British. Actual battle deaths of persons in the U.S. armed forces whose preservice residence was Hawaiʻi numbered six: seven others were wounded.[3]

These figures are not entirely correct: 101 names are listed on the memorial not 102; eight soldiers were "actual battle deaths," not six. Nevertheless, these figures raise questions about the purpose of the memorial. Since only eight Hawaiʻi residents died by enemy action under the U.S. flag—the others having died of other causes before and after the war's end—the Memorial obviously exaggerates the death toll, thus magnifying the sacrifices made by "Hawai'i's sons."

Memorials are an important way of remembering. They are not just part of the past; they help shape attitudes in the present and thus act as a guide for the future. Professor Charles Griswold, chair of the philosophy department at Boston University, argues that memorials are "a species of pedagogy" that seeks to instruct posterity about the past and, in so doing, necessarily reaches a decision about what is worth recovering.[4] In *Lies Across America,* sociologist James Loewen asks, "Where . . . do Americans learn about the past?" He argues persuasively that it is "surely most of all from the landscape."[5] One recurring theme of Loewen's analysis of American memorials is their importance as a political statement. Although many memorials outwardly project discourses of "remembering" or "honoring," they may also have covert and hidden meanings. Rather than simply paying tribute to the dead, the Waikīkī War Memorial actually promotes militarism. It is a triumphalist monument to the glory of war, which dishonors the dead by masking the horror of mechanized trench warfare behind a pretty façade and noble but misleading words.

Furthermore, when one adds the memorial's architectural style, which is so incompatible with its Pacific island setting, to the discrepancy between actual casualty figures and those listed by the memorial, it becomes clear that the Waikīkī War Memorial was built also to further the "100% Americanism" of Hawai'i. The memorial acted as a channel through which Hawai'i's American settler community could express its nationalistic pride. Patriotic groups used it to further the cause of Americanism and to glorify war as a noble and heroic sacrificial act. Conveniently forgotten in this narrative, however, are the soldiers actually named on the memorial. Details of why they enlisted, and how and where they died, are missing from the memorial's dedication. This paper will address how and why these soldiers are remembered by the memorial and evaluate if the extant structure is either the best or only way to remember their deaths.

Origin of the War Memorial

Local citizens formed a War Memorial Committee in 1918 in response to the promptings of a group called the Daughters and Sons of Hawaiian Warriors. There were a number of interested parties involved including the Daughters of Hawaii, the Rotary Club, the Outdoor Circle, the Pan-Pacific Union, Central YMCA, St. Andrew's Cathedral, Hawaiian Women's Guild, Kamehameha Alumni Association, Hawaiian Civic Club, Order of Kamehameha, Longshoremen's Mutual Aid Association, Knights of Pythias, and the Ad Club. Notable interested individuals included former territorial Attorney General W.O. Smith and territorial tax collector Colonel Howard Hathaway.[6] As historian Kirk Savage has noted, they were following a relatively new trend in monument building that began in the 19th century:

> In the expansive era of the nineteenth century, monuments were not bestowed by the state on the citizenry, or at least they weren't supposed to be. . . What gave monuments their particular appeal in an era of rising nationalism was their claim to speak for 'the people'. . . Most monuments therefore originated not as official projects of the state but as volunteer enterprises sponsored by associations of 'public-spirited' citizens and funded by individual donations. These voluntary associations often had direct links to officialdom, but they received legitimacy only by manufacturing popular enthusiasm (and money) for the project.[7]

The first designs for the memorial had no connection whatsoever to the extant construction. In fact, there was considerable support at one stage for either a memorial designed by architect Roger Noble Burnham[8] to be erected in Palace Square close to the statue of King Kamehameha, or for a Memorial Hall.[9] Burnham suggested that his design would "symboliz[e] Hawaii's contribution to Liberty. It consists of three figures, the central one typifying Liberty while beneath are a Hawaiian warrior and a Hawaiian maiden. The warrior offers his spear while the maiden extends in outstretched hands a lei."[10] This design would feature a rostrum enclosed on three sides by a wall. Unlike the extant memorial, Burnham wanted to honor both the military and Hawai'i's civilian population, which had contributed to the war by buying bonds and helping the Red Cross. One wall, therefore, would have inscriptions dedicated to Hawai'i's civilian population and the other walls would depict military activities.

Burnham's modest design was championed by Mrs. Walter (Alice) Macfarlane. She was born Alice Kamokila Campbell, daughter of

wealthy landowner James Campbell and Abigail Kuaihelani Maipine-
pine, who was from a mixed Native Hawaiian and *haole* (Caucasian)
family from Lahaina, Maui. When James Campbell died in 1900,
his estate was held in trust for his wife and daughters. Alice Macfarlane, who in later years would become a voice against statehood for
Hawai'i, was a respected and influential woman. She opposed notions
of a memorial hall, an auditorium, or civic center as she was concerned that a "memorial hall would commercialize the memory of the
men who had paid the supreme sacrifice." Supporters of the memorial hall design, however, believed that it would become a center of
civic life where "people could go and hear enlightening talks and
entertaining music."[11] One other suggestion at this time, by the
Chamber of Commerce, was for the memorial either to be placed in
a prominent position at the entrance to Honolulu Harbor or on Sand
Island, where "it would be the first thing that would greet the arriving traveler, and the last thing he would see."[12] These early deliberations over the placement of the monument, and its design as either
a traditional monument or as a usable, "living" structure, would characterize the nature of the debate for many months.

In early February 1919, further designs were considered; Burnham
exhibited sketches of a design that incorporated his original sculpture
into a larger design that also included a memorial hall.[13] The cost of
this project would be somewhere in the region of $750,000,[14] the
equivalent today of $7,674,333.33.[15] Another suggestion at this point
was for a very practical memorial that would comprise one new wing
of the Queen's Hospital.[16] Yet another design by T.H. Ripley & Davis
architects envisaged an impressive memorial hall surrounded by large
Grecian columns, which would feature a large rotunda filled with
"statuary tablets."[17]

On March 24, 1919 it was reported in the *Pacific Commercial Advertiser* that the War Memorial Committee was finally going to announce
that a general design had been agreed upon for a monument and
memorial hall to be situated on a "strip of land along Punchbowl
Street, between King and Queen Streets." This was to be the majority
report's proposal. A dissenting minority report, led by Alice Macfarlane, questioned the cost of the proposed memorial and suggested
once again that it be limited solely to a monument without the additional expense of a memorial hall. Macfarlane stated that the monu-

ment should "emphasize the spiritual side of victory, rather than . . . show the wealth of the community."[18] The next day, however, the *Advertiser* reported that the memorial would not be situated on Punchbowl and that proposals had been made to approach the Irwin Estate to buy property at Kapiʻolani Park instead. For some time John Guild, chairman of the Beach Park Memorial Committee, had been in correspondence with the Irwin Estate about buying the property for use as a Pan-Pacific Peace Palace. However, at the War Memorial Committee meeting, Guild suggested that the land be purchased for a war memorial park instead. It seems this was a compromise to ease the tensions raised between those responsible for the majority and minority reports.

The site of the memorial had now been resolved but the debate over its design had not. Guild's letter to the Legislature envisaged a memorial park with an "arch or statue" as opposed to a memorial hall.[19] Perhaps it was believed that the open spaces of the park would provide a natural amphitheatre and that a hall was no longer appropriate. Or perhaps there was no way to overcome the objections of Mrs. Macfarlane and still maintain a consensus. In any event, Guild was insistent that the memorial plans be given due consideration and that they should not rush into accepting a design. He worried that,

> We do not want to erect a monument which shall at some future date be looked upon as a thing of bad taste. Too many of the soldier's [sic] Monuments of the past have been of this character. I believe the memorial should take a form that will express the spirit of Hawaii and be in harmony with the wonderful tropical surroundings of the proposed site.[20]

Early deliberations over the erection, placement, and design of the memorial took place almost entirely within the American civilian community in Hawaiʻi. However, in August of 1919 the newly-formed American Legion entered the fray.[21] Colonel Theodore Roosevelt (son of the ex-president) and other senior officers created the American Legion in France to direct disaffected soldiers away from the lure of socialism. Journalist and author Marcus Duffield states, "The American General Staff was seriously concerned about how to keep up morale. American bankers and business men [sic] who visited Europe returned filled with anxiety. What would be the attitude of returning troops?"[22] By early 1921, the Hawai'i branch of the American Legion had wrested control of the memorial scheme out of the hands of the citizens' War Memorial Committee. There is no suggestion of conflict or dispute in the historical record—a *Paradise of the Pacific* editorial noted simply that the "American Legion . . . has charge of the projected War Memorial"—but it would have taken a very brave or foolish citizen indeed to stand up to military veterans who had so very comprehensively wrapped themselves in the U.S. flag.[23]

Despite many different ideas as to what design would constitute a fitting memorial and where it should be situated, by early 1921 the American Legion's views held total sway. For example, CJS Group Architects note in their *Final Historical Background Report* on the memorial, that, "This concept of having a memorial [i.e. one that included a swimming pool] was originally initiated by the American Legion Chapter of Hawai'i."[24] This despite the fact that the Legion was not involved, in fact did not even exist, when some of Hawai'i's citizens were submitting plans and raising interest and money for the memorial in 1918. Of course, arguments over control of projects such as memorials are not unusual: The Daughters and Sons of Hawaiian Warriors were complaining as early as January 1919 that "they proposed the memorial first and then later on another element steps in and crowds them."[25]

However, even given that expected bickering, the question still remains, why did such a new and untried organization quickly gain such a hold over the Memorial project? Perhaps the answer can be seen in the preamble to the American Legion's constitution, in which the Legion pledges not only to "preserve the memories and incidents of our associations in the Great War" but also to "foster and perpetuate a one hundred percent Americanism."[26] Coming so soon after the end of a devastating world war in which 116,000 Americans were killed,[27] it is hardly a surprise that a veterans' group would quickly attain a position of influence. However, what made the Legion so powerful was that its aims coincided with those connected to the powerful U.S. military presence in Hawai'i, with some of the *haole* elite who were pushing for statehood, and with others who did not want statehood but did want to make Hawai'i less alien to their American sensibilities.

At the Memorial Park's formal dedication on Armistice Day,

November 11, 1919, Governor James McCarthy symbolically handed over possession of the park to the American Legion whose Honolulu chapter had been formed barely two months earlier. The Legion's chaplain, Father Valentin, read prayers at what the *Advertiser* described as a "semi-military ceremony not without its lessons to present and future generations."[28] Although the Legion now had control over developing the park, it still had not solved the problem of the design of the war memorial itself. In that respect it had made no more progress than the war memorial committees from which it had assumed control. The Legion did, however, ignore all previous designs and schemes and published instead a rough outline of its own proposals:

> . . . an arch or other memorial feature at the shore. To the landward would be an open space under the trees, carefully landscaped and prepared for seats so that memorial exercises, band concerts or other similar events may be held with the arch or monument as the stage and background. To the seaward would be a natatorium, but with its concrete walls rising only high enough above the waterline to keep their tops above the surf. . . By the plan suggested the views along the beach would not be obstructed in any way and yet all the features of other plans, and more, would be preserved.[29]

Unlike Burnham's earlier design, this was to be a memorial dedicated only to the military, with no recognition of the contribution made to the war effort by Hawai'i's civilian population. It is telling that although the Legion was offering prizes for new designs, it had already established what the rough outline of the memorial should be. In fact, its outline is remarkably close to the extant memorial, the only real differences being the incorporation of the arch into the actual natatorium and the omission of the landscaped area on which now stands the Honolulu Stone and plaque.

In 1921, when the Territorial Legislature authorized the appointment of a "Territorial War Memorial Commission" to hold a competition to find an appropriate design for the memorial, Governor McCarthy asked the American Legion to put together the Memorial Committee, effectively handing it total control over the project. Governor McCarthy invited the Legion to submit names for the Memorial Committee and asked Louis Christian Mullgardt to be the Territorial War Memorial Commission's advisory architect.[30] In choosing

Mullgardt, the governor and the American Legion were virtually ensuring that a neoclassical-style *beaux-arts* memorial would be built. All of the architects favored neoclassical designs. For example, Mullgardt designed the Panama-Pacific International Exposition's "Court of the Ages" and "Tower of the Ages." The Territorial War Memorial Commission nominated three architects from the mainland to judge the competition: Ellis F. Lawrence of Portland, Bernard Maybeck of San Francisco and W.R.B. Wilcox of Seattle.[31] All three were practitioners of the neoclassical style of design. Furthermore, the winning design had to conform to Mullgardt's plan for the Memorial Park, in which the war memorial "was to consist of a temple of music, plaza, and collosseum [sic] with swimming basin."[32] It made no real difference, therefore, who actually won the design competition; it had already been decided that a neoclassical *beaux-arts* natatorium and landscaped park would be the outcome.

When the judges arrived in Hawai'i in June 1922 to award the prize, they were met by officials of the American Legion under whose auspices the memorial was to be built. Within a few days the judges awarded the first prize to Lewis Hobart of San Francisco.[33] Between

FIG. 1. Tentative Sketch of Memorial Natatorium proposed by the American Legion, ca. 1919–1922. War Memorial Commission. Hawai'i State Archives.

1922 and 1927, when the Waikīkī War Memorial and Natatorium was finally opened, Hobart's original design, described as a "dream plan" by Maybeck, was twice pared down to stay within the $250,000 budget. The original plan for a natatorium, temple of music, ticket booth, dressing rooms, and some very elaborate friezes, busts, and murals could not be built within the budget, and after attempts to appropriate more money failed, the temple of music became the cost-cutters' main casualty.

HOBART'S FOLLY

Like most *beaux-arts* constructions, the Waikīkī War Memorial Park and Natatorium is grandiose and pompous. The entrance is composed of a grand arch flanked by two pilasters projecting slightly out from the wall (pilasters are rectangular supports resembling a flat column). The top of the arch features typical classical ornamentation —a medallion and frieze topped with a round pediment in the Greek

B-1254-(1 PS/11/25/28)   WAR MEMORIAL NATATORIUM . HONOLULU, T.H.

FIG. 2. The Natatorium, 1928. Hawai'i State Archives.

Revival style. Two large symmetrical eagles on either side flank the medallion. Adjacent to the main entrance arch are two smaller arches, above each of which is a decorative cartouche set into the wall, topped with elaborate cornices. The effect of the entrance is to present a symmetrical façade, an imposition of order, structure, and planning into the natural disordered surroundings of sea, beach, and parkland. In its imperial grandeur, it means to instruct viewers of the benefits of the stability and order that European civilization can provide. Architectural historian William Jordy states "the idea of stability was . . . implicit in the traditionalism of the Beaux-Arts esthetic; in other

FIG. 3. Entrance Arch of the War Memorial, undated. Hawai'i State Archives.

words, its academic point of view which held . . . that the past provided vocabularies of form and compositional themes from which the present should learn."[34]

Memorials can only work as designed when the shared memory of the past is uncontroversial, Historian Kirk Savage points out, for example, that memorials to the American Civil War avoided controversy by memorializing soldiers from both sides but not the disputed causes for which they fought. In the process, these memorial makers erased from their reconstructed history images of slaves and slavery. Conversely, the Vietnam Veterans Memorial remains controversial because its design reflects the arguments over the war it commemorates. American World War I memorials avoided such controversy by narrating that war as a noble cause, a clear-cut fight between good and evil, freedom and despotism—the evil "Hun" verses the freedom-loving, democratic nations of England and the United States.

While comparisons between war memorials dedicated to different wars can be problematic, some use can be made of comparing and contrasting the Vietnam Veterans Memorial in Washington to the Waikīkī War Memorial. It should not be expected, of course, that the Waikīkī War Memorial should in any way resemble the Vietnam Wall: the former is a product of a victorious war with relatively few American casualties (compared to other Allied losses), the latter is a product of a bitterly divisive war that America lost. However, rather than making any comparison between the two memorials inappropriate, those differences in historical context can actually serve to illustrate the functions of war memorials in a society at any given time.

Unlike, the self-reflective Vietnam Veterans War Memorial, the imposing entrance of Hobart's structure has most of its decoration and inscriptions well above eye level, and thus demands that its audience step back, crane their necks and look up to the two American eagles. The Vietnam Veterans Memorial is made with black reflective granite instead of the triumphant white marble or stone of *beaux-arts* monuments. Whereas the façade of the Waikīkī War Memorial demands that viewers remain passive in contemplation of its majesty, onlookers at the Vietnam Veterans Memorial can see themselves reflected in the stone, which seems to mirror the self-reflective mood associated with the "Vietnam Syndrome." The names on the Honolulu Stone plaque are arranged in a rigid and anonymous way: top and center is an eagle holding laurel leaves. Below that there is a five-pointed star in whose center is a circle with the letters "US". Below that on a banner is the legend "FOR GOD AND COUNTRY." Below that is the legend "ROLL OF HONOR" and below that again is the quotation, "DULCE ET DECORUM EST PRO PATRIA MORI." Below that are the words "IN THE SERVICE OF THE UNITED STATES." The names are listed in three columns and split into Army and Navy. Below that, also in three columns, are the names of those who died "IN THE SERVICE OF GREAT BRITAIN."

These categorizations group the soldiers together as if they died in a common cause, and make them anonymous servants to the greater glory of war. Compare that to the Vietnam Veterans Memorial, where the soldiers' names are arranged chronologically by date of death instead of country, rank, or regiment. This has the effect not only of verisimilitude—making it real—but also of presenting a more democratic "people's" memorial rather than a regimented military monument. In order to find a name on the Vietnam Veterans Memorial, relatives of those killed would need to come prepared with a certain amount of historical information about the war, including the date of the death of their loved one. Whereas most war memorials function as designed only if they remain vague about actual details of a war and its causes, in contrast, the Vietnam Veterans Memorial works only when precise historical details are present. Unlike the interactive Vietnam Veterans Memorial, which asks visitors to reflect on the causes of the war and the folly and waste that war entails, the façade of the Waikīkī War Memorial and Natatorium means to inspire awe and respect for Euro-American achievements, to excuse warfare as a legitimate and honorable way of solving disputes, and to glorify the U.S. military and its role in the conflict.

The Waikīkī War Memorial and Natatorium is dedicated to war, not peace. However, it is also dedicated to victory. The memorial contains, for example, three triumphal arches (an entrance arch, flanked by two smaller arches). In a 1919 *Pacific Commercial Advertiser* article, architect C.R. Ripley had warned of the inappropriateness of utilizing such celebratory imagery. Ripley argued, "Surely we want no memorial arches. The watchword of the war has been, 'To make the world safe for democracy.' Where does the victory arch typify that inspiration? We want no memorials to glorify war and victory."[35] Hobart, however, relied heavily on the American Legion's arch-dominated design,[36] thus ensuring that the memorial would be dedicated to vanquishing America's enemies.

University of Kansas architecture professor James Mayo points out, "War memorials to victory are trophies that not only keep us mindful of who won, but also assure us that the war was honorable. God was on the side of the victors, and therefore their cause was righteous."[37] The Waikīkī War Memorial fits neatly into Mayo's analysis of victory monuments: it is made to be "steadfast and solid," of those good materials [that] are practical expressions of permanence." The main design on the *mauka*-facing wall is above head level, a technique, Mayo notes, that "works as a metaphor, since we look 'up' to people we respect."[38] A major theme of this memorial is the sacrifice that Hawai'i and its citizens made for the greater glory of America. Advocating "peace" instead of victory was seen as weakness; war was a rite of passage to manhood transmitted "through inscriptions on war memorials which lauded martial virtues by accompanying the names of the fallen with adjectives such as 'brave' or courageous."[39]

The Waikīkī War Memorial does not make any bold or precise statements about those it commemorates. There are no phrases, for example, like "killed in action" or "killed by enemy fire." Instead, the memorial is coy and evasive about where and why these soldiers died. It utilizes non-specific phrases such as "For God And Country," "Roll Of Honor," *"Dulce Et Decorum Est Pro Patria Mori,"* "In The Service Of Great Britain," and "In The Service Of The United States," all of which could refer to almost any war. Clearly the overall impression the memorial wishes to convey is that the soldiers died for a noble cause, which is why the legend does not linger on any specific reasons for the war, or mention any battles. The effect of this is, as Mayo notes, "facetious," as the high-minded and abstract ideals mentioned "are not grounded in the ugly realities of war."[40] In this respect, the memorial is ahistorical. This narrative is, as historian Paul Fussell points out,

> typical of popular histories of the war written on the adventure-story model: they like to ascribe clear, and usually noble, cause and purpose to accidental or demeaning events. Such histories thus convey to the optimistic and credulous a satisfying, orderly, and even optimistic and

wholesome view of catastrophic occurrences—a fine way to encourage a moralistic, nationalistic, and bellicose politics.[41]

By employing a rhetorical device known as enthymematic argumentation, the memorial gives the impression that 101 persons from Hawai'i died in France—79 died fighting under American arms, and 22 in the British Army. In enthymematic argumentation, the speaker builds an argument with one element removed, leading listeners to fill in the missing piece. Since it provides only limited information, one might assume from reading the text on the Honolulu Stone that all of those who died were killed as a result of enemy action. This is, however, not the case. For example, of the 79 who served in the U.S. armed forces, it can be ascertained that only eight were killed by enemy action—seven in France and one, Private Manuel Ramos, on the way to France, when his troopship was torpedoed in the Atlantic Ocean.[42] The causes of death of the other 71 soldiers and sailors are more mundane than the memorial would have us believe. Thirty-six died of flu and/or pneumonia in the great epidemic that ravaged the world in 1918, five in accidents, one of suicide, two of heart attacks, eight of unknown causes, and 19 of other natural causes including tuberculosis, cancer, appendicitis, meningitis, blood poisoning, peritonitis ulcer, intestinal obstruction, and brain hemorrhage. Eight of the 71 non-combat-related deaths occurred in France: four of those soldiers died of flu, two in accidents, and two of unknown causes.

Whereas the British public knew by the end of the war that the battlefields of Belgium and France were slaughterhouses, an epiphany which led to the disillusioned literary style of the period, Americans, who had suffered far fewer casualties, and had been fighting for only about six months, from March 1918 until the Armistice in November, were still inclined to think of the war as a "noble cause." Historian David Kennedy states, "Almost never in the contemporary American accounts do the themes of wonder and romance give way to those of weariness and resignation, as they do in the British."[43] This desire by Americans, to remember the war as dignified and purposeful is also why Latin was chosen as the language of the most forthright statement on the Waikīkī War Memorial's plaque. Such "'[R]aised,' essentially feudal language," as Fussell calls it, is the language of choice for memorials.[44]

By the end of the war, British writers left behind the "high diction" of 19th-century literary tradition—words and phrases like "steed" instead of "horse," "strife," instead of "warfare," "breast," instead of "chest," and "the red wine of youth," in place of "blood"—and instead described events in a more down-to-earth and realistic way.[45] However, memorials were a different matter: whereas it seemed appropriate, given the high death tolls and brutality of World War I, for writers to change to a more factual and graphic idiom, "high diction" remained the language of monuments and memorials. It seemed somehow inappropriate and disrespectful, given the solid dignified presence of a concrete or marble memorial, to tell the undignified truth about wartime deaths, a truth that would involve grisly descriptions of severed limbs, burst intestines, decapitations, and other bloody injuries. Moreover, if the purpose of the Waikīkī War Memorial was to inspire Native Hawaiian devotion to the greater glory of the state (the United States)—to be, as historian John Bodnar states, "reminded of 'love of country' and their duty to their 'native' land" —it would be self-defeating to remind Hawaiians of the butchery of Flanders.[46]

The purpose of the Waikīkī War Memorial and Natatorium is only superficially a tribute to Hawaiʻi's Great War dead. In fact, the dead were used in death as they were in life, as sacrifices to the gods of war, to militarism, colonialism, and nationalism. This is evident in the memorial's scale and in its deliberately vague and secretive inscription. James Mayo argues that war memorials "represent failure, the failure to prevent war."[47] However, the American Legion and its supporters chose to build a huge neoclassical structure that exaggerates Hawaiʻi's role in the Great War. Given the relatively small number of casualties and minor role played by Hawaiʻi, a more honest memorial would surely have been the small token affair envisaged by Burnharm and championed by Macfarlane.

Conclusion

The Waikīkī War Memorial and Natatorium represents a grand, overstated tribute to the relatively small number of casualties sustained by residents of Hawaiʻi. However, that, of course, is not its true purpose, as is evident in its design and scale. The message that it symbolizes is one of submission to imperial forces and glorification of both war and the American military. This is exemplified by the legend on the Honolulu Stone which reads (in Latin), *"Dulce et decorum est pro patria mori,"* or "it is sweet and noble to die for one's country," from Horace's Odes. This phrase would not only have been familiar to those with a classical education, but also to a wider audience who had read popular war novels. As historian David Kennedy points out, "one of Edith Wharton's characters [in her 1918 book *The Marne*] tearfully meditate[d] on the ancient phrase from Horace: 'dulce et decorum est pro patria mori.'"[48] However, at that time, the more topical and relevant use of that quotation was by British soldier and war poet, Wilfred Owen. His poem entitled *Dulce et decorum* cautions against the very same triumphant patriotism that the Waikīkī War Memorial Park and Natatorium represents:

> My friend, you would not tell with such high zest
> To children ardent for some desperate glory,
> The old Lie: Dulce et decorum est
> Pro patria mori.

Both Hobart and the American Legion probably knew of Owen's poem. Like Siegfried Sassoon, he was well known and widely publicized at that time. They chose, however, to use the quote in its original context—as an obsequious and jingoistic tribute to war.

One-hundred-and-one persons from Hawai'i died during the Great War. Who can know now what their motivations were in enlisting? Certainly for some it was not to defend the United States, as 30 or so of them enlisted with the British Army before the U.S. even entered the war. On July 31, 1918, a military draft was introduced that applied to all residents of the United States between the ages of 21 and 30, whether native born, naturalized, or alien. The draft was expanded in October 1917 to all male residents between the ages of 19 and 40. In total 4,336 of those who registered for the draft were called up to serve in the 1st and 2nd Hawaiian Infantry.[49] Of the 79 non-Navy U.S deaths recorded on the memorial, 40 men served with the 1st or 2nd Hawaiian Infantry. These units were, in effect, the Hawai'i National Guard, federalized and sent to Fort Shafter and Schofield Barracks, or garrison duty to release other more profes-

sional troops for war service. A soldier in these units had little chance
of being sent to France. Many of them worked as laborers in the sugar
plantations and, as scholar Charles Warfield notes, Washington recognized that Hawai'i's sugar was more important than any contributions in terms of manpower that it could make to the war:

> The National Guard had been organized with the idea that it would be
> used only for the defense of the Islands and would never be sent over-
> seas. A large proportion of its ranks was composed of men who were
> indispensable to the sugar industry of the Islands, which had been
> greatly expanded during the war in Europe. If the National Guard of
> Hawaii were mobilized when the United States went to war it would
> seriously cripple the sugar industry.[50]

Twenty-five of the non-Navy soldiers who are named on the memorial enlisted after July 1918, and 36 of the 67 men enlisted in non-
naval forces were attached to the 1st and 2nd Hawaiian Infantry. In
other words, nearly one third of those who died while serving in the
U.S. military may have been unwilling draftees, not volunteers, and
almost one half may have joined the Hawai'i National Guard to avoid
having to go overseas to fight in the World War.[51]

Of the 72,000 residents of Hawai'i registered for the draft as
eligible to fight, 29,000—or 40 percent—were *issei* and *nisei*. Of the
total that actually did serve in the U.S. Armed Forces, 838—approximately nine percent—were of Japanese descent.[52] Since Japan was at
war with Germany at this time, who can say with any certainty that
those from Hawai'i were fighting for either America or for Japan? If
they were fighting for the U.S., like the famous 442nd Regiment of
World War II, how many enlisted to prove their loyalty in an unwrit-
ten test that should never have been enacted? Undoubtedly, those
involved in the advocacy, planning, design, and building of the Waikīkī War Memorial were mostly *haole*. There is little evidence, for
example, of the involvement of Native Hawaiians or Japanese residents of Hawai'i. Indeed, it is ironic that 838 Japanese residents of
Hawai'i volunteered to fight in France yet the American military,
which in 1919 had asked the Hawai'i State Legislature to pass a bill
regulating Japanese language schools, and the American Legion,
which gave that bill its full support, were extremely antagonistic in
both rhetoric and action to Japanese culture in Hawai'i.[53]

Most newspaper accounts of Hawai'i during the Great War paint a picture of a dedicated, patriotic populace, eager to do "its bit" for the war effort. Occasionally, there is some slippage in this narrative. For example, a 1919 *Advertiser* headline complained that, "not enough Hawaiians are on hand at the railroad depot when the mustered-out soldiers arrive there each day from Schofield Barracks to form a real welcoming committee. Representative citizens are in a feeble minority in the crowds." This was in contrast to the U.S. mainland where "every town that has a railroad depot has its crowds on hand when a train comes in and the returning boys are given the biggest kind of welcome."[54]

Author and sociologist Albert Memmi has noted that it is the colonialist's "nation's flag which flies over the monuments" in a colonized country and that the colonialist "never forgets to make a public show of his own virtues, and will argue with vehemence to appear heroic and great."[55] Both of these descriptions aptly fit the Waikīkī War Memorial and Natatorium. It glorifies war and acts to consolidate the American imperialist presence in Hawai'i. Its celebration of the deaths of men for "freedom and democracy" masks the fact that World War I was fought between imperial powers, many of which were governed by unelected monarchies. Historian Jonathan Schell argues, "every political observer or political actor of vision has recognized that if life is to be fully human it must take cognizance of the dead."[56] But what is the proper way to remember the dead of a senseless world war? Should they be used, as the American Legion and others seemed to think, to perpetuate patriotic, pro-militaristic narratives? The architectural folly that is the Waikīkī War Memorial Park and Natatorium should remind us that, instead of glorifying war, nationalism, and militarism, there is no better tribute to those fallen than to remember war's waste and futility.

Notes

[1] See Robert R. Weyeneth, *Kapi'olani Park: A Victorian Landscape of Leisure.* (Honolulu: Dept. of Parks and Recreation, City and County of Honolulu, 1991) 48–52, 62, 67. Also "Heiau found at La Pietra," *HSB*, Feb. 16, 1968: A-8.

[2] Anne Burleigh, "Save the Natatorium," *Hawaii Architect* July 1973: 12–13.

[3] Robert Schmitt, "Hawai'i's War Veterans and Battle Deaths" *HJH* 32 (1998) 171–174.

[4] See Marita Sturken, *Tangled Memories: The Vietnam War, the Aids Epidemic, and the Politics of Remembering*. (Berkeley: U of California P, 1997) 48.

[5] James Loewen, *Lies Across America: What Our Historic Sites Get Wrong* (New York: New Press, 1999) 15.

[6] See Jeannette Murray Peek, *Stepping Into Time: A Guide to Honolulu's Historic Landmarks* (Honolulu: Mutual, 1994) 108; "Memorial Project Takes Real Shape" *PCA*, Feb. 19, 1919: 5; "Pan-Pacific Art Committee to Plan Memorial," *PCA*, Feb. 19, 1919: 4; "Statue Or Memorial Hall Issue Must Be Determined," *PCA*, Jan. 11, 1919: 5; "Proposes Aid for Memorial Funds," *PCA*, Jan. 9, 1919: 1; "Rotary Club To Honor Officials Of Old Republic," *PCA*, Aug. 12, 1919: 6.

[7] Kirk Savage, *Standing Soldiers, Kneeling Slaves: Race, War, and Monument in Nineteenth-Century America* (Princeton UP, 1999) 6.

[8] Burnham was a well-known architect responsible also for the design of the United Spanish War Veterans Memorial (also called The Spirit of '98) erected in 1950 at the Wadsworth Hospital Center, West Los Angeles. Text from the plaque on the memorial reads: "1898—To Those Who Volunteered and Extended the Hand of Liberty to Alien Peoples—1902."

[9] "Proposes Aid For Memorial Funds," *PCA*, Jan. 9, 1919: 1.

[10] "Proposes Aid For Memorial Funds," *PCA*, Jan. 9, 1919: 1.

[11] "Proposes Aid For Memorial Funds," *PCA*, Jan. 9, 1919: 1.

[12] "Promotion Body Talks Memorial," *PCA*, Jan. 15, 1919: 2.

[13] "Mass Meeting To Pass On Memorial," *PCA*, Feb. 12, 1919: 1–2.

[14] "Rotarians Interested In Plans For Memorial For War Dead," *PCA*, Feb. 22, 1919: 5.

[15] Economic History Services: http://www.eh.net/hmit/ppowerusd/

[16] "Mass Meeting To Pass On Memorial," *PCA*, Feb. 12, 1919: 1–2.

[17] "Proposed Memorials For War Heroes Are Widely Discussed," *PCA*, Feb. 15, 1919: 4.

[18] "Final Decision On Memorial Is Expected Today," *PCA*, Mar. 24, 1919: 6.

[19] "Memorial Park Proposal Wins Warm Approval," *PCA*, Mar. 28, 1919: 1.

[20] "Irwin Property Makes Ideal Site For Park As Memorial To Men Of Hawaii Who Served," *PCA*, Mar. 30, 1919: 1.

[21] "Veterans Plan to Launch a Post of Legion Here," *PCA*, Aug. 29, 1919: 1.

[22] Marcus Duffield, *King Legion* (New York: Johnathan Cape & Harrison Smith Inc, 1931) 5.

[23] "A Suggestion," *PP*, Feb. 1, 1921: 3.

[24] CJS Group Architects. *Final Historical Background Report Waikīkī War Memorial Park and Natatorium* (City and County of Honolulu, Dept. of Parks and Recreation, 1985) 2.

[25] "Proposes Aid for Memorial Funds," *PCA*, Jan. 9, 1919: 1.

[26] Thomas A. Rumer, *The American Legion: An Official History 1919–1989* (New York: M. Evans & Co, 1990) intro.

[27] Christina K. Schaefer, *The Great War: A Guide to the Service Records of all the Worlds Fighting Men and Volunteers* (Baltimore: Genealogical Publishing Co, 1998) 161.

28 "Beautiful Park Is Dedicated To Memory Of Men In Great War," *PCA,* Nov. 12, 1919: 1.

29 "American Legion Plans Memorials At Waikiki Park," *PCA,* Aug. 10, 1920:1.

30 Mullgardt was well-known both locally and nationally: he had designed the Honolulu Commercial Center (1919–1921) and, along with Bernard Maybeck, Mullgardt was on the Architectural Commission of the Panama-Pacific International Exposition in San Francisco (February 20–December 4, 1915).

31 "Memorial Architects To Look Over Plans," *HA,* June 14, 1922: 3.

32 Ralph S. Kuykendall, *Hawaii in the World War* (Honolulu: The Historical Commission, 1928) 451–452.

33 "Successful Architects Conception Of Hawaii's $250,000 Memorial," *HA,* June 21, 1921: 1.

34 William H. Jordy, *American Buildings and Their Architects: Progressive and Academic Ideals at the Turn of the Twentieth Century* (Garden City: Anchor Books, 1976) 279.

35 "Proposed Memorials For War Heroes Are Widely Discussed," *PCA,* Feb. 15, 1919: 4.

36 See "Tentative Sketch of Memorial Natatorium proposed by American Legion," McCarthy—Territorial Departments War Memorial Commission, AH.

37 James M. Mayo, *War Memorials as Political Landscape: the American Experience and Beyond* (New York: Praeger, 1988) 61.

38 Mayo 61.

39 George L. Mosse, *Fallen Soldiers: Reshaping the Memory of the World Wars* (New York & Oxford UP, 1990) 48.

40 Mayo 88.

41 Paul Fussell, *Wartime: Understanding and Behavior in the Second World War* (New York: Oxford UP, 1990) 21–22.

42 See United Veterans' Service Council Records, AH. The seven soldiers killed in action in France were Private Louis J. Gaspar, Sergeant Apau Kau, Private Antone R. Mattos, Private John R. Rowe, Private Henry K. Unuivi, Manuel G.L. Valent Jr. (rank unknown), and Captain Edward Fuller. There is contradictory information about Manuel G.L. Valent (or Valente), Jr. (rank unknown). His home address is listed as Aiea, Oʻahu, and he was attached to Co. L. 298th Infantry. He was either killed in action or died in service—on either July 18 or Sept. 30, 1918. The *Star Bulletin* says "Died in Service," in September 1918, but UVSCR card refers to him as "KIA." See also "Hawaii Men Who Wear Wound Stripes: War Leaves Its Mark on 14 Island Heroes," *HSB,* May 10, 1919: 3.

43 David Kennedy, *Over Here: the First World War and American Society* (Oxford: Oxford UP, 1980) 214.

44 Paul Fussell, *The Great War and Modern Memory* (Oxford UP, 2000) 21.

45 Fussell 22.

46 John Bodnar, "Public Place in an American City: Commemoration in Cleveland." *Commemorations: the Politics of National Identity.* John R. Gillis. (Princetown UP, 1994) 78.

[47] Mayo 58.

[48] Kennedy 179.

[49] Charles Lamoreaux Warfield, *History of the Hawaii National Guard From Feudal Times to June 30, 1935* M.A. thesis (U of Hawai'i, 1935) 78.

[50] Warfield 72.

[51] The figures may be underestimates: there was also a Naval Militia of the Territory of Hawai'i, which was established in 1915. At the outbreak of war with Germany, the Naval Militia was federalized and 50 enlisted men and officers were accepted into federal military service. See Warfield, 69–70.

[52] Franklin Odo and Kazuko Sinoto, *A Pictorial History of the Japanese in Hawai'i 1885–1924* (Honolulu: Hawai'i Immigrant Heritage Preservation, Department of Anthropology, BPBM, 1985) 208.

[53] Gary Y. Okihiro, *Cane Fires: The Anti-Japanese Movement in Hawaii, 1865–1945.* (Philadelphia: Temple UP, 1991) 108.

[54] "Weak Welcome Is Given To Soldiers: General Public Is Not Turning Out To Meet Trains From Schofield Barracks," *PCA,* Jan. 30, 1919: 1.

[55] Albert Memmi, *The Colonizer and the Colonized* (Boston: Beacon Press, 1967) 13, 54.

[56] Jonathan Schell, *The Fate of the Earth* (New York: Avon, 1982) 122.

NANCY J. MORRIS

Beatrice Patton's Hawai'i

"A splendor and a reverence gone forever from the world" [1]

GEORGE S. PATTON and his wife Beatrice Ayer Patton were stationed in Hawai'i from 1925 to 1928 and again from 1935 to 1937.[2] Patton's glory days as the famous and controversial general of World War II still lay ahead of him. During these years, however, Beatrice Patton came into her own as a person apart from army wife, and her Hawaiian experiences became the foundation for her achievements as a little known but accomplished published author. Beatrice's attachment to Hawai'i was the bonding of person to place that Joan Didion had in mind when she wrote: "A place belongs forever to whoever claims it hardest, remembers it most obsessively, wrests it from itself, shapes, renders it, loves it so radically that he remakes it in his own image...."[3] Didion had James Jones and the Hawai'i of *From Here to Eternity* in mind, but Beatrice Patton was another who remembered obsessively and, after her husband's death, reshaped her Hawaiian memories in an extraordinary and vengeful way.

Patton's family was wealthy, Beatrice's even more so. She was the daughter of Frederick Ayer, who had made his fortune in the patent medicine business and later in the textile mills of New England. Beatrice knew Patton from her girlhood and early on was determined to marry him. By the time he entered West Point, Patton returned her love. He courted Beatrice in the flamboyant style that was to become his trademark. Family members recall an elegantly dressed Ayer fam-

Nancy J. Morris is Librarian/Curator Emerita, University of Hawai'i Library.

The Hawaiian Journal of History, vol. 39 (2005)

ily gathered on the terrace of their mansion; Second Lieutenant Patton appeared on horseback, but instead of stopping in front of the house he rode right up the stairs of the terrace, where he dismounted to bow at Beatrice's feet.[4] Frederick Ayer objected to the match with Patton—he could not see his daughter married to a soldier, and soldiering was Patton's sole ambition—but a brief hunger strike on Beatrice's part settled the matter.

Their marriage had its ups and downs, but throughout the years Beatrice retained her devotion to Patton:

> Georgie, you are the fulfillment of all my ideals of manliness and high courage & bravery I have always held for you, ever since I have known you. And I have expected more of you than any one else ever has or will.

Patton copied this into his diary, adding, "I'm glad she likes me."[5] Patton's devotion was equally strong: "Beat," he would write long after their honeymoon days had faded,

> I had almost forgotten how soft you are even with corsets on, to say nothing of your softness in your wedding nightie. I love you so, Bea . . . I am not so hellish young, and it is not yet spring, yet still I love you much as if we were 22 again on the baseball grandstand at West Point the night I graduated.[6]

Living with this man she had chosen could not have been easy, and the shabby quarters and the frequent moves and the separations of military life were difficult, but Beatrice successfully transformed herself from pampered debutante to model army wife. She learned to win over other army wives who might well have resented the stables of horses and the nannies, cooks, and maids accompanying the Pattons in their moves from post to post.

"The Paradise of the Pacific" it was called, and for the wealthy, Hawai'i in the 1920s and 30s so it was. Fortunes made in pineapple, sugar, and commerce supported an indolent and extravagant life style for a small but influential elite. Cruise ships regularly brought interesting celebrities to enliven the local social scene. The beaded flapper gowns glittered and the gin flowed freely. A fading if exotic Native Hawaiian aristocracy, their blood over several generations mingled with that of the Caucasian elite, joined the parties. Life was not so sweet for an underclass of Native Hawaiians and immigrant workers. Sometimes ugly realities were exposed to all, as happened in the notorious 1932 Massie case. A naval family, not satisfied with the verdict passed down on five "local boys" accused of raping navy wife Thalia Massie, took justice into their own hands. Thalia's mother and husband arranged the beating of one of the youths and the murder of another, and for these crimes, served one hour in a judge's office. Mainland newspapers followed the lurid case avidly, and readers wondered just what was going on out there in the Islands.[7] Sociologists prefer to dwell on the huge—and real—gulf between rich and poor in the Hawai'i of this era, but still, by many accounts, many average people in Hawai'i enjoyed a simple life farming their taro fields, casting their fishing nets, and plucking 'opihi from the rocky coastlines. Half-buried in the social structure, battered but still alive, the culture of ancient Hawai'i managed to endure.

The Pattons found island life to their liking. They were outdoorsy people. Patton especially took to the polo set, and in the construction tycoon Walter Dillingham found a soulmate and lifelong friend. Both were men's men, handsome, driven, and both rode their polo ponies with furious abandon. "Goddamn it, Walter, you old son of a bitch, I'll run you right down Front Street," Patton would yell while careening down the polo field. It was one of the many occasions when Patton's hot blood landed him in trouble with his superior officers.[8] Both Beatrice and Patton joined the more sedate Piko Hiking Club, formed in part to mend the bad blood between the military and local communities so evident in the Massie case. They marched along the trails shouting out the club's motto, a familiar Hawaiian greeting: "Pehea kou piko—How's your belly button?"[9] To launch their second tour of duty in Hawai'i in 1935, they bought a yacht and sailed it from the West Coast to the Islands. Gamely, Beatrice signed on as cook, though she had never cooked a meal in her life. She took cooking lessons, but as it happened, she was so seasick en route that others had to take over her duties.[10]

Seduced by the Islands, Beatrice began a serious study of Native Hawaiian history and culture. Her interest in antiquities was longstanding. As a young girl traveling abroad, she once reached into a sarcophagus, broke off a toe from an Egyptian mummy, and carried it away as a keepsake.[11] When Patton was stationed in a desolate army post in Kansas, she found excitement in discovering marine fossils and in realizing that she was standing where eons ago there had once been a sea.[12] It was this ability to immerse herself in the life of varied far-flung posts that made her an exceptional army wife.

Near Schofield Barracks where the Pattons were first stationed, Beatrice began her encounters with the Hawaiian past. She had come to Hawai'i with the idea of researching some distant relatives who once served as missionaries to the islands, but she found that she was more attracted to the old ways the missionaries had tried so hard to eradicate than to the gospels they implanted. Hidden in the sugar cane fields, hiking distance from her quarters at Schofield, she found a scattering of large boulders buried in the red dirt. The stones do not match those of the surroundings and undoubtedly were dragged there from another locale. Beatrice was to learn that these are the birthing stones of Kūkaniloko where in ancient times *ali'i* women came to give birth. The stones, it was thought, not only relieved the pangs of childbirth but also marked the offspring as *ali'i* of the highest rank. Set in the plains of Wahiawā and ringed by the magnificent Ko'olau and Wai'anae mountain ranges, the mysterious, dramatic stones could not fail to impress the active mind of such a woman as Beatrice.[13] She began to seek out those who might help her understand what she was seeing. The Pattons' daughter, Ruth Ellen, remembered that some of her mother's new associates were not to the liking of the snobbish Patton and he called them her "nigger friends."[14]

A visiting relative of the Pattons marveled at the range of Beatrice's circle of friends. "I remember traveling in her company about the Hawaiian Islands where she knew, and was liked by everyone from the Big Four families and the governor to Japanese vegetable growers and native fishermen."[15] The Pattons lived in several worlds by establishing the pleasant habit of living on base during the week and decamping to the elegant tourist hotels of Waikīkī for the weekends.

A particular friend was the respected Hawaiiana expert, Emma Ahuena Taylor. This chiefly woman (in fact, Beatrice wrote, descended through incarnation from Pele) shared with Beatrice her store of Hawaiian history and legends.[16] Hawaiians call elders such as Taylor *kupuna* and from ancient times, continuing still today, *kupuna* have passed on stories of the past to future generations with an immediacy that cannot be matched by book knowledge. Another good friend was Bishop Museum director, Sir Peter Buck. Buck (Te Rangi Hiroa) was a Maori, and as such, able to place Beatrice's understanding of Hawaiian culture in the larger context of Pan-Polynesian society.[17] The half-Hawaiian man of letters, John Dominis Holt, provided additional insights. At the time the Pattons were in Hawai'i, Holt was a young man, and this was long before he escaped to the Mainland to explore being a *haole,* a Caucasian, and long before he returned to the islands to become an authority on being Hawaiian.[18] The acquaintance was a fruitful one, and years after Beatrice's death, Holt was to publish a collection of her short stories and memoirs set in Hawai'i. The families of Taylor, Buck, and Holt were tangled mixtures of Polynesian and Caucasian, typical, then as now, of Hawaiian social patterns and ambivalences. The tensions and conflicts of Hawaiian interracial relations and the clash of old Hawaiian ways with *haole* culture intrigued Beatrice, and she was to draw on these themes in her writings.

Spend a little time in high-rise, high-tech Hawai'i today and you will sense that Hawai'i oldtimers relish their ghosts. "I don't believe a word of this stuff of course," the *kama'aina* will say "but . . ." and then will follow the stories. Pele walks on the road in the guise of a beautiful young girl dressed all in red. Ghosts congregate as "night marchers" at a certain treacherous corner on Old Pali Road where there have been many fatal accidents. Better not buy an apartment in this condo—it's haunted and there have been many suicides.

In her day, Beatrice Patton heard the stories too. She wrote them down with care and in detail, and she wove them into her writings. One of her spooky stories came from an evening at the Royal Hawaiian Hotel when the Pattons entertained some military friends. In 1936, she would write, a lava flow threatened Hilo. To divert the flow, Air Force pilots bombed it. Pele was furious. Of the three pilots involved, one was killed in a plane crash shortly after the flow. A second pilot was a guest at a dinner party hosted by the Pattons. After too many cocktails, the pilot rose to shout: "Phooey to Pele. They say I should give her a pig, but I gave her a bomb. That's what I did—I gave her a bomb!" Hawaiian guests present at the party shuddered, and a local waitress predicted the pilots' imminent deaths. The pilot, Beatrice was later told, was killed in the war, as was the third pilot involved in the bombing.[19]

Beatrice's collection of tales grew. A *pueo*, the Hawaiian owl said to be a messenger of death, flew into a Queen's Hospital ward. None of the patients were on the critical list, but in the morning, seven of the eleven Hawaiian patients were found unexplainably dead.[20] The black magic arts of the *kahuna*, accorded some credence by a plantation doctor acquaintance of the Pattons, especially seized Beatrice's imagination. The doctor told Beatrice that at least six of his patients had been prayed to death. Beatrice took the stories seriously—very seriously, as she would later demonstrate.[21]

She began to publish her impressions: some poetry in the magazine *Paradise of the Pacific*, retellings of Hawaiian legends, and a novel. Years later, a collection of her short stories interwoven with her memoirs of Hawai'i would be issued posthumously.

Of her books, the partly autobiographical *Love Without End* is the most revealing for the biographer. The book traces her growing attachment for old Hawaiian ways. At mealtimes she forced breadfruit on her unwilling family. When she suffered from aches and pains, she called in the *lomi lomi* practitioner, the Hawaiian masseuse, and for her bronchitis, the *kahuna lapa'au* or medical practitioner came with *noni* leaves and ground-up *kukui* nuts.[22] She was given a Hawaiian name. "This name," she wrote, "is a sacred thing to be treasured with love and reverence, a secret not to be shared."[23] It seems clear that in time she came to believe in the power of Hawaiian gods. She was given a small *'aumakua*, a carved piece intended as a family god. With the gift came instructions: "When you unpack him, make him a lei, and give him a little oke ['*okolehao*, a liquor made from the roots of the Hawaiian *ti* plant], but do it only once. He will then know that you have aloha for him but he must not be spoiled." It was a figure of a soldier, and she reported that she gave it to someone who carried it off to the war.[24] Whether or not this someone was her husband is not known, but it is intriguing to think of Patton going off to battle protected by a Hawaiian *'aumakua*.

With archaeologist friends she traveled to the outer islands for excursions to the complex of burial caves that lay half-hidden in the rocks. In her time, collectors showed no hesitation in entering Hawaiian burial caves and removing objects found there for display in museums. This practice led in the late 20th century to a campaign by Native Hawaiian activists to prohibit such activities, and federal legislation, the Native American Graves Protection and Repatriation Act, calls for the return of Hawaiian funeral objects to their original locations. Beatrice's sensibilities to the wanton desecration of Hawaiian artifacts put her ahead of her time. She made a point of stating that she never took anything from the caves and was aware that Hawaiian guardians stood watch over ancestral sites and often succeeded in bringing back objects improperly taken.[25] She mentioned one of the several images of the poison god Kalaipahoa "glowering from behind a case at the Bishop Museum . . . . a captive behind lock and key." Beatrice might be gratified to know that today a number of such captive museum objects have been repatriated, though not without controversy, to their original sites.

Beatrice was fluent in French, and she put this accomplishment to use in a privately published work, *Légendes Hawaiiennes* (Paris, 1932), a collection of translations into French of a number of Hawaiian tales. Book connoisseurs value the book not only for the stories but for Juliette May Fraser's beautifully drawn illustrations, each one a careful vignette of some aspect of Hawaiian life. Fraser was a local artist, little known outside the Islands but well loved and regarded in Hawai'i. Few copies of the work exist.

Blood of the Shark, published by Paradise of the Pacific in 1936, is a fully realized novel. "Oh, it's just another of those romantic South Sea novels of the '30s," said a Hawaiian historian when the book came up for discussion. True, there is rather too much talk of silvery moonbeams in the novel, yet Beatrice was a writer capable of turning many pretty and imaginative phrases. Here is the voice of her heroine, calling out while swimming by moonlight: "See those drowned stars looking up through the water. Watch me scatter them!" The book is a passionately sincere effort to communicate all the stories Beatrice had absorbed, all the unique beauty of green valleys and mountains surrounded by a cobalt sea, all the conflicts brought about by colliding cultures. It was begun during the Pattons' first Hawai'i tour in the 1920s, simmered for several years and was completed during their second tour. The plot concerns the unlikely marriage of a young British seaman who travels to Hawai'i with the explorer Vancouver, and a chiefly island beauty. Beatrice takes on two themes: first, an exploration of Hawaiians clinging to old ways and beliefs in the face of encroaching western contact, and, second, the story of a cross-cultural marriage, a saga of a couple who fall in love, marry, battle furiously, fail totally to understand the myths of one other, and yet emerge after years of marriage as two trees of different species whose roots have grown together. Her hero is Adam, a difficult man who swears fulsomely, kills easily in battle, rides a horse with a furious intensity, and yells at his wife ("You god-damned black wahine."). He has a taste for poetry and sometimes quotes long passages remembered from his childhood. Beatrice's model for this man is not hard to guess.

The book's tour de force is a chapter called "The Net," in which Beatrice dares to enter the mind of a Hawaiian sorceress intent on doing what she can to stop the flood of foreign influences converging on Hawai'i. Prominent in the chapter are mentions of the shark, the owl, and the lizard, all creatures, as Peter Buck put it, guaranteed to make the flesh of a Polynesian crawl "for they are the incarnations of the family gods throughout Polynesia and in far south New Zealand. Through these mediums the deified ancestors gave signs and warning to their living descendants."[26] The chapter is a long rant of the sorcerer against the evils brought by the foreigners—diseases that have decimated the native population, and prompted the fading of a culture. "We live in rags, and splendor and reverence are gone forever from the world." Beatrice takes the sorcerer's lament as the theme of her novel. It is a lament that continues to be voiced in the 21st century by Native Hawaiians.

Bishop Museum director Sir Peter Buck wrote an appreciative introduction to *Blood of the Shark*. It received excellent reviews in the Honolulu press, and the first printing sold out in a week. There were three additional printings. Beatrice was given a proper Hawaiian-style book party. Peter Buck sprinkled the four corners of the room with salt water in a Polynesian blessing, and Beatrice's friend Emma Taylor, the cultural consultant for the novel, further blessed the novel with a traditional Hawaiian prayer. "How could the book not be a success?" Taylor said. "The prayer was completed."[27]

In all three of her books Beatrice returns repeatedly to one particular element of Hawaiian culture, the art of black magic. She had learned a chant used by Hawaiian sorcerers to pray their enemies to death, and she quotes from the chant repeatedly: "May the Great

Worm gnaw your vitals, and may your bones rot, joint by little
joint. . . ."

Patton too tried his hand at writing about Hawai'i and produced
a poem about the Hawaiian god Lono. Patton's poem, reproduced
here in an appendix, tells the reader much about his passion for war
and weapons, his disdain for Native Hawaiians, and even something
of his interest in reincarnation, but in contrast to Beatrice's writings
so densely packed with the color and characters of Hawai'i, it says little about Hawaiian culture.[28]

Beatrice's novel was published in 1936, but she was not allowed to
enjoy the glow of authorship for long. Family troubles intervened.
George Patton had turned 50. All his achievements seemed behind
him: he had placed fifth in the pentathlon competitions in the 1912

FIG. 1. Beatrice Patton at Thomas Nickerson's bookstore at 175 South Queen Street,
Honolulu, ca. 1936–37. Her book, *Blood of the Shark* is prominently displayed in the
store's wondow. Hawai'i State Archives.

Stockholm Olympic Games. He and his men had tracked and killed several of Pancho Villa's bandits during the U.S. Mexican Punitive Expedition of 1916. He had served honorably in combat for three days during World War I. Was this to be all? Patton was morosely afraid that he would be too old to be in the next war he knew was coming. When Beatrice's niece, Jean Gordon, visited, Patton began a flirtation with the girl. Gordon was a recent Boston debutante, pretty, lively, and the best friend of Ruth Ellen, the Pattons' daughter. Unwisely, Beatrice did not accompany Patton and Jean on a horse-buying trip to a neighbor island, and when the two returned, it was clear to Beatrice that the flirtation had become an affair. Beatrice forgave Patton, and the marriage survived. Beatrice talked to her daughter about all this, and what she said is an indication of both character and enduring love. The quote comes from Patton biographer Carlo D'Este, who had access to the memoirs of Ruth Ellen:

FIG. 2. Beatrice Patton signing copies of *Blood of the Shark* at book party at Thomas Nickerson's bookstore, Honolulu, ca. 1936–37. Hawai'i State Archives.

Your father needs me. He doesn't know it right now, but he needs me. In fact, right now, he needs me more than I need him. Perhaps there is a reason for all this. I want you to remember this; that even the best and truest of men can be bedazzled and make fools of themselves. So, if your husband ever does this to you, you can remember that I didn't leave your father. I stuck with him because I am all he really has, and I love him, and he loves me.[29]

Not long after the Pattons left Hawai'i, the long and bloody war came, as Patton knew it would. He was not denied the victories and the glory he had sought for so long. On the home front, Beatrice, as the wife of the famous general, was in demand as a speaker for the war effort. She remained fiercely loyal and proud of her warrior: "I am so full of his triumph that I just glow with pride. . . . He is twice the man and twice the commander that he has ever been."[30]

Toward the end of the war, the niece who had betrayed Beatrice, Jean Gordon, traveled to Europe as a Red Cross "doughnut girl." These were young women who cheered up the troops with home-style snacks and social evenings, all very respectable, of course. Jean was reunited with Patton and sometimes played hostess at his social functions. but whether or not their affair continued remains their secret. Learning of Jean's presence in Europe, Beatrice had her suspicions and wrote a fretful letter to Patton. He replied that she should not worry, that he "was no fool."[31]

Short months after the end of the European war, while on a bird shooting expedition in Germany, Patton's car was involved in a collision with another vehicle. Others in the car were not seriously injured, but Patton's spine was crushed and he was paralyzed. "A hell of a way for a soldier to die," Patton said. There was time before his death, 12 days after the accident, for Beatrice to fly to his side, and they had a few last days together. She read to him from his favorite military histories, Armand de Caulaincourt's memoirs of Napoleon and the like, and he dictated portions of his memoirs. He drifted in and out of consciousness and once as he drifted, he said to his wife: "It's too dark, I mean too late." Beatrice had used this strange and haunting phrase for the death scene of one of her characters in *Blood of the Shark*.[32] A blood clot, undoubtedly related to the accident, ended Patton's life.

Patton was buried in Luxembourg on Christmas Eve, 1945. Beatrice returned home on Christmas Day. There remained some unfinished business. Beatrice had never forgiven Jean Gordon, and in the weeks after Patton's death, arranged for a meeting with her niece. Pointing her finger at Jean, Beatrice delivered the ancient Hawaiian curse: "May the Great Worm gnaw your vitals and may your bones rot joint by little joint . . . ." Present at the scene was Beatrice's brother, Fred Ayer. Horrified at the malevolence of the scene, Fred ran from the room. Within weeks, Jean Gordon put her head in the oven of a New York apartment and was declared a suicide. She was 30. Various explanations for the tragedy have been offered by the Ayer and Patton family and friends. Two aunts said that when they claimed Jean's body, they found a note: "I will be with Uncle Georgie in heaven and have him all to myself before Beatrice arrives." A conflicting story has it that Jean was in love with a married officer who decided to return to his family.[33]

What can be made of this bizarre incident? A case can be made that Beatrice truly believed in the efficacy of the chant she hurled against Jean Gordon. Mysticism and paranormal experiments were strong elements in the family cultures of both Patton and Beatrice. According to one of his finest biographers, Carlo D'Este, Patton genuinely believed that he had lived before, as a marshal under Alexander, fighting as a Viking, as a cavalryman under Napoleon, and that he would live again. Both families experimented with Ouija boards and seances. Dead relatives appeared to the families in visions. After her mother's death, Beatrice consulted a medium in order to apologize for some perceived misdeed. In the weeks following Patton's death, Beatrice gave a glove worn by Patton at the time of the accident to a sister for a seance in which Patton was called upon to reappear. It is clear that Beatrice was enthralled by the Hawaiian spiritual world. The shark was her 'aumakua, her protector, and because of this she swam without fear in the open ocean (though her nervous husband stood by with a rifle just in case).

She did not make up the words of the chant she used against Jean Gordon. It is part of the kahuna 'anā'anā lore well documented by Hawaiian specialists. Kahuna 'anā'anā were members of a larger order of Hawaiians priests. Some kahuna were medical practioners, some interpreted signs and omens, some specialized in knowledge of the earth and sea, but *kahuna ʻanāʻanā* were best known for their ability to pray people to death. As late as the turn of the 20th century, evangelical missionaries to Hawaiʻi were railing against the power exercised by the *kahuna ʻanāʻanā*. In Beatrice's time, specifics as to *kahuna ʻanāʻanā* practices were mostly to be found spelled out in Hawaiian language oral traditions and in Hawaiian language texts; today the published works of such native Hawaiian writers as Samuel Kamakau and David Malo are widely available in English language translations. A text corresponding to the fragments of the chant she used is to be found in Samuel Kamakau's *Ka Poʻe Kahiko: the People of Old*.[34]

In 1953, Beatrice fell from her horse while riding in a race and died at once. She had previously been diagnosed with an aneurysm, and quite possibly this was the cause of her death rather than the fall.

Beatrice Patton emerges, for all her personal charm, literary ability, and inquisitive intelligence, as a woman who crossed forbidden boundaries. Hawaiian chants were not hers to invoke. Though her Hawaiian encounters were only part of a long and adventurous life, they were indelible. Her family and friends mourned her and for years after her death, when they saw a porpoise they would call out, "Hi Bea!" There she was, arching in the sea, living her next life as she always said she would.[35]

NOTES

[1] A lament and the theme of Beatrice Patton's *Blood of the Shark: A Romance of Early Hawaii* (Honolulu: Paradise of the Pacific Press, 1936) 350.

[2] Patton biographies consulted in preparing this article include:

Frederick Ayer, *Before the Colors Fade: Portrait of a Soldier, George S. Patton, Jr.* (Boston: Houghton-Mifflin, 1964).

Martin Blumenson, *The Patton Papers* 2 vols. (Boston: Houghton Mifflin, 1972–74).

———. *Patton: The Man Behind the Legend* (New York: Morrow, 1985).

Carlo D'Este, *Patton: A Genius for War* (New York: HarperCollins, 1995).

Ladislas Farago, *The Last Days of Patton* (New York: McGraw-Hill, 1981).

Stanley P. Hirshson, *General Patton: A Soldier's Life* (New York: HarperCollins, 2002).

Robert H. Patton, *The Pattons: A Personal History of an American Family* (New York: Crown Publishers, 1994).

[3] Joan Didion, *The White Album* (New York: Simon and Schuster, 1979) 146.

[4] D'Este, *Patton* 108.

[5] Blumenson, *The Patton Papers* I: 669; D'Este, *Patton* et al 276.

6 George S. Patton to Beatrice Patton. Quoted by Blumenson, *Patton Papers* I: 505.

7 Historian Gavin Daws devoted an entire chapter of his one-volume history of Hawai'i to this significant case (*Shoal of Time,* Toronto: Macmillan, 1968), 317–327. The latest of several books on the case are Cobey Black's *Hawaii Scandal* (Waipahu, Hawai'i: Island Heritage, 2002) and David Stannard's *Honor Killing: How the Infamous "Massie Affair" Transformed Hawai'i* (New York, N.Y.: Viking, 2005.)

8 See, among other biographers, Hirshson, *General Patton* 214.

9 On the Piko Club and the participation of the Pattons in this group, see Stuart M. Ball, "The Piko Club: Hiking O'ahu in the 1930s," *HJH* 37 (2003): 179–197.

10 D'Este, *Patton* 358.

11 Robert H. Patton, *The Pattons* 109–110.

12 D'Este, *Patton* 147.

13 For background information on Kūkaniloko see, for example, "Kukaniloko: Famed Birthplace of Aliis," *Hawaiian Annual,* 1912, 101–105.

14 Robert H. Patton, *The Pattons* 228. Robert Patton based much on his family history on conversations with the Pattons' daughter Ruth Ellen.

15 Ayer, *Before the Colors Fade* 43. Ayer was Beatrice Patton's nephew.

16 For a biographical sketch of Emma Taylor, see Barbara Bennett Peterson, ed., *Notable Women of Hawaii* (Honolulu: U of Hawai'i P), 1984) 369–373.

17 Buck's biographer is John Bell Condliffe's *Te Rangi Hiroa: The Life of Sir Peter Buck* (Christchurch: Whitcombe and Tombs, 1971.)

18 The historian Michael Slackman interviewed Holt and documented Holt's friendship with the Pattons. Michael Slackman, "The Orange Race: George S. Patton, Jr.'s Japanese American Hostage Plan," *Biography* 7 (Winter 1984): 17.

19 Beatrice Patton, *Love Without End* (Honolulu: Ku Pa'a, 1989). This book is a collection of Hawaiian stories intermixed with Beatrice Patton's memoirs of her Hawai'i years.

20 Beatrice Patton, *Love Without End* 98.

21 Beatrice Patton, *Love Without End* 96. Some of Beatrice's stories came from her friend, Dr. Hubert Woods, a respected plantation doctor.

22 Beatrice Patton, *Love Without End* 96–97.

23 Robert Patton, *The Pattons* 231, quoting from Beatrice Patton's "Thought Book." The "Thought Book" is retained by the Patton family and seemingly not available to researchers.

24 Beatrice Patton, *Love Without End* 31–32.

25 Beatrice Patton, *Love Without End* 92.

26 Peter Buck's unpaged foreword to *Blood of the Shark.*

27 Beatrice Patton, *Love Without End* 46.

28 Patton's 1927 poem is attached to this article in an appendix. The poem is included in the Patton Papers at the Library of Congress, Washington, D.C.

29 Quoted by D'Este, *Patton* 359. D'Este based the quote on the unpublished biography of Beatrice Patton compiled by the Patton's daughter Ruth Ellen. The biography is seemingly not available to most researchers.

30 Blumenson, *Patton Papers, 1940–1945*, 151, quoting a letter (date not noted) from Beatrice Patton to her brother Fred Ayer.

31 D'Este, *Patton* 744, quoting a letter of Patton to his wife, March 31, 1945.

32 Beatrice Patton, *Blood of the Shark* 87.

33 D'Este, *Patton* 805–807; Blumenson, *Patton* 307.

34 Samuel Kamakau, *Ka Po'e Kahiko: the People of Old* (Honolulu: BPBM, 1964) 123–125.

35 Beatrice Patton's wish to return to life as a porpoise is mentioned by a Patton family friend, Roger H. Nye, quoted by Hirshson, *General Patton* 704.

APPENDIX

The Sword of Lono

Long have I wandered since, in far castle,
Fire and the anvil joined to give me birth
And I appeared a vivid thing of steel
To 'grave my fame in blood o'er half the earth.

First in a soldier's hand I felt the thrill
Of ringing combat as we stormed a town
And drank my fill of blood as through the dawn
We slaughtered Moors to give our Queen her crown.

Again in memory I seem to feel
My keen point bite the Unbelievers' mail
The kiss of frenzied parries as he strove
Toward my lunge and strove to no avail.

There on a ship I wandered many a day
Stopping at times to drink some savage gore
Until at last I came, all white with brine,
Strapped to a corpse, to rest on Maui's shore.

A rescued sailor polished there my blade
And long I served him Lono, white and fair
While as a god he ruled a savage race
Nor failed I, in his hand, his fame to share.

And many a field I slashing led our van
And many a dark-skinned chief to carrion sped
In every isle I quenched my baleful thirst
Great was my fame, great as the list of dead.

But glory passes and in Lono's death
The clumsy savage little knew my worth
My blade was shattered and in evil hour
I came to stand the sign of God on earth.

Yet soon their childish memory failed to link
My twisted hilt with that white blade of yore
And cast to earth in miserable disgrace
My rusty grip was trampled by the shore.

But though a shapeless wreck I now appear
Midst spear and adze for crowds to look upon
I still am Lono's sword and in his hand
I was the means to all the fame he won.

George S. Patton
1927

JANINE A. POWERS

Worlds Beyond Medicine:
Nils P. Larsen's Impact on Hawai'i

INTRODUCTION

Nils Paul Larsen (1890–1964) was a significant transitional figure in Hawai'i as it changed from a plantation society to a modern Pacific community. Larsen lived in Hawai'i from 1922 until his death in 1964, and was recognized in varying degrees as a physician, director, researcher, writer, historian, politician, artist, playwright, inventor, association president, decorated war hero, Swedish consul, honorary *kahuna,* and congressional delegate.

This article focuses on Larsen's biographical information, contributions to the field of medicine, and his appreciation for both progressive and traditional medical practice in Hawai'i. His work included milk regulation, better nutrition, improved care for tuberculosis patients, studies on aging, population control, industrial medicine, decrease of infant mortality, healthier lifestyle for plantation workers, and improved housing for nurses. He also sought to preserve Hawaiian herbal remedies and medical knowledge.

Dr. Janine A. Powers has taught psychology and American studies at the University of Hawai'i–Mānoa, and received her Doctorate of Philosophy in December 2003. Publications and research studies include: "From Medicine to Art: Nils Paul Larsen (1890–1964)," "Emotional Contagion: Gender and Occupational Differences," and "Contemplating Campion: Representations in Motion Picture Film." She is currently working as an Intensive Instructional Services Consultant and is certified to teach behavioral science and general studies for the University of Phoenix in Hawai'i.

The Hawaiian Journal of History, vol. 39 (2005)

EARLY YEARS

Larsen's father, Emil, was a tailor from Sweden. He changed the spelling of the family's last name from L-A-R-S-O-N to L-A-R-S-E-N when he became an apprentice in Norway because of animosity between the countries. He kept the spelling upon his return to Sweden and started his own tailor business. Emil married Maria Friman when he was twenty-four and she was twenty-six years old. Their seven offspring (eldest to youngest) included: Joseph, Samuel, Mary, David, Dan, Nils, and Elisabeth.

Facing bankruptcy, Emil borrowed money to move to New York. Emil and Samuel traveled to Peeksville, New York, and arrived in early October 1892. In June 1893, the rest of the family donated their belongings to the local church and joined them. Larsen was three years old when his sister lifted him up from the ship to see the Statue of Liberty. They moved to Bridgeport, Connecticut, when Emil was asked to help start a Swedish Mission Church. The three eldest siblings quit attending school to help support the family, while the youngest boys (Dave, Dan, and Nils) were encouraged to pursue higher education.[1]

The family had a "stern ethical" upbringing by his father whose church services were always conducted in Swedish. On one occasion Emil asked his youngest son, who was known by his middle name, "Paul," to give a sermon. The heart of the young Nils Larsen's sermon was built upon the belief that the "greatest glory is not in never falling, but in rising every time you fall."[2] In nightly readings to her family from Christian teachings, his beloved mother passed on a belief that "you are responsible for your soul and the joy of living is the fight against oppression and evil."[3]

Nils Larsen began working for hire in grammar school cutting grass, washing windows, and shoveling snow in winter, or cleaning yards every day after school and all day on Saturdays. During vacations in high school he worked in a steel mill as a box carpenter and made big wooden boxes wrapped in steel bands for steel shipping. "He could drive an eight-penny nail in one blow and sink it to the hilt." Larsen recalled "there was always a group of twenty to thirty men outside the gate looking for the job if you couldn't keep up."[4] During football season Larsen would cajole his brothers to take over his share of the work.

Larsen considered himself an American, even though he was born in Sweden and the family spoke Swedish at home. After giving his high school graduation speech, his German teacher called his attention to his thick Scandinavian accent. Larsen became self-conscious and worked hard to get rid of the "dis/dat, dese/does/weat/weter and so on" to no avail.[5] A critique written by his teacher on this paper warned him, "Do not fear feeling strongly, or expressing your feelings; but let judgment and reasonable restraint tone down any excess in feeling or language."[6] Despite his aggressive and obstinate character, Larsen proved to be a well-rounded person in both academic and extracurricular activities .

COLLEGE YEARS

Larsen studied agriculture when he entered the University of Massachusetts (known then as Mass Agee), to become a forester. As an extracurricular distinction, he was offered the presidency of the campus Young Men's Christian Association (YMCA). He refused on the grounds that it would not allow people of other religious affiliations to hold office, and instead formed a group (the College Christian Association) that fought against fraternity fixing of campus elections.[7]

In college Larsen wrote a soul-searching paper entitled "A Confession." In it, he questioned the believability of the fire and brimstone language of Biblical events that did not portray a forgiving spiritual father. Debates such as the "creation" versus "species evolution" models of the origin of the world made it difficult for him to decide to choose a life of "works over faith." He simply believed God symbolized the highest ideal for humans and he concentrated on acting in a righteous manner with the interests of ordinary people in mind.[8] As a college representative at a Christian Northfield Conference, Larsen learned that there was only one doctor for every million people in China, and he felt compelled to pursue this career; he decided to become a physician.[9]

Larsen lacked money when he was in college. His brother, Sam, assisted him by providing him with a home and a summer job. Larsen received a Bachelor of Science degree from Mass Agee in 1913 and a medical degree from Cornell Medical School in 1916. Even in medical school, Larsen displayed the kind of community service that would characterize his medical career by organizing two Boy Scout troops in New York.

MILITARY COMMISSION

In 1916, Larsen finished his graduate work in biological chemistry at Columbia and was granted a fellowship at New York Hospital.[10] He served as an assistant pathologist there until April 1917. During World War I, Larsen received a commission as first lieutenant in the Medical Corps 106th, United States Infantry.

FIG. 1. Nils Larsen in military uniform, ca. 1918. Lila Larsen Morgan Collection.

First Lieutenant Larsen went overseas on active service to Belgium and France in May 1918. He wrote a letter to his sister, Mary, in May 1917 on a field typewriter on his way to France, which reflected his wartime apprehension. When the troops were awaiting orders in safe places, he worried that "at any moment we will be called away again and be put into a concentration camp and there is no telling what will happen even five minutes ahead."[11]

While he was overseas, Larsen's younger sister Elisabeth developed tuberculosis. In 1918 his sister Mary wrote that she had accompanied Elisabeth to a farm in the country in New Hampshire where she "could live in the open." When the disease advanced Elisabeth lamented to her sister, "Oh, how terrible it is to die and how long it takes."[12] She was twenty-six years old when she died.

Larsen did, in fact, face combat duty. In the infantry he was promoted to major in 1919 and received the Silver Star Citation that read:

> ...While directing the evacuation of wounded from the front line trenches under a heavy concentration of machine gun and artillery fire, constantly exposing himself to such fire with utter disregard for his own safety. Five of his seven litter bearers being killed or wounded, he crawled well forward of the front elements of the 106th Infantry and finding a wounded soldier who had lain in an exposed position for 36 hours, he carried him upon his back to safety; afterward searching the shell holes in front of the lines until all the wounded or killed of his regiment had been found.[13]

After military service, Larsen re-embarked on his medical career at the University of Cornell as an instructor in medicine and bacteriology and as an assistant visiting physician in pediatric service at Gouveneur Hospital.[14]

MARRIAGE AND CAREER

In the summer of 1919 Larsen went on vacation to Hawai'i and brought along his eleven-year-old niece. He visited his brother, Laurentius David Larsen, who had come to Hawai'i in 1908 to work as a plant pathologist. By then David Larsen was an established manager for Kilauea Sugar Plantation. It was through Dave that Larsen met Sara "Sally" Lucas of Honolulu, a member of Dave's circle of friends from his bachelor days.

Unlike Sally's jovial and sociable manner, Larsen's character showed evidence of a strict upbringing in his puritanical beliefs about women. He claimed that dancing was something he never indulged in, nor did he engage in much dating. After his vacation, Larsen returned to New York, with no intention of further contact and he and Sally went their separate ways.[15]

At Bellevue Hospital in New York, Larsen continued his medical research, writing, and working with other prominent physicians, focusing on pneumonia and asthma. He published in *The Journal of the American Medical Association* and *The Journal of Immunology*. Larsen conducted ambitious research on respiratory disorders. Additionally, he held the post of commanding officer of the First Field Hospital of the New York National Guard.[16]

Some two years after Larsen and Sally Lucas met, Sally traveled to New York, with the intent of starting a candy business. She had been impressed with the doctor, who had brought his young niece to Hawai'i with him, and was urged by a friend to call him. When he called on her, with the lining of his jacket hanging out, she offered to mend it. This impressed him greatly, and the two embarked on a fast-paced romance. They wed on September 1, 1921 in Kensington, New Hampshire and lived in New York City. Meanwhile in Hawai'i, Sally's mother, Lydy Lucas, sought out employment for her son-in-law so she could keep her daughter nearby. Lydy discovered that Queen's Hospital needed a pathologist. Larsen was offered the appointment in July 1922 and accepted it.

Larsen and Sally left New York and traveled to Hawai'i by train and ocean liner when she was six months pregnant. When the newlywed couple first moved to O'ahu they initially resided with Sally's parents on Lunalilo Street in Honolulu. Their daughter, Lila Elizabeth Larsen, was born on September 18, 1922 in the Lucas' home. The following year, the Larsen family moved into a cottage near Diamond Head. Jack Lucas Larsen was born on May 30, 1924. Nils Larsen worked and studied his new environment, eager to prove himself as a physician.[17]

QUEEN'S HOSPITAL THURSDAY MORNING ROUNDS

When Larsen joined the Queen's Hospital, it had been in existence for about 60 years. Upon becoming its first medical director, he went to work examining the population and local medical maladies and pushing for modernization. He also initiated the often-heated Thursday morning clinic, called "round-table discussions," vigorously conducted instructional sessions, mainly for interns. In January 1923, Larsen wrote:

> ...Thursday morning rounds are now made by the Honorary Board of Physicians. These are weekly conferences at which interesting cases, undiagnosed conditions, therapeutic problems are presented for discussion. The response by the members of the Board to the number of 10 to 20 each week has been very gratifying. Their interest and discussion has helped materially to improve the service and stimulate to more thorough work. At these conferences the deaths of the week are also discussed. The cooperation by the members of the Honorary Board through constructive criticism and helpful suggestions make it possible to more speedily check defects and errors which results in better service to the patient.[18]

The meetings were held in the spacious nurses' classroom with large windows. The sills were wide enough so that latecomers could sit on them and passersby could humorously see the long row of participants' rear ends from outside the building. Interns would present their cases, and locally established physicians, like Dr. Fennel from Straub, would lecture. Prominent visitors added to the appeal of the meetings. The "1928 Report of the Medical Director" noted:

> ... The Thursday Morning Clinics have continued without a break and with increasing attendance. Many mainland visitors have expressed wonder when they find over 50% of the whole medical profession gathering weekly to discuss their medical problems. We have also been most fortunate in having with us some of the very best men in the country. . . . It sounds like the top of Who's Who in Medicine. These men have each taken part in the discussion and helped us with our problems. Few people realize the value thus reverted by the hospital to the community.[19]

Annual progress reports were generated and continued until 1936. As the discussion group increased in size, the meetings moved into even larger classrooms that held more attendees.

Milk Campaign

The "milk campaign" in Hawai'i, as it came to be known, began in November of 1922. The medical community was alarmed because the infant mortality rate was unacceptably high, with 366 deaths per thousand births. Learning of milk campaigns on the U. S. East Coast exposing potential health problems with milk, Larsen suspected Hawai'i had similar problems. A surprise inspection of Honolulu dairies uncovered unsanitary conditions, leading him to spearhead a drive against spoiled, unsanitary milk. The test samples from "baby milk" sold in Honolulu showed a dangerously high bacterial count. In one inspection Larsen found a man sieving milk through a mosquito net, claiming it would, "strain out them germs you've heard about." Another found a milker, "squatted before a cow whose ulcerated udders were distended three times their normal size with streptococcus infection." Honolulu milk, Larsen claimed was, "as safe as drinking a swig of water from a stagnant pool."

Larsen, along with Army Medical Corps Commanding Officer Colonel Craig; President of the Board of Health, John Trotter; Territorial Food Commissioner Bairos; and Chief Sanitary Inspector Schultz, set about correcting the situation. A coalition of Queen's and Tripler hospitals and the Board of Health became involved in a cooperative drive to analyze Honolulu milk. When all laboratories confirmed a problem, the matter was taken to the public via the editor of *Honolulu Advertiser,* Lorrin P. Thurston. After Thurston was shown the relationship of milk to infant diarrheas, septic sore throats, and other milk-born epidemics, due to the high bacterial count and dirty handling of the milk, he began a media campaign to clean up the milk. The Medical Society formed and passed a resolution for standard milk regulations and laws.

On April 28, 1923, *Honolulu Advertiser* headline news aimed to warn and incense the public stating: "Children of Honolulu are Perishing as a Result of Germ-Laden Milk." To expedite change, individual dairy sites and their bacteria counts were mentioned in articles.

Some of the bacterial counts ranged into the millions. Dairies were up in arms over the negative publicity. When Trotter, the president of the Board of Health, asked that the publicity be ended because of the damaging effect on the industry, Colonel Craig responded by banning any further purchase of milk for the military unless the campaign was continued

The *Honolulu Advertiser* headlines finally improved for the milk industry in August, 1925 with stories like "Health Board's Drive Results in Better Milk," and "Removal of Tubercular Cows from Dairy Herds Insures Better Milk." On January 14, 1926, it was officially announced that the milk in Hawai'i ranked as well as mainland milk; later that year Honolulu had more certified and pasteurized milk than other comparable cities in the United States. An article entitled "Plantation Babies Okay Now," which appeared in *Reader's Digest,* made national news.[20]

PREVENTORIUM

Larsen, along with other prominent Honolulu physicians, as George Straub of Straub Hospital, worked on many health programs and clinics at Palama Settlement on the outskirts of downtown Honolulu. Larsen was a member of the Board of Trustees that provided specialty care to the economically disadvantaged. Programs like milk stations, prenatal clinics, public health nursing, and camps were developed to teach health, hygiene, and stress management. A tuberculosis committee was developed and branch dispensaries were established, with the first at Palama Settlement.

The purpose of settlement houses like Palama Settlement was "to allow social workers, health care providers, and community leaders to gain an understanding of the geographical neighborhood they lived in—and to enlist the aid of the more fortunate to improve these conditions." They did so by living with the people in the communities who were not able to afford medical care.

While Palama Settlement had operated a tuberculosis day camp since 1910, and a summer camp for children at its Fresh Air Camp at Waialua, these were not sufficient for the total care that children with tuberculosis required. Local interest in Hawai'i preventoriums ("twenty-four hour, twelve month institution for the care and observation of children sub-standard in health") arose in the early 1920s.[21] In 1926, Dr. A. L. Davis, Bureau of Tuberculosis Director, wrote: "There is an urgent need for a preventorium where pre-tubercular children can be treated."[22] The tragedy of Larsen's sister's death drove his desire for premium medical care for people with this affliction.

On July 19, 1927, Larsen, a member of the Health Committee of the Chamber of Commerce, once again called for the creation of a preventorium; he also brought up the matter with the trustees of Leahi Home. The proposed site was estimated to cost $140,000 and serve up to one hundred children. The cost was considered excessive.

The College Club finally renewed its commitment to create a treatment facility. In 1929 it encouraged local welfare and public health agencies to add their support. In 1930 the director of Palama Settlement offered to lease, free of charge, three settlement residences for preventoriums. The trustees of Leahi Home secured the attorney general's support. In July 1930, a five-year lease was signed between Leahi Home and Palama Settlement for use of the buildings. The memorial fund of Dr. Francis R. Day, who was the first to "outline a definite crusade against the spread of tuberculosis in Honolulu," donated money to recondition the buildings and equip them for caring up to 39 children. Larsen was appointed to the advisory committee to assist in directing the preventorium with medical director, Dr. A. N. Sinclair. They conferred on such topics as nutrition, weight, follow-ups, intelligence quotients, dental conditions, and family relief. Eventually, because preventative shots and outpatient treatments diminished severe cases of tuberculosis, preventoriums were no longer needed.[23]

HARKNESS HALL

When Larsen first visited Hawai'i in 1919, he was a guest at the first graduating class from the Queen's nursing school, which was made up of women who had been recruited from plantations. Women had few opportunities other than plantation life; nursing was one of them. Some of them had witnessed their mothers dying in childbirth and left plantation life in favor of hospital life, even though that meant working twelve hour days for about ten dollars a month, and living in facilities that were in shambles.[24]

Nurses were housed in the Supervisor's Cottage, Graduate Quarters and Probationers' Cottage. Living conditions there were crowded and not very pleasant. In the wooden dormitory termite droppings were said to have fallen on them.[25]

In 1924 when Larsen became the director of the hospital he prompted better living conditions for nurses. In 1931, Mr. Louis Lapham of Chicago visited the meager cottages and, through his efforts, Mr. Harkness of New York donated $125,000 towards a nurses' home. Dr. James Judd, E. Faxon Bishop (chairman of the board of trustees of Queen's), as well as nineteen contributors raised the money needed for Harkness Hall, designed by noted architect C. W. Dickey. It was a substantial building with a sizeable lobby; in places it was a two-story and others a three-story structure. Each nursing superintendent had a suite consisting of a bedroom, living room, bathroom, and a petite kitchen. The housemother had a similar suite and supervisors had connecting baths between each pair of rooms.[26]

Queen's & Plantation Health

In his research of plantation diseases, Larsen learned about deaths from beriberi and gastroenteritis—both preventable ailments. Larsen blamed the condition on neglect and ignorance. In 1928, he was invited to speak at the annual meeting of the Hawaiian Sugar Planters' Association (HSPA) on recent developments in medicine. To the members' dismay, instead Larsen described the worrisome health conditions found on some of the plantations. He argued for the creation of a plantation health center and for good medicine delivered in an economic manner: "At your experiment station, scientists have demonstrated that it pays to improve crops. Let me show that it also pays to improve human conditions." When one irate Planters' Association member replied that they were not in the business of public health, Larsen responded, "How much cane can a sick man cut?" Larsen offered an eighteen-month trial health improvement program to prove its effectiveness in reducing the costs of producing cane. "If it does not lower the cost of producing cane, we'll abandon the project." The HSPA agreed to a trial period based on these terms.

Larsen suggested improving nutrition on plantations first. Fruit trees and other edible plants were brought in and cultivated on the plantations so that workers could enjoy a variety of fresh food. After seventeen months, Larsen proved to the directors that "workers who ate twice their former amount of protective foods suffered less than half as many sick days as had the other laborers."[27] Plantation stores began to sell protective food at cost, and nutritious lunches were served to school-aged children for five cents. Well-balanced, afford-able meals were provided for workers that offered a better nutritional option than rice only. The plantation store began offering chocolate milk. Colored charts and comic books were used to teach children the importance of a balanced diet. The meal program fluctuated because the workers simply did not like all of the food provided.[28] Dr. P. Howard Liljestrand discussed the results of the trial period:

> I am now completely convinced that the population in general gets far less medical care than it needs and can use, because of fee for service payment. It is true that plantations have a high rate of office calls and a high rate of hospitalization, but Dr. Larsen's figures indicate that it pays off in good health.[29]

In 1929, Larsen took on the job of creating the Ewa Health Cen-ter that would become a hub for medical improvements.[30] Infant mortality rates on the Ewa Plantation were tragic. Physicians initiated a diet regimen for newborns that included local, fresh ingredients. Beta lactose, unsweetened evaporated milk, and cane syrup were given to infants prior to breastfeeding. After a few weeks, cod liver oil, and orange juice were introduced into their diet. At three months infants were given *poi* and strained vegetable soup. The health center also prepared formulas for babies in sterile bottles that were deliv-ered daily for a year and then supplemented by soup.

Larsen analyzed records at the Ewa Health Center. He believed that women were having too many children too close together and this resulted in maternal deaths. In one instance a thirty-five-year old mother gave birth to her twelfth child after having lost six others. Larsen recommended birth-spacing and birth-control on plantations for the well-being of mothers and infants. Condoms became available for three- to ten-cents despite strong religious opposition. Pregnant women were given rides to the health center for examination and prenatal education, and encouraged to deliver at the hospital rather than in unsanitary camp shacks. Post-natal care included home visits by nurses. Larsen's interest in population and birth-control later brought about his alliance with Margaret Sanger (also a visiting patient of his) and he accompanied her to international Planned Parenthood conferences. This led him to give sex education lectures at McKinley High School.

Larsen used his prolific writing skills in various arenas, such as in *The Queen's Bulletin*. He published his research findings in medical journals and took on the editorial role for *Plantation Health Bulletin*. The bulletin contained articles for and from plantation doctors regarding interesting cases, new findings in medicine, and transmitted information. Doctors wrote on subjects such as deaths, diseases, industrial accidents, births, or anything else of concern. *Plantation Health Bulletin* became a history of plantation health over its twenty-five years.

Industrial accidents, another major concern of Larsen's, were high on Oʻahu. After 1937, when specialists were assigned to minimize this figure, Oʻahu's rate of accidents on the job plummeted from 2450 per hundred thousand to 930, and the death rate was significantly lowered as well. The number of appendicitis operations was also studied in Hawaiʻi. The plantation records showed a comparison of 1.2 per hundred thousand deaths from appendicitis as against the mainland number of 10.8. This, Larsen commented, suggested good methods and "vigorous record keeping."[31]

With regard to plantation health, Dr. L. L. Sexton, Sr. asserts that:

> A discussion of plantation medicine would not be complete without the highest commendation to Dr. Nils P. Larsen whose name is synonymous with plantation medicine. His encouragement to the inexperienced young intern, or words of restraint to the over-aggressive has brought plantation medicine up from its crude beginnings to a degree of efficiency second to none in any other agricultural area in the world. He molded the disorganized, inefficient system of plantation medicine into the modern association of plantation physicians whom today we salute.[32]

Larsen spoke out about civil rights for plantation laborers, their need for advanced medical services, and access to better nutrition. By the 1940s, major epidemics had been curtailed. With the use of sulfapyradine, death from pneumonia had decreased close to threefold. The plantations became the most healthful places to live in Hawai'i. Tuberculosis cases were generally confined to sanitariums and that lowered the number of tuberculosis cases on the plantations. Larsen's efforts in the creation of a better health, welfare, and living environment for plantation workers had paid off.[33]

QUEEN'S EXPANSION & MEDICAL GROUP

During Larsen's tenure at Queen's, between 1922 and 1942, the hospital grew in many areas. The intern program was approved by the American Medical Association, the Liholiho Wing was constructed, a department of physiotherapy was initiated, mental health and diabetic clinics were opened, the Mabel Smyth building was dedicated, and a blood bank was established. In 1927, and again in 1946, Larsen

FIG. 2. Dr. Larssen at the Medical Group, ca. 1955. Lila Larsen Morgan Collection.

served as president of Honolulu County Medical Society; in 1929, he became chairman of the first Pan-Pacific Surgical Congress; in 1930, he became medical advisor to the HSPA. Additionally, Larsen acted as a consulting physician for Tripler Hospital.[34]

In addition to his work at Queen's and other associations, in 1934, Larsen became part of a medical coalition. The Medical Group was established on South Beretania Street in Honolulu. Doctors James Judd, Arthur Molyneux, Peter Halford, and R. L. Mansfield decided to create the joint venture in order to share expenses and profits. Larsen, who rented office space for his consulting practice, joined in. According to "The Medical Group of Honolulu" brochure, it behooved the group to be part of a team, affording them relief from such things as bookkeeping and paying for expensive equipment individually. It additionally advanced their knowledge of medicine as they could easily consult each other and provide better patient care. In 1939, they formed a formal partnership and decided to construct their own air-conditioned building on Punchbowl Street in Honolulu.[35]

TYPHUS AND VAGOTOMY

In 1939, at the age of 49, Larsen is believed to have contracted typhus as a result of a fleabite that he obtained while developing film in a darkroom under his home in Diamond Head.[36] On November 25, 1939, he came down with a mild case of diarrhea and minimal abdominal cramps. He developed a slight headache and loss of appetite on the second day. On the third day his temperature reached 102 degrees and symptoms increased to "general malaise, excessive peristalsis, and a wide-awake state." When admitted to the hospital, Larsen felt chilly, had increased headaches, experienced pain in the lower lumbar region with aches in his legs, and had "severe diaphoresis."

After four days Larsen's temperature dropped to normal and he felt much better. However, on the fifth day his temperature rose again. It soared to 104 degrees and averaged 103 degrees. On the sixth day of typhus, he developed a rash of small red spots on his abdomen. As they covered his whole body, "part of the rash was hemorrhagic." His symptoms grew to "a chilly sensation, a constant and severe headache, painful eye movements, sensitivity of his spine, and aches in his legs. He experienced extreme fatigue, with insomnia even after given A.S.A. [acetylsalicylic acid] compounds, morphine, dilaudid, and pantapon." Inhalations of pure oxygen gave headache relief, but he had no appetite and loose bowels.

On the ninth day of the disease, Larsen developed an irregular arthritis that involved his ankle, knee, hip, left shoulder, both wrists, and several finger joints. They were painful, red, and the swelling lasted from two to three days. He was also jaundiced and had an "acute nephritis." Larsen lost 22 pounds during this time period. It was not until the fifteenth day that his temperature dropped to the normal range. His pulse remained consistently below average. He was hospitalized for 20 days.[37]

After his recovery, Larsen initiated correspondence with Dr. Hans Zinsser of Harvard Medical School, professor of bacteriology and immunology at Columbia and author of *Rats, Lice and History*. Larsen wrote: "I had occasion recently to meet your good friend with whom you have been so intimately associated with throughout your professional life—namely typhus fever." He documented an increased number and severity of cases in Hawai'i: four cases of typhus in 1933, fourteen in 1934, nineteen in 1935, fifteen in 1936, thirty-four in 1937, forty-six in 1938, and thirty-five in the first six months of 1939.

Larsen informed Zinsser the disease seemed to frequent drier, more affluent sections of the community. In parched areas, dry fine dust naturally occurred under homes. An entomologist's report noted that after rats were killed in traps, they were often left indefinitely in this powder. The fleas that escaped off dead rats then lived for some time in these dry, dusty areas. Even Larsen's double-walled home was a breeding ground for rats, "whose scampering can be heard at any time, night or day."[38]

As a result of typhus, Larsen suffered from severe angina. On December 5, 1941, Larsen boarded the Matson luxury liner *Lurline* with his wife on a medical trip to help cure his angina. They went to Boston where he was to have an experimental surgery called a vagotomy, cutting the vagus nerve on the back to rid the heart of pain. He was one of Dr. Paul Dudley White's first patients to undergo this procedure.[39] The operation did not aim to resolve the source of his pain, only the sensation of it. The *Lurline* zigzagged its way to San Francisco, before Pearl Harbor was attacked on December 7, 1941. Fortunately, the Larsen children were away at college when the bombs hit Hawai'i. After the surgery Larsen contracted an infection and developed a large carbuncle; he recuperated for several weeks in New York, working on etchings. Upon returning to Hawai'i, his interests in medicine took a turn towards preserving traditional Hawaiian medical practice.[40]

HAWAIIAN HERBAL MEDICINE AND *KAHUNA*

Larsen believed Western doctors discounted Hawaiian medical practices because of "Anglo-Saxon prejudice and pompousness, the usual trimmings of the superiority complex." Larsen considered the system of traditional Hawaiian experts or *kahuna,* who were influential in all aspects of life, had been dismantled after Western influence took hold. Information about the *kahuna* and their belief system was either ignored or disparaged by newcomers, who focused mostly on the grisly stories about the "low-brow *kahuna*" who practiced "black magic" according to medical literature. The mystifying of Hawaiian herbal medicine may have been purposeful on the part of missionaries because slandering *kahuna* made all Hawaiian medical knowledge seem "primitive" and, therefore, insignificant to "real" medicine or Anglo-Saxon importance. Larsen found that modern Hawaiians only had fragments of knowledge about traditional Hawaiian medicine from which to piece together a "mosaic."

Larsen advocated for much of the *kahuna* system. Generally, Hawaiian children were trained as early as five years old to study in certain chosen areas that they showed a propensity for. According to Larsen, the *kahuna* was near the top of the traditional Hawaiian social hierarchy and the *kahuna lapa'au* and the *kahuna hā-hā* were the most respected of the *kahuna* class. They sat on the chief's council. They served as expert diagnosticians and therapists respectively, and possibly both. He pointed out that *kahuna* varied their pharmacopoeia according to what worked for them and were selective about disclosure of their remedies to even their own interns.

In Hawaiian medicine, the *kahuna lapa'au* was the authority qualified to perform the "highest form of healing." They were trained to relieve pain and suffering through medicinal herbs. In dispensing medicine, they carried herbs, scrapings from pumice stone, and earthen powdered roots in *lau hala* baskets. Larsen found *kahuna* believed in observation, animal testing, autopsy, the practical usage of many herbs, and the end result. Larsen noted there was experimentation in this learning process, as in all medical knowledge. Hawaiian medicine at the point of European contact understood the workings of the human heart, that the head controlled the body, and that disease responded to herbs and/or healing through the spirit. As Hawaiian medical knowledge increased through practical experience, it overcame superstitious beliefs. In comparison to traditional Hawaiian medical practices, Larsen claimed much of what missionary doctors practiced at this time was not considered acceptable medicine today (such as blood-letting, or using calomel, and sulphur). Hawaiian medicine, he asserted, "is still logical."[41]

In a divergence from the Hawaiian oral tradition, upon the demand of the king in 1868, a *kahuna lapa'au* and *kahuna hā-hā* had written their medical knowledge in a book entitled *Kua'ua'u*. Larsen found this to be a prime reference tool to validate the difference in medical practices prior to 1800. He contended green leaves and vegetables Hawaiian *kahuna* put on wounds could be compared to later uses Caucasians found for garlic, yeast cell extractions, and leaf chlorophyll—all useful in inhibiting the growth of bacteria.

In 1922 Larsen found that the Territorial Board of Health published a list of 191 known Hawaiian medicinal herbs, their method of preparation, and use. The best known of these included: the *kukui* nut (a purgative and strong physic), *'awa* (a sedative), *kalo* sap (a blood-clotting astringent), *noni* applied with hot Epsom salt packs (to abscesses and bring boils to a head), *uhalao* (to chew for sore throats), *pahoehoe,* (for eye inflammation), fine *pia* or starch mixed with certain smooth clays (for stomach disorders), *laukahi,* a broad green leaf containing chlorophyll with vitamins and minerals sterilized by the sun (to heal wounds), and saline water (a cathartic). The *popolo* plant, related to deadly nightshade, was the backbone of the *kahuna laupa'au* armamentarium.[42]

Larsen became so well known for his advocacy of Hawaiian herbal medicine that, by the 1950s, William Totherow, an assistant physician from the Lanai Plantation, referred to him as "medicine man of Hawai'i."[43] Larsen emphasized Hawaiian remedies were effective only when they were prescribed by the *kapuna lapa'au*. However, Larsen had such a strong belief that taro was one of the reasons why Hawaiian children had such healthy teeth (as opposed to the white rice diet of other cultures found in Hawai'i) that he developed a supplement he called "tarolactin," which he gave to his grandchildren, who were fond of it.[44] In 1951 Larsen showcased an exhibit at Bishop Museum featuring information on practices Larsen deemed valuable in his investigation of medicine among Hawaiians.[45]

Larsen's interest in preservation of ancient medical Hawaiian practices prompted him to become an active member in the restoration of an ancient Hawaiian *heiau*. In 1953, at a Hawaiian Historical Society meeting, Clarice Taylor suggested a small, newly rediscovered *heiau* in Keaiwa could easily be preserved and the committee concurred. Per Larsen's request, a retired forester in the 'Aiea area, Thomas K. McGuire, confirmed that the abandoned *heiau* was, in fact, a medical center that had maintained a large herb garden. After Hawaiian cultural experts Mary Kawena Pukui, Anna Peleiohaolani Hall, and Emily Taylor verified the *heiau*, the committee went to work on the idea.

The *heiau ho'ōla* (or "heiau of healing") was simple in construction: "A stone wall surrounded an area in which there was a grass house for the medical master who lived there and practiced his art there."[46] It was where:

> ... the kahuna of old dispensed their powers. They prepared herbs with stone pestles and mortars, seen, now, only on the shelves of Bishop Museum or in an occasional family collection.[47]

Ill or injured Hawaiians either traveled to the *heiau* for medical help or assistance was dispensed to those who were too sick to journey. Larsen conducted a study of the *kahuna-lapa'au* and found that after patients entered the gates of the *heiau*, they met an intern for the *kahuna-lapa'au*. The patient took bundles of food or clothing as payment. Salt water stood in a bowl at the entrance for all to sprinkle on for purification. Green *ti* plants were grounded around the walls to keep out the contamination of evil spirits. The medical master kept intern *kahuna* busy as they gathered plants and herbs and helped the master make medications. Women *kahuna* were restricted to the area outside the walls.

Healing centers were dedicated, so a rededication, quasi-reenact-ment ceremony was planned for the *Keaiwa heiau*. The Board of Agri-culture and Forestry set aside the land as a park and assigned a crew to clean the site. About 40 plant varieties used by Hawaiian ancestors were planted. The Outdoor Circle of Ewa and 'Aiea laid a path of *ti* leaves from the roadway to the *heiau* entrance. The rededication on 'Aiea Heights was held on Thursday, November 15, 1951, at 3:00 p.m. Hawaiian community leaders honored Larsen, saying "we want our friend who has studied medical lore, to come inside the *heiau* as a *kahuna lapa'au*."[48]

AGING

Throughout his professional life, Larsen studied aging. In Novem-ber, 1956, Larsen wrote an article entitled "On Deferring Old Age." He told of his "first angina symptom at 39 and severe angina until 51 when a coronary thrombosis floored me for a while." In January 1941, he wrote:

> The world has come into a realization that we are in the midst of a great change. 'The wave of the future' as Anne Lindbergh calls it, is a mighty force which is engulfing us. When it has passed, it will leave a washed and different world. To fight that wave and try to keep every-thing as it is, is like trying to deceive ourselves as individuals into believing that we are not growing old.[49]

At a symposium in Philadelphia regarding aging, Larsen declared the current problem was how "to keep the step firm, and creative effort active until one is about to disappear into the golden sunset of an active, happy life." He was ahead of his time in discovering ways to remain healthy into old age; they included a low fat, low salt diet, no smoking, daily exercise, and moderate alcohol consumption which lessened the chance for a hardening of the arteries.

Larsen was the medical director at Queen's for 20 years, until 1942. He retained his partnership in the Medical Group up until 1955 when he retired and continued to treat only a select number of patients in his Kāhala office. He analyzed the difficulties of growing old, describing the cramps in his calves, the tightening of the chest, pains in the jaw—all of which, he said, were evidence of hardening and stiffening of the blood vessels. He insisted that by 69 years of age the idea of death had "lost all its terrors." Life was still full of fun, but for him there was no longer any fear for him connected with the "step beyond."[50]

Despite his best efforts, on March 19, 1964, Larsen suffered a heart attack and died at the age of 73. Dr. Marvin A. Brennecke reported:

> You can see him—and this he did—sitting in the waiting room (of the Medical Group office in Waialae-Kahala), two hours before his death, holding an oxygen mask over his face and reading a current lay magazine. He was waiting to receive the report on his EKG that a colleague had just taken. He had just finished writing a note to Dr. Paul White of Boston describing his symptoms, believing that this may be of value in the study of heart diseases in the future.[51]

FIG. 3. Nils Paul Larsen, ca. 1955. Lila Larsen Morgan Collection.

It was typical that Larsen was at work not only on his own needs, but also in pressing new research for those who had yet to face the aging process. Larsen took the same practical medical approach as did his venerable Hawaiian counterpart, the *kahuna lapaʻau.*

NOTES

I would like to thank Lila Larsen Morgan for encouraging the preservation of Nils Paul Larsen's memory and for providing many references used in this article from her private collection. Helen Wong-Smith has also been instrumental in editing and offering valued suggestions.

[1] Lila Morgan, notes on NPL ancestors, 5 June 1998.

[2] Nils P. Larsen, "Looking Back," *The Pharos of Alpha Omega Alpha,* 1958, p. 24.

[3] Lila Morgan, letter to her children, 30 Sep. 1996.

[4] Morgan, notes on NPL and money, 30 Dec. 2000.

[5] Nils P. Larsen, letter to his children, 1 Aug. 1959.

[6] Nils P. Larsen, English paper, 30 Sep. 1909.

[7] Lila Morgan, notes on Mass Agee, 17 Aug. 1998.

[8] Nils P. Larsen, "A Confession," 1914.

[9] Lila Morgan, notes on Mass Agee, 17 Aug. 1998.

[10] Margery Hastert, Mamiya Medical Heritage Center, Nils P. Larsen, M.D. Queen's Historical Room. http://hml.org/mmhcexhibits/larsen/fngaid.html. 1 April 2001.

[11] Nils P. Larsen, letter to Mary Larsen, 2 May 1918.

[12] Mary Larsen, letter to Nils P. Larsen, (circa 1918).

[13] *Sanitary Detachment 106th Infantry History and Roster Pamphlet,* 1919.

[14] Hastert, "Nils P. Larsen, M.D. Queen's Historical Room."

[15] Morgan, letter to her children, 30 Sep. 2002.

[16] Hastert, "Nils P. Larsen, M.D. Queen's Historical Room."

[17] Lila Morgan, letter to her children, 30 Sep. 1996.

[18] Nils P. Larsen, "House Physician's Report," 30 Jan. 1923.

[19] Nils P. Larsen, "1928 Report of the Medical Director."

[20] Nils P. Larsen, "History of the Campaign for Better Milk in Hawaiʻi, 1947, 9–11.

[21] Paula Rath, "Palama Settlement: 100 Years of Serving a Neighborhood's Needs," *Hawaiʻi Medical Journal,* Nov. 1955, 774–5.

[22] A.L. Davis, *Annual Report for the Board of Health,* 1926.

[23] Rath, "Palama Settlement," 774.

[24] Ruby LoRaine Carlson, "A Case Study of Queen's Hospital School of Nursing (1916–1968)," Diss.U of Hawaiʻi, 1991.

[25] *Ka Hakaupila* School of Nursing Yearbook, 1934.

[26] Carlson, "A Case Study of Queen's Hospital School of Nursing."

[27] Nils P. Larsen, "Hawaiian Sugar Plantation Speech of 1928," 4.

[28] Nils P. Larsen, "Twenty-Year Review of Health Work on Hawaiian Sugar Planta-

tions," Address Before the 74th Annual Meeting of the Hawaiian Sugar Planters' Association, 7 Dec. 1954.

29 Howard Liljestrand, "100 Years of Plantation Medicine," 1956.

30 Larsen, "Hawaiian Sugar Plantation Speech of 1928."

31 Larsen, "Twenty-Year Review of Health Work on Hawaiian Sugar Plantations."

32 L.L.Sexton, Sr., *Plantation Health Bulletin,* April 1961, 43.

33 Larsen, "Twenty-Year Review of Health Work on Hawaiian Sugar Plantations."

34 Margery Hastert, "Nils P. Larsen, M.D. Queen's Historical Room."

35 "Medical Group Brochure." [Honolulu] n.d.

36 Lila Morgan, notes on typhus, 28 Feb. 1999.

37 "Case Report—Typhus Fever," 1939.

38 Nils P. Larsen, letter to Howard Zinsser, 4 Jan. 1940.

39 Jane Thomas, *My Hawai'i, 1938–1962.* (Philadelphia: Xlibris, 2002) 50.

40 Janine A. Powers, personal interview with Lila Morgan, 27 April 2001.

41 Nils P. Larsen, "Medical Arts in Ancient Hawaii," *53rd Annual Report of the Hawaiian Historical Society,* Honolulu, 1944, 27–44.

42 Nils P. Larsen, "The Highly Developed Art of Medicine in Old Hawaii," *CIBI Journal,* Winter 1962.

43 William Totherow, "Doctor in the Sandwich Islands," *Harvard Medical Alumni Journal,* April 1954, 17.

44 Janine A. Powers, personal interview with Lila Morgan, 17 April 2001.

45 E.H. Bryan, Jr., "Kahunas' Means for Curing on Exhibition," *HA,* Nov. 1951.

46 Clarice Taylor, "Heiau Hunting," *The Saturday Star Bulletin,* 17 Oct. 1953, 8.

47 Nils P. Larsen, "Rededication of Healing Heiau Keaiwa," *Annual Report of the Hawaiian Historical Society,* Honolulu, 1953, 7.

48 "Park Rededication Tomorrow," *HSB* 10 July 1953.

49 Nils P. Larsen, "On Deferring Old Age," Social Sciences Association, 5 Nov. 1956. Unpublished speech.

50 Larsen, "On Deferring Old Age."

51 Marvin A. Brennecke, "Dr. Nils Paul Larsen," *Plantation Health Bulletin,* April 1964.

ALBERT S. BROUSSARD

The Honolulu NAACP and
Race Relations in Hawai'i

HAWAI'I DREW almost no attention among African American leaders or protest organizations such as the National Association for the
Advancement of Colored People (NAACP) or the National Urban
League prior to World War II. However, the onset of global conflict
changed the racial landscape of Hawai'i in profound ways. For the
first time, tens of thousands of African American servicemen and war
workers passed through Hawai'i, admittedly a fraction of the nearly
one million American soldiers, sailors, and marines who traversed this
Pacific paradise or were stationed on one of Hawai'i's military bases.
Yet the 30,000 African Americans who came to Hawai'i during World
War II, wrote David Farber and Beth Bailey, "found themselves in a
racial hothouse."[1]

Although World War II marked the first large in-migration of African Americans to Hawai'i, blacks had settled in the islands for more
than a century prior to 1941. Anthony Allen, a fugitive slave from
Schenectady, New York, arrived in Hawai'i in 1810. Allen was attempting to escape the oppressive conditions of that both slaves and free
blacks faced in northern states such as New York. In Hawai'i, Allen

Albert S. Broussard is a professor of history at Texas A&M University. He is the 2005
Langston Hughes Professor of American Studies at the University of Kansas. He is the
author of five books, including Black San Francisco: The Struggle for Racial Equality in the West, 1900–1945, *and* African American Odyssey: The Stewarts, 1853–
1963. *Dr. Broussard is a consultant to the National Park Service on its Underground Rail-*
road project. He is currently writing a history of African Americans in the Far West from
1945 to the present.

The Hawaiian Journal of History, vol. 39 (2005)

succeeded beyond his wildest expectations, becoming a respected merchant, marrying a Hawaiian woman, and serving as one of the advisers of Kamehameha the Great. Yet Allen was not alone. Betsey Stockton, the first African American female reported in Hawai'i, had arrived in 1823 to work with Christian missionaries. Yet neither Allen's nor Stockton's presence in Hawai'i stimulated a sizable movement of African Americans to Hawai'i in the nineteenth century, save several dozen Black missionaries, laborers, and seamen. In 1898, however, T. McCants Stewart, a prominent African American leader from Brooklyn, New York, arrived in Hawai'i with his family. Stewart had hoped to take advantage of the economic and political opportunities in Hawai'i during the formative stages of American settlement. But Stewart, like Anthony Allen, was also attempting to escape racial discrimination in the United States. Although Stewart remained in Hawai'i for only seven years, his daughter, Carlotta, graduated from Oahu College (Punahou School) and became a respected teacher and principal on the islands of O'ahu and Kaua'i.[2]

By 1900, only 233 African Americans lived in Hawai'i, and they represented but 0.2 percent of the total population. A modest attempt to import African American laborers had been made in the early 1900s by the Hawaiian Sugar Planters' Association. In 1901, the association successfully recruited at least 200 African Americans from Tennessee, and six years later about 30 Black families were recruited from several southern states. Yet the number of Black workers imported to Hawai'i remained relatively modest and, for a variety of reasons, including its distance from the mainland and the absence of established African American communities, the islands had not served as a magnet for Black migrants.[3]

The relatively tolerant and tranquil racial atmosphere that African Americans such as T. McCants Stewart and his daughter Carlotta had encountered in Hawai'i during the early decades of the twentieth century changed dramatically with the importation of American service personnel. White servicemen and their commanding officers attempted to recreate the segregated policies and practices that had existed on the mainland for nearly a century, and, to a large extent, they succeeded. White servicemen, for instance, spread vicious rumors about black people in general and black soldiers in particular, portraying them as thieves, rapists, murderers, criminals, and carrying a multitude of diseases. Black men could not be trusted under any circumstance, and were a particular menace to the islands' female population.[4]

These vicious racial attitudes, as well as the widespread pattern of segregation directed against African American servicemen in hotels, dance halls, and public accommodations, served as pivotal factors in the earliest attempt to establish an NAACP branch in Hawai'i. As early as February 1941, a small group of multiracial residents inquired about the prospect of organizing a NAACP branch in Honolulu. The request clearly took the NAACP's national leadership by surprise, for no branch had ever been chartered outside of the continental United States and Hawai'i contained a small black community in 1940. Approximately 255 African Americans resided in the islands in 1940, a number that could be found on any given night occupying a pool hall on Chicago's South Side or a barbershop in Philadelphia or New York. Yet these Hawai'i residents persisted. "Never before in the history of your people was there a greater need to organize than today. With the ever growing prejudice, and especially among the service men here, I feel that a group with your backing could protect their rights," wrote Jacob Prager to William Dean Pickens, director of NAACP branches in New York.[5] In subsequent correspondence, Prager, a native of Boston of Jewish faith residing in Hawai'i, informed Pickens that discrimination in defense industry jobs was just as prevalent in Hawai'i as in west coast cities. "I have noticed that on the defense projects, Negros [sic] still get the small pick and shovel jobs, not because they cannot fill other jobs, but, because of prejudice," wrote Prager.[6]

William Dean Pickens remained unconvinced that Hawai'i's racial problems were as serious as other locales on the United States mainland. He lamented that Hawai'i, to his recollection, had been free of racial prejudice when he had visited the islands previously, a misconception shared by numerous observers of all races who came to Hawai'i. The Hawaiian Islands, Pickens opined nostalgically, was "undoubtedly the freest place and freer from color prejudice of any part of the US territory. But even in such a condition, we would need organized cooperation to prevent the development of discrimination."[7] Thus Pickens concurred, albeit reluctantly, that in spite of Hawai'i's relatively benign racial past, organizing a branch of the

NAACP as sort of a preemptive strike made perfect sense. Although Roy Wilkins, then assistant director of the national NAACP, displayed far less enthusiasm than Pickens regarding this idea, and he queried the NAACP field secretary about the background of H. Parke Williams, an African American resident in Hawai'i and the principal booster of the Honolulu branch, he and other national NAACP leaders encouraged Hawai'i's leadership to continue their organizing efforts. H. Parke Williams gave the national NAACP office even more reason to praise their zeal when he requested that Pickens send "at least 150 [membership] application blanks, grant him permission to solicit funds in behalf of the NAACP, and mail at least twenty-five copies of the *Crisis* magazine so that some may be sold at meetings." Pickens assumed, in kind, that Williams would keep him informed about both the group's organizing efforts and the racial climate in Hawai'i. "At any early date I shall forward a more comprehensive picture of inter-racial conditions on those islands," wrote Williams.[8]

These early organizing efforts by a committed group of interracial leaders in Honolulu fizzled almost abruptly as they began after H. Parke Williams suddenly left the islands in the spring of 1941. Roy Wilkins had been correct to inquire about Williams's reputation, for he proved less interested in racial betterment than in filling his own coffers. Williams pocketed membership funds from 53 people and failed to mail them to the national office. Despite repeated attempts by the NAACP national office to contact him, Williams has not been heard from since.[9]

Although discouraged, local activists in Honolulu continued to press the NAACP national office to organize a local branch, as racial attitudes grew even more vicious and discrimination more pernicious against African American servicemen. By early 1944, these local leaders, led by Kenneth Sano and William C. Page, both Hawai'i residents, took the initiative and passed a resolution, "requesting charter and establishing of local branch in Hawai'i from the NAACP."[10] Yet mindful that H. Parke Williams had absconded with the initial funds that were raised for memberships, these new activists, a bit wiser three years removed, designated Henry J. Green, deputy of the Territory of Hawai'i for the Elks, an established African American fraternal society, to serve as the group's liaison to the NAACP's national office.

Under the authority of the organizing committee, Green mailed an application to NAACP headquarters with 102 memberships to Ella J. Baker, who now served as director of branches.[11]

Yet rather than welcoming the Honolulu branch with open arms, the NAACP's national leadership was cautious and reserved. Walter White, the executive director, and the NAACP board of directors, were uncertain if their charter permitted it to establish branches outside of the mainland United States. Ella Baker had no such reservations, and, like William Pickens before her, encouraged Kenneth Sano and others in Honolulu to press on. The NAACP board of directors, however, did not share Baker's enthusiasm, and voted instead to postpone the request for an official NAACP charter until Walter White visited Hawai'i in December 1944, when the NAACP's executive director had proposed to tour the Pacific war zone. Ella Baker, clearly disappointed with the board's decision, fired off a memorandum to Walter White, requesting that the board of directors reconsider its decision. The decision stood. In the meantime, 102 people from Hawai'i were granted NAACP membership, but not the authority to organize a formal branch, a situation that the national office did not find the least bit awkward.[12]

This decision, however, was reversed following Walter White's whirlwind visit to Hawai'i in December 1944. Before a large public gathering, which numbered more than 250 people, White discussed the proposed chartering of a branch of the NAACP in Honolulu. The majority of those in attendance were African American servicemen, who had a particular stake in both the war's outcome and the creation of a local NAACP branch in Honolulu, which they viewed as one vehicle to protect their rights. That these servicemen possessed a strong racial consciousness, there can be no doubt, for Walter White attempted to answer questions on such important topics as the Port Chicago mutiny trial of African American sailors, black postwar unemployment, and "possibilities of racial wars following World War II."[13] That black servicemen would query White about the prospects for racial wars in the United States at the conclusion of this global conflict, reveals a keen awareness of the race riots and wave of racial violence that swept across America following World War I in dozens of American cities. Unlike their World War I counterparts, who had expected a new racial order upon their return to the United States after fighting for democracy abroad, these African American service-men were far less naive.[14]

From the onset, the drive to charter an NAACP branch in Hono-lulu was interracial, and Walter White, as well as Ella Baker, were pleased with this fact. Kenneth Sano, for instance, a pivotal figure in the drive to charter a local branch, was of Asian ancestry. Sano had served as a local distributor of *Crisis* magazine, an indication that he was keenly aware of the NAACP's goals and objectives and how a local branch of the NAACP could potentially assist the local populace in minimizing racial conflict. It was an example, too, of the NAACP's reach that the *Crisis* magazine had made its way across the Pacific to Hawai'i. Yet Sano was only one of many non-African Americans who supported the establishment of a local branch. Irving Townsend, a white ensign in the United States Navy Pacific Fleet, wrote the NAACP national office and pledged his unqualified support. "I would like to enlist myself in your case and give it all the support of which I am capable, if my services can help you at all in the future. I have great faith in the future of the Colored Race and hope to have some part in helping them get their future recognition as soon as possible," wrote Townsend.[15]

This groundswell of multiracial support, White's concern for the welfare of black servicemen, and Kenneth Sano's boast that as many as 500 people in Honolulu were interested in joining the NAACP, convinced Walter White that a local branch was necessary and worth whatever risk that creating a branch this far removed from the United States mainland might entail. After consulting with his board of directors and receiving their assurance that the NAACP could legally charter a branch outside of the continental U.S., White rec-ommended that the national office issue a charter to establish a branch of the NAACP in Honolulu.[16] As Ella Baker informed Henry Green, "you perhaps note there was some difference of opinion as to the feasibility of establishing a branch so far from our national head-quarters," a reservation that persisted at the NAACP national office for many years. These reservations notwithstanding, the Honolulu branch received its official charter in June, 1945, and Kenneth Sano promised Ella Baker that "we intend to make our branch an example of efficiency and intelligence, for we feel that only in that way can a worthwhile cause be given proper emphasis." The Honolulu branch had the distinction of being the first NAACP branch chartered out-side of the mainland United States and the first branch established in United States territory rather than in a state.[17] Given its diverse membership, which included African Americans, whites, Japanese, Chinese, and members of Hawaiian ancestry, the Honolulu NAACP may well have been the most racially and ethnically diverse of any NAACP branch.

Despite its prestige, the Honolulu branch was just one of several organizations working to achieve racial justice in Hawai'i. For many years, the Inter-Racial Committee had worked to promote equality and fair play, and with the onset of World War II, the Hawaii Asso-ciation for Civic Unity was established.[18] Councils for Civic Unity existed in numerous American cities during World War II in an effort to improve the racial climate after the large wartime migration of African Americans. In some cities, where few blacks had lived prior to 1940, such as San Francisco, Seattle, and Los Angeles, civic and community leaders viewed these organizations as vehicles to lessen racial friction and, in some instances, to prevent race riots. Thus these interracial organizations, which comprised the major civic, business, and community leaders, played important roles in many western cities. They often worked in tandem with more established civil rights organizations such as the NAACP and the National Urban League.

The Honolulu NAACP wasted little time in presenting a slate of officers, and elected Fleming R. Waller, who resided on South King Street, as its first president, and Kenneth Sano, whom Katharine Lackey called the "moving spirit of this organization in the Islands" as secretary-treasurer.[19] Indeed, Sano, one of the many unsung figures in the national records of the NAACP, played a pivotal role in the branch's founding and during its formative years. Sano, for example, consistently pressed Ella Baker on the urgent need for a branch in Hawai'i, despite the territory's small African American population and its distance from the mainland. Sano also took the initiative to prepare a meticulous outline of the branch's "proposed plan of action," and he contacted all interested persons and organi-zations in Honolulu, including local newspapers, announcing the creation of a new NAACP branch in Hawai'i. Finally, Sano, as well as other local leaders, organized a small dinner for those individuals, he believed, would, "take an active part in the Branch."[20] Nor did Sano, a careful organizer and a meticulous leader, act in haste. He cautioned Ella Baker that the newly formed branch would purposely delay taking part in the national drive for new members until the branch had explained the purpose of the NAACP to local residents and promoted sufficient interest in the Honolulu community. "We want a carefully considered plan with influential citizens behind us and our proposals presented to the public before any membership drive is undertaken," he informed Ella Baker.[21]

During its formative years, the Honolulu branch, like all new NAACP chapters, struggled to gain members and attempted to forge an identity. Since this type of civil rights organization had never existed in Hawai'i, local residents did not know exactly what to expect. Yet the local branch set the tone early when it vigorously protested racially offensive advertisements that appeared in the *Honolulu Advertiser* and the *Honolulu Star Bulletin* for the sale of "20-inch Nigger Dolls." Although this type of grotesque caricature of African Americans had been sold for over a century, and was particularly prevalent in the southern states, they were relatively new to Hawai'i, perhaps a product of the large in-migration of white servicemen from the South. Katharine Lackey, who succeeded Fleming Waller as branch president, seized the initiative and joined with the Inter-Racial Committee to protest this indignity. Lackey organized an intensive letter-writing campaign directed to the editors of both daily newspapers in Honolulu, and the racially offensive advertisement was removed immediately. "I am sure that this advertisement does not indicate the policy of the management of either the *Star-Bulletin* or the *Advertiser*," Lackey informed Madison Jones, Jr., an administrative assistant at the NAACP's national office. In reality, both newspapers had occasionally run racially offensive headlines and editorials, maligning both African Americans and Asians, although this practice had become less frequent by World War II.[22]

The Honolulu branch also pushed for a systematic investigation of racial discrimination in the islands, particularly in the areas of housing and employment. While discrimination had been uncommon in these areas prior to World War II, it was practiced more frequently as the African American population increased between 1941 and 1945. Thus it came as no surprise when Lackey informed Ella Baker that the Honolulu branch would conduct a comprehensive survey to reveal the types of racial discrimination most commonly practiced in Hawai'i.[23] The branch also passed a resolution in 1946 endorsing statehood for Hawai'i, 13 years before the territory officially joined the union. The Honolulu branch's executive committee unanimously approved of Hawai'i becoming a state and the branch president appointed a statehood committee to meet with the governor and the local press. Fleming Waller also mailed a copy of the branch's resolution supporting Hawai'i statehood to African American Congressman Adam Clayton Powell, Jr., in the hope of gaining an ally in the United States Congress. There is no record, however, that Powell ever replied to this request.[24]

Although statehood was the most sensational issue that the Honolulu branch addressed, the quest for fair employment was a more urgent matter. The majority of African Americans who lived in Hawai'i between 1941 and 1950 were members of the armed forces, and were, therefore, unaffected by employment discrimination in the civilian sector that African Americans faced daily. Since Hawai'i had no laws prohibiting employment discrimination, the Honolulu branch had little recourse except to investigate allegations and exert moral suasion on an employer.[25] Elizabeth Rademaker, president of the Hawaii Association for Civic Unity, encouraged the NAACP's national office in New York to "excite the interest" of the Honolulu branch and join forces with the Civic Unity Council to pressure the legislature to pass a Territorial Fair Employment Practices Act. This was precisely the kind of interracial alliance that the NAACP national office had encouraged the upstart Honolulu branch to seek, for Hawai'i's racial makeup, they noted frequently in their correspondence, was different from most states on the mainland. Thus Madison Jones spoke for all national NAACP officers when he directed the Honolulu NAACP to "entertain a philosophy of boldness in their approach to the racial question linking up the cause and program of the other groups."[26]

Multiracial alliances offered another benefit to the Honolulu branch: the opportunity to expand its membership base beyond the islands' small African American population. Many servicemen, irrespective of race, such as Irving Townsend, a white naval officer who supported the formation of the Honolulu branch, terminated their membership when they were discharged from the military and shipped home. Thus any alliance, however tenuous, permitted the Honolulu NAACP to enlist whites, Japanese, Chinese, Portuguese, Filipinos, and Hawaiians on their membership rolls. Given the historically small African American population in Hawai'i, it was critically important for the local branch to reach out and serve the needs of other racial and ethnic groups as well as blacks.[27]

As officers of the Honolulu branch attempted to address the concerns of a diverse membership and allegations of increasing discrimination in the islands in the postwar years, they faced a challenge to their leadership. Branch president Fleming Waller revealed that serious dissent existed within the Honolulu branch, and just five months after his reelection as branch president submitted his resignation to the board of directors. Confident of Waller's capable leadership, the branch's executive board refused to accept it and encouraged their embattled president to persevere. Waller had found it personally frustrating to work with James Neal, the branch's vice-president, who he described as possessing an "incongrous [sic] Dr. Jekyll and Mr. Hyde personality—a personality that renders it impossible for others to work for long with him."[28]

Leadership squabbles, to be sure, in NAACP branches or in any civil rights organization, were commonplace, and the NAACP's long established policy had been to allow its branches to sort out these disagreements among themselves. Occasionally, if a dispute seemed beyond the ability of local leadership to resolve amicably, it was not uncommon for either a regional director or the national director of branches to pay the branch a visit and attempt to mediate the dispute. Yet the Honolulu branch posed several unique challenges to the national office. Hawai'i's sheer distance from the mainland made a trip by a national official, such as Walter White or Gloster Current, very expensive and time consuming. Not surprisingly, yet to the dismay of local leaders, the Honolulu branch did not have an official visit from the NAACP's branch department during its first three years of existence.[29] When branch officials in Hawai'i complained of feeling disconnected from the affairs of other NAACP branches and the national office in New York, Current encouraged the Honolulu branch secretary to send delegates to the annual meetings. Although this was sound advice and within the purview of branch leaders, Current's unwillingness to visit Hawai'i only distanced the Honolulu branch further from the national office.[30] Current's remark also illustrated an insensitivity that the national office displayed toward the Honolulu branch and its membership.

By 1949, the Honolulu branch faced a far more serious crisis: allegations that members of the Communist party were current members or seeking membership in the branch.[31] Since the conclusion of World War II, the NAACP had taken a firm stand on members of the Communist party and individuals in other radical organizations applying for membership in their branches: they were not welcomed. This may explain the urgency of Gloster Current's tone when he asked the president and executive broad of the Honolulu branch to clarify this matter for the national office. Yet, James Neal, the outgoing branch president, turned Current's question on its head and demanded that the national office, not the local branch, clarify its own policy on membership. "If no national policy exists regarding this problem [we] desire [the] authority [to permit] Honolulu Branch to set their own policy," wrote Neal. Gloster Current informed branch officials that in neither the Branch Constitution nor the National Constitution were individuals required to sign a loyalty oath in order to join the NAACP, to hold office, or to vote in branch elections. To do otherwise, argued Current, constituted discrimination based on one's political views, clearly a violation of NAACP policy.[32]

Yet the director of branches couched his words very carefully in clarifying the NAACP's position on this matter, attempting to walk a fine line between censorship and freedom of association. "There should be no discrimination," stated Current, "in offering membership to any person on account of race, color, creed, religion or political views. However, we do urge branches to be diligent in carrying forward the program of the NAACP and to be alert to check the indoctrination or course of action not consistent with our program." In a word, Current informed the Honolulu branch that any *new* policy would require approval from the NAACP national office as stipulated in the branch constitution.[33]

On the more urgent matter of Communist party members who also held membership in the Honolulu branch, Morris Freedman, a branch officer, was direct and unwavering. At least thirty members of the Honolulu branch, Freedman informed Gloster Current, including branch officers and members of the executive committee, were openly affiliated with the Communist party in Hawai'i. These individuals, noted Freedman, had gained such a foothold in the branch that its work had virtually come to a standstill. Freedman urged Current to either suspend the Honolulu branch's charter on a temporary basis or, "send someone here from the National Office so that he can make an investigation of the situation.[34]

The NAACP's national office, showing their indifference to the affairs of the Honolulu branch, once again declined to visit the branch, citing inadequate finances to make a trip of this magnitude. But Current added an important caveat. "I doubt whether the [Honolulu] branch can carry out the program of the NAACP anyway as it has been outlined here," he exclaimed, in his frankest statement regarding the troubled branch. Within a month, Current informed the new branch president, Catherine Christopher that, "if the Honolulu Branch is unable to settle its differences amicably at the next election we shall have no other recourse than to consider possible suspension or revocation of its charter."[35] In the space of four years, the work of the Honolulu branch had become a comedy of errors, crippled by leadership struggles and the infiltration of at least one radical political party. These problems, regrettably, eclipsed more significant issues such as employment and housing discrimination or improving race relations, issues that the Honolulu branch had grappled with successfully between 1945 and 1947. However, contested branch elections and voting irregularities had become commonplace by 1949, as Eleanor Agnew and Robert Greene, two branch officers, informed Gloster Current and Lucille Black at the national office.[36] To an outsider such as Frank Davis, executive editor of the Associated Negro Press, who had come to Hawai'i in 1948 to write a book of poetry and a series of articles about the islands, "a temporary suspension of [the] charter is the most logical step if a [branch] president cannot be elected." Davis also corroborated the opinions of others that Communists and Communist sympathizers had considerable influence within the branch. Yet Davis urged Roy Wilkins and other NAACP officials to approach this matter cautiously, for he believed that the NAACP could potentially, "run into difficulties in the matter of keeping control away from Communist or Communist sympathizers in these days of growing reaction when even mild liberals are red-baited."[37]

These suggestions notwithstanding, both Gloster Current and Roy Wilkins had lost faith in the Honolulu branch's leadership, its ability to hold fair and impartial elections, and with the harm that Communist party affiliation could bring to the NAACP's image. Thus in June, 1949, the Committee on Branches at the national office voted to recommend to the board of directors that the Honolulu branch's charter be revoked.[38] This highly unusual move by the national office had been expected by many branch members and welcomed by some. Yet acting branch president Catherine Christopher remained obstreperous despite Roy Wilkins's warning. Christopher denied in a truculent tone that either she or any officer had failed to follow NAACP policy to the letter. "I strongly resent, however, the implication of intent to prejudice the NAACP in the phrase guilty of conduct inimical to the NAACP," she protested. Attempting to assume the high ground, as well as to preserve her reputation, Christopher lectured Wilkins: "It ought to be clear to you that my conduct was motivated solely by the desire to protect the NAACP and protect it zealously from the undermining process to which it is being subjected in Honolulu."[39]

Neither Wilkins nor Current, however, were convinced, and they pressed their recommendation to the NAACP board of directors to revoke the Honolulu branch's charter. The board of directors agreed with this assessment and voted at their November 1949 meeting to formally revoke the branch's charter. Roy Wilkins informed a clearly discouraged Catherine Christopher of the board of director's final decision and requested that she, as acting president, "kindly forward the charter of the Branch, all records, property and monies of this notice."[40] Those individuals in Hawai'i who wished to continue their affiliation with the NAACP would be considered as members at large, independent of any local branch affiliation.[41]

So what went wrong? How did a branch of the NAACP that began with such promise, enthusiasm, and a committed local leadership dissolve within four years? And what could Hawai'i's local leadership or the NAACP national office have done differently to have prevented this outcome? Part of the answer lies in a letter that Gloster Current wrote to Anita Flynn in 1950, who had requested general information on the local NAACP branch in Hawai'i. "I am afraid that there is very little that I can tell you about the situation in Hawai'i," wrote Current. "We did have a Branch in Hawai'i but because of internal friction and the fact that the National Office could not supervise the Branch in any way because of the distance[,] the charter was revoked by the National Board of Directors."[42]

In reality, Current could have revealed a great deal more to Flynn regarding the Honolulu branch's demise and implosion, and his lack of candor is surprising just nine months after the NAACP board of directors had voted to revoke the branch's charter. Current failed to acknowledge, for example, that the NAACP would not tolerate any radical political party to take control of the leadership of its branches, and it found the Communist party the most repugnant of all. He might have also revealed to Flynn that in the entire four years that the branch was in existence, not one official from the national office ever visited Hawai'i, despite the severity of its internal strife and the leadership crisis within the branch. Nor did the branch's lack of members serve as the pivotal reason for the NAACP board of directors in terminating this branch, for the Honolulu NAACP reported a membership of 194 in 1946 and 215 in 1947, a highly respectable membership for any new NAACP branch and a larger NAACP membership than in some western cities on the mainland.[43] And while factionalism and leadership struggles were evident in the Honolulu branch, the same could be said regarding numerous NAACP branches throughout the country, none of which were in danger of having their charters revoked.

What especially hurt this branch's image and standing in the eyes of national NAACP leaders was the association of branch activities with the Communist party, the inability of the branch to attract a strong president after 1947, and the distance between the Honolulu branch and the national office. This final point deserves closer scrutiny, because the NAACP's West Coast Regional Office, based in San Francisco, had Noah Griffin, a capable regional director, as its head. Yet instead of taking an aggressive posture to correct turmoil within the branch, the West Coast Regional Office and the national office permitted the Honolulu branch to self-destruct as it viewed the carnage from afar. Neither Gloster Current, Roy Wilkins, nor Noah

Griffin ever seriously entertained visiting the branch to offer their guidance, at the very time when NAACP officials would have been hard pressed to locate a branch in greater need of their services.

Yet the Honolulu branch deserves most of the blame for its dissolution, for it attracted strong leadership between 1945 and 1947, but only leaders who were obstinate, inflexible, and confrontational between 1948 and 1949. As Hubert H. White wrote in the *Atlanta World*, an African American weekly newspaper, after it appeared imminent that the Honolulu branch would lose its charter, "it seems to this writer that the real trouble with the Honolulu branch has been its lack of trained, intelligent leadership."[44] Neither Catherine Christopher nor James Neal, who served as branch presidents of the Hawai'i NAACP between 1947 and 1949, possessed the leadership qualities that were necessary to quell dissent within the branch or to work effectively with the national office. Consequently, by 1949 the NAACP in Hawai'i was a dead letter, and in April, 1951, Edward Cox, former branch treasurer, mailed a check in the amount of $238.70 to the NAACP national office, officially terminating the relationship between the defunct branch and the oldest civil rights organization in the nation.[45]

The NAACP, despite its inauspicious start in Hawai'i during the 1940s, ultimately gained a foothold in the islands and became an important civil rights organization. More than a decade would pass before African Americans and their supporters in Hawai'i attempted to organize another NAACP branch in the islands.[46] In 1960, Willie Moore, an African American sergeant in the U.S. Marines, who had transferred to Hawai'i from Camp Pendleton in California, imbued with the same zeal and commitment of Jacob Prager and Kenneth Sano, requested permission from the NAACP to organize a branch in Hawai'i. If Moore had been aware of the obstacles that previous supporters of the Hawai'i branch had faced, he may have had second thoughts. Undeterred, he pressed on, and on May 9, 1960, the NAACP national office granted Hawai'i a branch charter for the second time. By the mid-1960s, the Hawai'i NAACP branch had emerged as a major civil rights organization in the islands, but it also aligned its own struggle with the broader campaign for racial justice led by Dr. Martin Luther King, Jr. and the Southern Christian Leadership

Conference. Working collectively with an array of multiracial organizations in the islands, the Hawai'i NAACP would play a vital role in pushing for civil rights and racial equality for all Hawai'i residents throughout the twentieth century.[47]

NOTES

[1] David Farber and Beth Bailey, *The First Strange Place : The Alchemy of Race and Sex in World War II Hawai'i* (New York: Free Press, 1992), 133.

[2] Katherine Takara, "Who is the Black Woman in Hawai'i?, in Nancy Foon Young and Judy R. Parrish, eds., *Montage* (Honolulu, Hawai'i: General Assistance Center for the Pacific, 1977), 86–87; R. A. Greer, "Blacks in Old Hawai'i," *Honolulu* 21 (November 1986): 120–121, 183–184; Marc Scruggs, "Anthony Allen: A Prosperous American of African Descent in Early 19th Century Hawai'i," *HJH* 26 (1992): 55–93; Constance K. Escher, "She Calls Herself Betsey Stockton," *Princeton History* 10 (1991): 71–101; Bobette Gugliotta, *Nolle Smith: Cowboy, Engineer, Statesman* (New York: Dodd, Mead, 1971); Albert S. Broussard, "Carlotta Stewart-Lai, A Black Teacher in the Territory of Hawai'i," *HJH* 24 (1990): 129–154; *PCA*, November 29, 1898, May 2, 1900.

[3] Eleanor C. Nordyke, "Blacks in Hawai'i: A Demographic and Historical Perspective," *HJH* 22 (1988): 241–255; *Report of the Commissioner of Labor on Hawaii*, 1901, Senate Document 169 (Washington, D.C.: Government Printing Office, 1902), 147, 152, 166, 174, 212; Farber and Bailey, *The First Strange Place*, p. 164; *Hawaiian Almanac and Annual for 1902* (Honolulu, 1901), p. 164; Eleanor C. Nordyke, *The Peopling of Hawai'i*, 2d ed. (Honolulu: U of Hawai'i P, 1989), 71–73.

[4] Farber and Bailey, *The First Strange Place*, 134; Broussard, "Carlotta Stewart Lai: A Black Teacher in the Territory of Hawai'i," 133–34.

[5] J. Prager to William Dean Pickens, July 28, 1941, carton 42, Hawai'i branch files, Part 2, NAACP Papers, Library of Congress, hereinafter cited as Hawai'i branch files, NAACP Papers. Although Pickens served as the national director of NAACP branches in 1941, he would later serve as the NAACP field director.

[6] Prager to NAACP, September 20, 1941, carton 42, Hawai'i branch files, NAACP Papers; Memorandum, Lucille Black to Walter White, December 4, 1944, carton 42, Hawai'i branch files, NAACP Papers.

[7] Pickens to Prager, May 14, 1941, carton 42, Hawai'i branch files, NAACP Papers. For examples of racial prejudice in Hawai'i prior to World War II, consult Broussard, "Carlotta Stewart Lai, A Black Teacher in the Territory of Hawai'i," 130.

[8] H. Parke Williams to Pickens, March 20, 1941, carton 42, Hawai'i branch files, NAACP Papers.

[9] Wilkins to Pickens, April 15, 1941, and Pickens to James P. Russell, April 24, 1941, carton 42, Hawai'i branch files, NAACP Papers.

10 Resolution, William C. Page to Ella Baker, June 22, 1944, carton 42, Hawai'i branch files, NAACP Papers. Kenneth Sano, who played the most active role in pushing for a local branch of the NAACP, resided at 1188 Nuuanu Avenue in Honolulu, although I was unable to determine his occupation. I was also unable to find any biographical information on William Page.

11 "Application to Join NAACP," August 4, 1944, carton 42, Hawai'i branch files, NAACP Papers.

12 Ella J. Baker to Walter White, September 7, 1944, and Baker to Kenneth Sano, September 23, 1944, carton 42, Hawai'i Branch files, NAACP Papers.

13 *Honolulu Star-Bulletin*, December 20, 1944; *Honolulu Advertiser*, December 20, 1944.

14 On racial violence during the First World War era, see William Tuttle, *Race Riot: Chicago in the Red Summer of 1919* (New York: Atheneum, 1974).

15 Irving Townsend to NAACP, July 24, 1944 and Assistant Secretary, NAACP to Townsend, July 31, 1944, carton 42, Hawai'i branch files, NAACP Papers.

16 Oscar C. Brown to NAACP, August 1, 1944; Lucille Black to White, December 4, 1944; Ella Baker to Roy Wilkins; Telegram, Ella Baker to Henry J. Green, March 22, 1945, carton 42, Hawai'i branch files, NAACP Papers.

17 Ella Baker to Henry J. Green, March 26, 1945; Kenneth Sano to Baker, June 8, 1945, carton 42, Hawai'i branch files, NAACP Papers.

18 Katharine Lackey to Ella Baker, February 22, 1946, carton 42, Hawai'i branch files, NAACP Papers.

19 "Membership," August 1944, carton 42; Memorandum from Katharine Lackey regarding Hawai'i Branch NAACP, August 14, 1945, carton 42, Hawai'i branch files, NAACP Papers.

20 Sano to Ella Baker, carton 42, Hawai'i branch files, NAACP Papers.

21 Sano to Ella Baker, carton 42, Hawai'i branch files, NAACP Papers.

22 Katharine Lackey to Madison S. Jones, Jr., February 19, 1946, carton 42, Hawai'i branch files, NAACP Papers.

23 Lackey to Baker, March 24, 1946, carton 42, Hawai'i branch files, NAACP Papers.

24 Fleming Waller to Madison Jones, Jr., June 22, 1946, carton 42; "Minutes of Branch Meeting," February 21, 1946, carton 42, Hawai'i branch files, NAACP Papers.

25 Henry J. Fugett to NAACP, August 28, 1946, carton 42, Hawai'i branch files, NAACP Papers.

26 Memorandum, Madison Jones to Branch department, July 29, 1946; Memorandum, Julia E. Baxter to Gloster Current, February 27, 1947, carton 42, Hawai'i branch files, NAACP Papers.

27 Madison Jones to Department of Branches, July 16, 1946 and July 29, 1946, carton 42; Irving Townsend to NAACP, July 24, 1944, carton 42; Townsend to Ella Baker, February 11, 1946, carton 42, Hawai'i branch files, NAACP Papers.

28 Report of Election, Honolulu branch, January 5, 1947, carton 42; Fleming Waller to Executive board, June 1, 1947, carton 42; Charles T. Mackey to

Gloster Current, June 18, 1947, carton 42; Waller to Current, August 29, 1947, carton 42, Hawai'i branch files, NAACP Papers.

29 Gloster Current to Lucille Neal, May 27, 1948, carton 42, Hawai'i branch files, NAACP Papers.

30 Current to Neal, July 28m 1947, carton 42, Hawai'i branch files, NAACP Papers.

31 Telegram, Current to Honolulu branch, February 5, 1949, carton 42, Hawai'i branch files, NAACP Papers.

32 Transcript of telephone conversation between Current and Morris Freedman, February 7, 1949, carton 42, Hawai'i branch files, NAACP Papers.

33 Transcript of telephone conversation between Current and Freedman, February 7, 1949, carton 42, Hawai'i branch files, NAACP Papers.

34 Transcript of telephone conversation between Current and Freedman, February 7, 1949, carton 42, Hawai'i branch files, NAACP Paper.

35 Current to Christopher, March 2, 1949, carton 42; Current to Alfred Stacy, March 2, 1949, carton 42; Stacy to Current, February 10, 1949, carton 42, Hawai'i branch files, NAACP Papers.

36 Eleanor Agnew to Current, February 8, 1949, carton 42; Robert Greene to Black, February 5, 1949, carton 42, Hawai'i branch files, NAACP Papers.

37 Frank Davis to Roy Wilkins, April 7, 1949, carton 42, Hawai'i Branch files, NAACP Papers; *Honolulu Advertiser,* December 14, 1948. On Davis's varied career as a journalist and poet, see John Edgar Tidwell, ed. *Livin' the Blues: Memoirs of a Black Journalist and Poet* (Madison: U of Wisconsin P, 1992). On the repression of American civil liberties during the Cold War era, see Richard Fried, *Nightmare in Red: The McCarthy Era in Perspective* (New York: Oxford U P, 1990). I wish to thank professor John Bracey for bringing the papers of the Associated Negro Press to my attention.

38 Roy Wilkins to Catherine Christopher, June 20, 1949, carton 42, Hawai'i branch files, NAACP Papers; *Atlanta World,* July 16, 1949.

39 Christopher to Wilkins, June 25, 1949, carton 42, Hawai'i branch files, NAACP Papers.

40 Memorandum, Current to Wilkins, November 18, 1949, carton 42; Wilkins to Christopher, November 29, 1949, carton 42, Hawai'i branch files, NAACP Papers.

41 Edward Cox to NAACP, April 17, 1951, carton 42; Current to Cox, May 31, 1951, carton 42, Hawai'i branch files, NAACP Papers.

42 Anita Flynn to Current, August 15, 1950, carton 42; Current to Flynn, August 30, carton 42, Hawai'i branch files, NAACP Papers.

43 "Membership Status of Branches," n.d. [1947], carton 42, Hawai'i branch files, NAACP Papers.

44 *Atlanta World,* July 16, 1949; On Noah Griffin, see Broussard, *Black San Francisco,* p. 227.

45 Canceled check, $238.70 to NAACP, April 14, 1951 and Edward Cox to

NAACP, April 17, 1951, carton 42; Current to Cox, May 3, 1951, carton 42, Hawai'i branch files, NAACP Papers.

46 See Tarea Hall Pittman to Gloster B. Current, May 3, 1960, carton 29, Hawai'i branch files, NAACP Papers.

47 Current to Willie Moore, May 24, 1960; "Petition for Charter [Hawai'i] NAACP, 1960;" Current to Pittman, May 25, 1960; Moore to Current, June 16, 1960, carton 29, Hawai'i Branch files, NAACP Papers; *Advertiser,* February 6, 1962; *Honolulu Star-Bulletin,* March 22, 1965; *Ka Leo O Hawaii,* March 16, 1965.

HAROLD S.Y. HEE

The Tachibana Incident

MARCH 1, 1954 was a fateful day for both Haruo Tachibana and
Hutchinson Sugar Company. On that day, Tachibana became agi-
tated over what he thought was the severity of the punishment
imposed on him by the company for failing to turn out to work on
the previous workday. When he lost his temper and tried to pick a
fight with his bosses and failed, and then coaxed his fellow mill workers to walk off from their jobs, the penalty of a one-day suspension
was extended to a full discharge the next day, March 2. That was not
the end of the Tachibana Incident. What was to follow was a near
calamitous strike at the company, the longest ever in the history of
the relationship between the International Longshoremen's & Ware-
housemen's Union (the ILWU) and the sugar companies.

Nā'ālehu in 1954 was a remote, small and quiet sugar plantation
village in the Ka'u District on the southernmost part of the island of
Hawai'i. It sits on the lower slope of Mauna Loa, some 670 feet in ele-
vation and was home to about 1700 residents. It was a friendly and
pretty town, a model for its harmonious and cooperative spirit on the
Big Island. As union leader William Silva from the neighboring plan-

*Harold S.Y. Hee was vice president of industrial relations at C. Brewer before retiring in
1987 after nearly 36 years of service with the company in various capacities. He began his
employment in 1951 as a management trainee following completion of his undergraduate
studies at Cornell University. He was first assigned to Hutchinson Sugar Company, a
C. Brewer affiliated company, in December 1951, and became acquainted with all of the
individuals (both union and company personnel) mentioned in "The Tachibana Incident,"
but he left before the conflict occurred, having been assigned in 1953 to Paauhau Sugar
Company. "The Tachibana Incident" is a chapter from a book he is writing on labor relations in the sugar industry. This piece is his first contribution to the Journal.*

The Hawaiian Journal of History, vol. 39 (2005)

tation town of Pāhala said, "Here, everybody seems to pitch in at the same time on a community project. In Pahala, it's more like you wait for the other fellow to go ahead. This [Naalehu] is a nice town."[1] There had not been a labor walkout or any dispute of the least magnitude at Hutchinson since the industry-wide sugar strike of 1946. How then could this strike have ever happened in this peaceful and quiet town? And why did it last so long?

Profile of Tachibana Who Felt Unjustly Treated

Haruo Tachibana was a local boy of Japanese ancestry from a family of six children. Of slender and medium build, he was regarded in the community as a leader and "generally well thought of as a person."[2] To some, however, he was a contentious person who was inclined to be defiant towards plantation authority and even arrogant.[3] He was known for his occasional, tempestuous run-ins with management and others. A good friend and a retired electrical supervisor, Tokuichi Nakano, grew up living next door to the Tachibanas in the Honu'apo upper camp before all the outlying camps were consolidated into a single camp in Nā'ālehu sometime in the late 1940's.[4] The two attended the Naalehu Elementary & Intermediate School where they completed the 8th grade, then the highest grade taught there. Tachibana was always fighting in school and the only way Nakano remembered gaining his respect was by beating him in a fight one day. Nakano also recalled how Tachibana went after Nakano's brother with a hammer and ended up with a black eye instead. Yet, Nakano had only kind words for Tachibana as a person. He was "a good friend and he had a good heart."

Tachibana went to work for Hutchinson in 1934 right out of school. During World War II he served with the famed 442nd Regiment Combat Team having joined as a volunteer, along with his older brother, Harry, also from Nā'ālehu. He earned two Purple Heart awards in combat in the European theater as a member of "M" Heavy Weapons Company, 3d Battalion.[5] When he was discharged from the army, he had attained the rank of staff sergeant, a sign that his leadership attributes were recognized in the military. He returned to Nā'ālehu and his job at Hutchinson as a shop machinist. In 1954, together with his years in the military, he had been employed for 20 years with the same company. He was 35 years old and married with two children.

A penalty of a one-day suspension was not by any means a harsh form of punishment. In reality it was the typical measure of discipline meted out by most sugar firms for an infraction such as an unauthorized absence. It was strange for Tachibana to have felt that he should have been treated otherwise, unless he thought there were mitigating circumstances. After all, he had absented himself for a legitimate union activity and had given the company advance notice of his absence. That he was denied permission by the company didn't seem to be a big thing. In an interview with Jack Burby of the *Honolulu Advertiser*, dated June 6, 1954, Tachibana explained that he was angry because he felt that a one-day suspension for his absence was too steep for a man with 20 years of service. Besides, he explained, on the day he was absent the mill was closed and it was raining. (The mill did not grind that day, but the shop in which he was working was functioning and the mechanics were busy doing repairs.) He recalled the times he had been awakened from bed by calls from the mill to fix machinery. Of the two machinists in the shop, he was recognized as the more skillful, and thus was relied on more heavily for emergency repairs. Had his remarks stopped there, it would have been an explainable defense of his behavior. But his darker side was revealed when Burby quoted him saying, "I told them if this is the way you folks are going to treat me after all that time, let's go out on the road and settle this. Some haoles think they can push us around, but they pick on the wrong guy."

The incident had its origin on Thursday, February 25, 1954 when Tachibana asked for two days off from work to attend an island-wide ILWU caucus of union leaders on Friday and Saturday, February 26 and 27. The ILWU represented sugar workers at 26 companies in Hawai'i. The only unorganized plantations were Waimea Sugar and family-owned Gay & Robinson, both on Kaua'i and both small. Tachibana wanted to attend the meeting as one of the representatives of the Hutchinson unit to listen to a briefing on the progress of the industry-wide sugar negotiations then ongoing in Honolulu. At the same time, Tachibana asked that Robert Kamakura, the only other machinist, be excused for the Saturday meeting. The chief engineer said he couldn't allow both of them to be off on the same day, suggesting one go one day and the other the next day. Tachibana told his boss that he could excuse Kamakura on the 27th but he, Tachibana, would not show up.[6] The chief engineer warned him that an unauthorized absence was grounds for disciplinary action. Tachibana took off from work and went to the meeting on both days anyway.

FROM A MINOR SUSPENSION TO OUTRIGHT DISMISSAL

When he reported to work on Monday, March 1, Tachibana was greeted by his immediate supervisor, Benigno Salvador, who told him he was suspended for the day and handed him the written suspension notice. Tachibana was beside himself as he raced to talk to the mill engineer, Bob Wilkinson, a young, mainland, college-trained engineer who had been at the company for only a short time, to complain about the suspension. When told that the suspension was not going to be withdrawn, he swore at Wilkinson and is alleged to have laid his hands on Wilkinson (while the original statements by the company included this charge, in subsequent statements the company did not repeat this allegation) and in anger, he asked Wilkinson to step outside to settle the matter. Wilkinson, a much larger person and a boxer in college, declined. Tachibana then rushed into the office of the mill superintendent to confront John Jarman about the suspension. Jarman, a small and wiry person of Scottish origin, was an experienced sugar factory head of the old school. After an exchange, Tachibana flung the suspension notice on Jarman's desk, swore at him and challenged Jarman to go outside and fight. When Jarman refused, Tachibana stomped out of the office and went to talk to his co-workers. Shortly afterwards, they all walked off the job. The mill was shut down for the remainder of the day when the mill employees for the other two shifts failed to show up for work.

Tachibana was fired for his actions the next day, March 2. The mill workers returned to work that same day and all company operations returned to normal. On that afternoon, the ILWU Hawaii Island division director, George Martin, drove in from Hilo to meet with the manager of Hutchinson Sugar Company, James S. Beatty. Martin, 29, was a local boy raised in Hilo, an intelligent and a smooth-talking union leader. In the short time he had been the island director he developed a haughty bearing. Those who had dealt with him stated that he was arrogant about the power he and his union wielded over management, and that he had no compunction in showing it. So Beatty's remarks about the conversation he had with Martin had to be given some credence. "Beatty said that Martin told him that unless Tachibana was taken back, the workers might not ratify the industry-wide contract now being negotiated and he intimated that there might be a strike."[7] The report continued, "Martin denies a strike threat. He says his remarks were in more general terms about recognizing workers' rights or there would be a strike."

Profile of the Manager Who Stood His Ground

James S. Beatty, 57, was an experienced sugar manager. Born in Rochester, Minnesota of Irish and German descent, he completed his high school education in Vancouver, Washington. He worked as an ice delivery man, and in Portland, Oregon as a lineman. Seeking adventure, he came to Hawai'i at age 19, along with a friend. Instead of a short stay as intended, he remained in Hawai'i for the rest of his life. He became a lineman with the electric company in Honolulu, went to Laupāhoehoe on the island of Hawai'i for a short time, and joined the army during World War I, where he was assigned to lineman duty. After finishing his service in 1919, he returned to Laupahoehoe Sugar Company. He was restored to his job as a field *luna* or overseer and later moved to Hutchinson where he worked himself up over the years to become manager, first at Paauhau Sugar Company for a year, then back to Hutchinson, both subsidiary companies of C. Brewer. When he was confronted with the Tachibana case, he had been in the sugar business for 35 years and had been manager at Hutchinson for nearly 17 years.

Beatty was a tall, trim, and big man, who always wore a white shirt and a tie tucked into it. The cuffs of his khaki pants were rolled into the high leather boots he wore daily. On top of his mane of gray hair he wore a straw hat. With dark glasses, which he often did not remove inside his office, he had a stern appearance. He spoke with a firm, but modulated, voice, never raising it even when his ire was raised. He looked like a manager. Kazuo Ikeda, who was then the principal at Naalehu School, described him 50 years later as "a regular sugar plantation manager" and "human," but he added, with his workers he was "quite a boss."[8] In short he was fair and tough, a no-nonsense manager. Most people in the community thought he was friendly and a good manager. A former resident, a woman now living in Honolulu who spent her childhood days in Nāʻālehu, remembered Beatty thusly, "he was a good and nice man." Her father was a union member.[9] A life-long resident of Nāʻālehu said Beatty knew the family members of the workers, calling them by their names even when she, for example, as a young woman was recognized and greeted by him in Honolulu.[10] A former Hawaiian Agricultural Company supervisor remembered him as "a good and fair manager, although a stern disciplinarian."[11] These comments reinforced reporter Jack Burby's observation of Beatty:

> He is an austere man, aloof, but not the haughty whip-cracker that has been painted in the ILWU's stories of 'Beattyism'. He demands a job be done right. He believes that only one man can run a plantation at a time. He is a plantation manager up from the old school, but he is no martinet.[12]

Beatty turned down Martin's request to reinstate Tachibana.

The Lull Before the Storm

For the next seven weeks, like the proverbial lull before the storm, everything seemed normal in Nāʻālehu. Work progressed as if nothing had happened. There was some grumbling when Tachibana was fired, but not too much.[13] Yet, if there was no tension in this peaceful town, there were misgivings about the probability of some form of concerted action by the workers, since there was no process in place for the resolution of the Tachibana discharge. He remained fired, did not file a grievance, and started collecting his unemployment compensation payments. And he left his tool box and tools at the workshop. No meetings were held between the company and the union. In Honolulu, negotiators were wrestling over a new industry-wide labor contract when Jack Hall, the regional director of the ILWU, after being advised of the discharge, passed the word along to Dwight Steele, lead industry spokesman, that there was some trouble brewing at Hutchinson involving, "this union leader who was recognized as a hothead, but he has 17 years and the union would try to do something about him."[14] Agreement on the sugar contract was reached on March 21. The contract was ratified by all of the sugar units except at Hutchinson, where according to a union official then, a vote was taken at a union meeting and ratification lost out.[15]

A union business agent, Elias Domingo, out of the Hilo office was assigned to Nāʻālehu to interview workers for the purpose of gathering information on past unresolved grievances, ostensibly to prove the union's allegation that union-management relations had been strained in the past and that the Tachibana incident brought management's bad attitude to the forefront.[16]

On April 20, seven weeks from the day of the discharge, Beatty, sensing renewed activity by the union, sent a letter to his employees:

> We have heard that some of your union leaders have said there will be a strike of all employees if Tachibana is not taken back. Threats of a strike certainly won't help this situation and a strike won't get Tachibana back. We feel sure that all of you will think this over carefully before taking any action that may hurt you and the company.

The letter had no effect. Two days later, on April 22, the strike began.

WHY WAS START OF STRIKE DELAYED?

When the strike started the town was not surprised. Most had already gotten word that it would take place. But why was there such a long delay of seven weeks before the strike was called? The answer is open to conjecture. No one would give a rational explanation, at least not in 2003, almost 50 years later when the author revisited Nāʻālehu. A few reasons come to mind.

As previously mentioned, the ILWU leadership, whose authorization for a strike was required, was preoccupied in industry-wide contract negotiations in Honolulu and could not attend to this local issue.

Tachibana was not "a highly popular rallying point for a strike." While he had been a loyal union leader, he was not an elected union official. No immediate groundswell developed over his discharge.

Too many members considered him "cocky"or "hot tempered" and something of "a troublemaker."[17]

The field workers, comprised largely of Filipinos, were not interested in the politics of the situation. Long after the strike, in an interview conducted in 2003, an active Filipino union leader said, "it was a stupid thing to go on strike for one man," a man who was not well liked. Why then did they go on strike, he was asked? "The majority voted for it. After all, the union's motto was 'An injury to one is an injury to all.'"[18]

The Hutchinson unit did not and never had strong leadership. Whether this was due to its remote location, or due to the dominant leadership of its manager, who had served as manager there for more than 16 years and made the unit leadership looked impotent, the perception held by the island and local ILWU leadership was that it was weak. Because potentially capable leaders (and that included Tachibana) were not eager to assume the unit chairmanship, the job was passed on to whoever wanted it. The then-current leader was George Beck, Jr., a small and quiet person, not given to union militancy. He was a truck driver in the harvesting department; the more aggressive union members were found in the shops.

While the final decision to wage a strike rested with the international offices in Honolulu and San Francisco, speculation was that Martin, the Hawaii Island division director, played a key role in making a strong plea to get Tachibana reinstated. Martin was known for his style of intimidating management with strike threats, as he surely did with Beatty on the day Tachibana was fired. Despite Martin's denial, the words expressed by him at the meeting with the manager at Hutchinson, as reported by Beatty, were characteristic of Martin's nature in harassing employers. No one in sugar management underestimated the power and sway he held over them. Martin may have felt that to permit a company to fire a militant union leader with impunity would undercut the power he had so relentlessly built up for himself.

Hall's approval had to be obtained before a strike could be called and he needed the time to make that decision. It is not clear who in the San Francisco office had authorized this action, but if it was not Harry Bridges, the head of the ILWU, he was informed before it happened. Both were influenced by Martin's strong plea to engage in a strike to undo the discharge of a rabid union leader. By pushing for the strike, Martin's aggressive and very successful tactics on the Big Island would continue to weigh heavily on management.

COMMENCEMENT OF THE STRIKE, APRIL 22

It was the garage employees who led the work stoppage on April 22nd. The 19 workers from the automotive garage department on that morning demanded at a meeting with H. Alfred Hansen, the company industrial relations superintendent, that the company drop its employee testing program, which had been ongoing for over a year. The employees received the expected "no" as the answer, asked for a caucus, and failed to return to work at the garage. The mill employees followed with a walkout. Later all of the shifts of both the garage and mill workers failed to turn out. All told, 56 employees went on strike on that day. The company shut down the harvesting operations immediately. On the following day no work was offered to the cultivation and other employees. With the strike in full swing there were in all 277 workers who were out.[19]

On the next day the union, led by Martin, held two meetings with company officials at Nāʻālehu. At each meeting the company told the union that it was willing to skip the lower steps of the grievance procedure and have the Tachibana grievance submitted directly to arbitration, provided the employees returned to work. Each time, the union spurned the offer, replying that Tachibana was not the only issue, but the testing program was, along with other matters.[20]

One day later, Saturday, April 24, Jack Hall, flew in from Honolulu to meet with Beatty. He asked Beatty whether all of the matters, including the Tachibana discharge, the testing program, and other matters that the union had brought up, could be mediated instead. Hall said an arbitrator could only deal with Tachibana's firing, but a mediator could dig into Hutchinson's labor-management history and find the root of the trouble. Mediation had the merit of having an outside third-party intervene, using his persuasive powers to resolve the differences between the two sides in dispute, but not possessing the authority to make a binding ruling. One side in the process could walk away from a proposed settlement offered by the mediator. The union was fearful of a binding arbitration ruling that would not reinstate Tachibana. Most observers felt that the facts of the case would more likely result in an award upholding management. On the other hand, the union felt that with a skillful mediator, the company could be moved to compromise on the issue with only a suspension, not a discharge.

Beatty said no, the grievance was to go through the procedure as provided by the labor contract. The meeting broke off and the status of the new labor contract at Hutchinson remained in doubt. Hall was quoted in the newspaper that the contract, "was neither ratified nor unratified."[21] The company said the old agreement remained in effect until the contract expired on August 31, 1954, acknowledging that while the August 1953 contract opening had been exercised and resulted in a settlement for all the companies in the industry, that settlement had not been ratified by Hutchinson nor the local union.

Recognizing that the strike could be protracted, the company decided on Monday, April 26, to salvage the cane on the ground that had been cut before the strike began. Supervisors drove four haul cane trucks into the field and, with the field crane, also operated by a supervisor, loaded the cut cane stalks into the truck beds. They brought the 300 tons of cane into the mill yard where the mill, also run by supervisors, processed it. The union did not interfere with the recovery operation. After this salvage operation was completed, the company said it planned no further attempt to operate the mill.

Three days later, in a *Honolulu Advertiser* news item dated April 29, 1954, Beatty said, "the trouble was stirred up by ILWU leaders who don't live in Naalehu." Beatty said that most of his workers were against the strike. It was true that outside union leaders had come to Nāʻālehu to abet the strike. Yoshito Takamine, an experienced business agent from Honokaʻa, (later to become an elected representative in the legislature) spent almost full time in Nāʻālehu helping to organize the strike activities. Yasuki Arakaki, a radical union leader from Olaa Sugar Company, was also a frequent visitor who worked to shore up the spirit of the strikers.

Jack Hall said that Beatty and his supervisors had been trying to undercut the union since the first contract was signed in 1946. Beatty replied,

The record of Hutchinson grievances speaks for itself. There are personality clashes, certainly between militant union leaders and management representatives everywhere. It's quite normal. But if Hutchinson had a conflict in this sphere, there certainly would have been a flood of work stoppages and grievances. No grievance in Hutchinson's history has ever had to go to arbitration. It should be remembered that there has not been a single picket, there has been no violence, no threats, no heated tempers, no indication whatsoever that feelings are running high. The company's operations of the mill went off without the appearance of a single picket and without a protest by the union. There is no better indication that this dispute is unpopular with the vast majority of the rank and file, and that it is rather an artificial dispute engineered by union leadership outside Naalehu.[22]

HARRY BRIDGES TRIES TO INTERVENE AT THE TOP

Two more weeks went by without any movement by either side. In fact, during this time, the ILWU had begun a behind-the-scenes attempt to settle the dispute. According to Sanford Zalburg, author of a biography of Jack Hall, *A Spark is Struck,* Harry Bridges, head of the ILWU in San Francisco, secretly contacted James Blaisdell, the former president of the Hawaii Employers Council, who after leaving the Council in 1947 had started his own law firm in Honolulu, to propose that the matters in dispute be mediated. Blaisdell, in turn got in touch with Alan Davis, CEO of C. Brewer & Company, the parent company of Hutchinson, to convey Bridges' concern that the strike could intensify unless something could be worked out, perhaps through mediation. Davis did not budge, supporting his manager, Beatty. His answer was that the company's stand was based on the right of management to manage the company. If the union felt that the company had violated its labor agreement, the contract provided redress: arbitration. To Davis, adherence to the labor contract was a matter of principle.

By the time Davis issued a statement to the stockholders of Hutchinson Sugar Company on May 12, the strike had gone on for three weeks. In it he said that the walkout was a test of "vital principle" which could not be compromised. He reasserted his belief that it was "management's right under the contract to discharge an employee for cause without the approval of the union leaders." He accused the ILWU officials of calling the strike at Nāʻālehu to force rehiring of

Tachibana because he was a strong union man. He continued his statement,

> Numerous indirect approaches were made to your company by top union officials to reinstate the discharged employee. These officials at first threatened to withhold ratification for Hutchinson of the industry agreement when concluded and later added the threat of a strike. In an attempt to divert attention from the real issue, union leaders hastily sought to attribute the walkout to grievances which they alleged to exist between the company and its employees. Since then, their tactics have taken a new turn and they are presently engaged in a personal attack directed against J.S. Beatty, manager of your company.
>
> These leaders have been told that your company will not bow to their threats of force and surrender to them the right to manage. I am confident that you will agree with me that this vital principle cannot be compromised. The situation is developing into a very serious one. A prolonged strike can produce nothing but dire results. The very existence of a peaceful little community of some 1700 people depends upon a return to work and a fair and impartial settlement of this dispute in accordance with this contract. For these union leaders to recklessly destroy an enterprise that has taken the better part of a century to build and for them to deliberately create suffering and hardship for so many people seems incredible. Should the action of the leaders preclude the ultimate resumption of operations at Hutchinson, the responsibility will rest squarely upon the leadership of the ILWU.[23]

Davis was referring to the campaign to impugn the character of Beatty. It was Robert McElrath who coined the term "Beattyism" in his attack against the manager. McElrath was the public relations spokesman for the ILWU. He said,

> Beattyism is a whistle or a roar instead of courteously calling a person. Beattyism is an 'I'm the boss' attitude,' and 'You'll watch your step if you want to keep your job around here.' Beattyism is a militaristic approach to labor relations.[24]

McElrath also called Beatty the "King of Naalehu." In fact, every manager of a sugar plantation was like a mayor, if not a king. He arranged for rubbish pickup in the community; he usually ran a plantation store where workers shopped on credit; he paved the roads on which workers traveled; he fixed the houses that the workers rented from the plantation; he provided a water and sewage system for the workers in the community; he provided the use of the only assembly rooms and halls in the community without charge; he provided the workers and their families the use of the only athletic fields for recreation; he provided medical services for the worker and his family. But plantation workers were not subjects; they were all members of an active union. So the title "king" did not reflect adversely on Beatty; his response to the charges was that they were "not worth answering."

The workers started preparing for the eventuality of a long strike. But there was only a handful of people in the community who predicted that the strike would endure that long—129 days, the longest strike ever directed at a sugar company by the ILWU. (It even surpassed the length of an industry strike that would come later. In 1958 the union would strike all of the sugar companies for 126 days.) Without monthly paychecks and store credit, the workers formed a committee to establish a soup kitchen. Canvas tops, wooden supports for tent posts, tables and benches normally used for the annual Nāʻālehu 4th of July carnival, were all used to set up an outdoor kitchen and dining tables where workers and families could get their meals. Hunting and fishing parties were organized to obtain wild game and fish to be turned into meals. Vegetable gardens were planted. Union committees were formed to go "bumming," that is, asking for donations of produce from sympathetic owners of shops and markets. Women volunteers helped in the mobile kitchen to prepare each meal. Monetary donations were sought from the treasuries of supporting ILWU units and from local merchants and business firms on the island that had been patronized regularly by the workers.

House rental payments were deferred and the company made no attempt to collect them from the workers during the strike. But most employees prepaid their medical plan premiums to be certain of continued medical services, alleviating the fear that the company would suspend services for non-paying workers. (Medical services under the plan were provided directly by a company-hired physician and staff, and hospital costs were billed to and paid for by the company. The sugar companies never discontinued medical or hospital services in any work stoppage, although on occasion, when strikes were of long duration, such as in the 1958 strike, they threatened the workers of that eventuality because the companies subsidized the major portion of the cost.)

Union and management rhetoric escalated. The union attack was pointed at Beatty. Caricatures of the manager drawn by the union cartoonist in union and affiliated publications depicted him as a Simon Legree using his whip on his workers. The company responded with its own bulletins to refute the claims made by McElrath. Beatty told his employees they were being shuffled around like checkers on a checkerboard. It was a foolish strike that could only hurt them, he said. And for what?

> Ask yourself this question: will I get more wages, or benefits or anything else when the strike is over? Is the strike for more wages? No. Is the strike for more benefits? No. Is the strike for better working conditions? No. Is the strike for any reason that will help me? No.[25]

A Strike About Principle and Power

There would be no winners at the end of this strike. At least, not economically. The workers in the end gave up over $300,000 in lost wages.[26] The company lost at least that much financially. From the beginning each party knew that the goal was not increased wages or benefits, nor was it to resolve alleged gripes and grievances. While it was about the reinstatement of Tachibana, it was about something more than that. Simply put, the strike was about the struggle for power. Could the union place restraints on management's ability to manage its workforce to the extent it could dismiss with impunity a militant union leader for misconduct? Would the union lose its power not only at Hutchinson, but at all the other sugar companies, that it had successfully accreted and harnessed for itself in the few short years since 1945 when it organized the sugar industry in Hawai'i? Did the union have the power to whittle away management rights that were agreed to in the labor contract through threats of, or actual acts of, an illegal job action?

In 1953 Waialua Sugar Company had established a wage incentive program for cane haul drivers operating the newly purchased Tournahaulers, mammoth truck trailers, with which the union did not agree. The union preferred a group-wide incentive to include not only the drivers but the crew members in one inclusive gang incentive. The harvesting crew began a slowdown that ultimately ended up as a company lockout that ran for over 100 days. Waialua finally capitulated when it became too costly to continue the strike, although Waialua explained that an unfavorable arbitration ruling at another company, Oahu Sugar Company, on a similar issue, was the reason it gave in and agreed to withdraw the incentive plan.

The history of the ILWU and the sugar industry relationship was replete with such illegal job actions. From the advent of unionization with the first industry-wide contract in 1945, until 1954 there were 19 recorded instances when the union engaged in illegal work stoppages. The length of the strikes ranged from 1 day to 129 days.[27] The union usually won out with rare exceptions to that rule. These job actions were illegal when engaged in during the term of the contract because they were banned by a clause agreed to by the company and the union. Between contracts, the union could *legally* exert economic pressure by engaging in a strike in order to gain better contract terms, but once a contract had been agreed to, such concerted activity was banned by the no-strike clause.[28]

THE STRIKE ENTERS THE FOURTH MONTH

There was no open line of communications between the union and management as the Hutchinson strike entered the fourth month. Wives were feeling the pinch of the loss of income. Meals continued to be eaten at the union's soup kitchen in the ball park. The striking workers showed their dismay at the prospect of a strike with no end in sight and with no economic gain. The sugar company was counting its loss of cash revenues and found that loss to be threatening its future survival. Clearly both sides wanted a solution to this dispute. Both wanted to see an end to the strike. But a compromise did not appear possible. The union sought nothing less than the rehiring of Tachibana. Management, on the other hand, would not countenance his return to the job. Even the company's offer of arbitration as a means of resolving the dispute was no longer on the table.

Life in the village went on, but it was humdrum. A few workers would picket the company's main office and garage facilities. But picketing was not essential since the company had made no attempt to resume operations and there were few visitors to inform of the strike. The union was unhappy over the salaried employees who showed up daily at the company office. Many of the women who worked at the office, and who were paid in full throughout the strike, as was the entire management staff, had spouses or family members who belonged to the union. A decision was made by the union to coerce (by management sources) or to invite (by union sources) the office workers to walk the picket line for a week. These clerks were in a quandary. They summoned enough courage to ask their department head (Archibald Johnson, office superintendent) what they should do. One remembered that Johnson was not happy about this turn of events, but said that if she must, then the company would not stand in her way. She joined the picket line reluctantly for a full week. She was surprised and pleased that the company continued her pay during the week she was absent picketing against her company.[29]

Beginning of the End

Sometime in early August it was surmised that Bridges and Hall, as had happened in past strikes that seem to go on interminably, concluded that the union had to cut its losses. The strike was not winnable.[30] Certainly, talk on ending the strike did not emanate from the local unit, which lacked the leadership to initiate action. Likewise, the decision to begin the strike four months before had not been made by the local unit. Talks between the top leadership of the union and the C. Brewer corporate office commenced over a return-to-work settlement. Off-the-record meetings were held in Honolulu between the principals of the two parties. Beatty and Martin also joined in the talks. But the meetings broke off without any meeting of the minds. Then, "Hutchinson announced it had lost so much money that it would have to withdraw its offer to sign on the same terms as the industry–wide contract now in effect for the rest of the industry unless the dispute were settled by August 31."[31]

In the fourth week of August, talks were resumed with Tachibana in attendance. Progress was made in the second round of negotiations and soon a settlement was announced on August 26. The membership at Nāʻālehu voted in favor of the settlement the following day. About 200 workers took part in the vote and the unofficial tally as given by the union was about five to one in favor of accepting the terms. After 129 days, the strike was over. Joy was subdued in Nā‘ā-lehu at the end of the strike. The patience of the community had been tried and found wanting as the dispute dragged on so long. A calm prevailed with little or no excitement generated among the residents. Full resumption of work ensued after a weekend of work by small crews to start up the long unused boilers in the factory, and to do the preparatory maintenance of the idle trucks and tractors parked in the garage or left in the fields.

Tachibana Did Not Get His Job Back

As part of the settlement the two parties agreed to the terms of the industry-wide agreement that was arrived at in March 1954. All employees on the payroll as of April 21, 1954 would be put back to work, which excluded Tachibana. All grievances raised by the union were dropped, except in one case where the employee involved would be permitted to process it in accordance with the contract. The complaint about providing an ambulance to the hospital in case of emergency was settled by a company pledge to work out arrangements for such transportation when it was ordered by the doctor. Employees would be permitted a reasonable time to work off their debts to the store or the company. And the parties signed on to a policy that upheld the employee testing program with specified guidelines on its application in filling job vacancies and promoting within the trades.

The union conceded Tachibana's dismissal as final. Some alluded to an unstated *quid pro quo* in the final settlement. The speculation was that Alfred Hansen, the industrial relations superintendent, who, along with Beatty, bore much of the brunt of the union's attack for the mishandling of grievances, would be retired after he returned from a three-month vacation. Dwight Steele, president of the Hawaii Employers Council, in a memo to member companies, categorically denied any such agreement had been made, stating that Hansen would return to his job after he completed his vacation. The company announced "the hiring of an assistant to Hansen, filling a vacancy created [about a year ago] by the promotion of Harold Hee to the

position of industrial relations superintendent at Paauhau Sugar Co."
He was Roy Replogle, who succeeded Hansen after the latter's retire-
ment the following year.

Beatty sent a memo to the employees at Hutchinson in which he
urged the employees to work together and to do all they could to
make Nā'ālehu a pleasant, happy place to live. "I know all of us are
glad that we are going to work and earn our wages. It is a very happy
thing to be working again.[32]

Davis issued a statement on behalf of the company,

> The long costly strike at Naalehu is now ended. It would have been
> avoided if the union had followed the regular, lawful procedures pro-
> vided for in our collective bargaining contract. The position taken by
> the company in upholding the observance of contractual obligations
> and refusing to submit to pressure or to bow to expediency has been
> vindicated.[33]

The union offered no official statement. Hall said in response to
Davis' remarks, however, that "vindication came pretty high for
Hutchinson."[34] It was abundantly clear that the union had lost the
strike, but in doing so, it had inflicted severe financial strains on the
company. This was the lesson the union wanted to bring home to any
sugar plantation that dared in the future to discharge a militant union
leader, or to challenge the union during the period a contract was in
effect. But unstated was the price paid by the workers at Hutchinson
Sugar who went without a paycheck for over four months. At a Honolulu meeting of the heads of the industrial relations departments of
the Big Five firms, C. Brewer's Howard Babbitt was congratulated by
the rest of the companies for the way the strike wound up.[35]

POST-STRIKE NĀ'ĀLEHU

The cooperative spirit which marked the Nā'ālehu town never diminished. Any rancor arising from the disastrous strike that might have
lingered for a while between individuals could not be detected a few
months later. Nā'ālehu once again assumed its neat, friendly, small
town status. People on both sides in the community remained friendly
with one another.

At the plantation level, the relationship between the union and management was unchanged and remained good. Kuniyoshi Arakaki, then the ILWU unit secretary, noted that the attitude on the part of management was improved, citing as an example, how under Replogle, the new industrial relations superintendent, union-management relations seemed to be better than before the strike. Hansen was criticized by many for being too one-sided and not balanced in resolving employee complaints. Another claimed that he gave the union a bad time. Hansen had been a field department head before being assigned the personnel position, a job he probably felt uncomfortable at and unsuited for.

Outside of some name-calling and a single incident where an outside agitator allegedly punched or tried to punch Beatty during the strike, things remained calm in the main. There were no nasty confrontations or violence committed by either side. Except for engaging in aerial fertilizing through a service contractor, the company had not tried to work the fields or the factory during the strike; it did not provoke the strikers with some overt action, such as demanding rental payments or collection of overdue payment of store debt. The rhetoric expressed in bulletins churned out by the union and management might have appeared inflammatory, but neither party was so offended as to take the matter to another level. Each took to the written (or in the case of the union, in addition, the over-the-air spoken) medium to respond. Both the company and the union had suffered too much from the strike to want to create a situation that could restart another confrontation. Both sides were eager to get back to work.

Tachibana was gone, never to return to his hometown. He was appointed an ILWU official, representing the east side of the Big Island. Tachibana's tenure with the union was short. By then he was disillusioned and felt betrayed by the union leadership for not backing him up to the end.[36] After a brief stint as a salesman of cemetery plots in Hilo, he left for Honolulu where he became an independent sales agent for a line of pots and pans, a job at which he reportedly was highly successful.

Beatty retired from Hutchinson in 1962 at age 65 and moved to Honolulu as well. Both he and Tachibana passed away in the 1990's. There are a couple of anecdotes that circulate today among the survivors of the strike in Nāʻālehu. One involves an incident in which the outside "agitator," Yasu Arakaki from Ōlaʻa, allegedly struck Beatty with his fist when they met in the village camp during the strike. This account was widely talked about during the strike and aroused some community members in Nāʻālehu to retaliate against Arakaki.[37] The other involved an alleged post-strike visit by Tachibana to Beatty, while the latter was convalescing at a Hilo hospital, to apologize for having caused the turmoil at the plantation. Those who knew Tachibana well said that this could have taken place because "he was a nice guy inside."[38] Both dramatic events, if true, demonstrated the stress and pathos that the record-long strike had evoked.

There is no more sugar in Nāʻālehu. Its last cane was milled in 1996 when Kaʻu Sugar Company ceased production. Hutchinson had merged with its neighboring sugar plantation, Hawaiian Agricultural Company, to form Kaʻu Sugar Company in 1973. Today the ILWU represents the workers in the macadamia orchards located in Pāhala. The monkeypod trees are still found along the *mauka* or mountainside, of the highway through the town, but now there are banyan trees as well. There is a fence in place of the stone wall that fronts the Nāʻālehu School. Large plots of untended and uneven cane growth are visible from the highway. The homes with the corrugated iron roofs are still there, but a number of them have new tenants/owners. A few of he younger families have left for other places with more job opportunities. Those who remain find work at Oceanview or in Kona. Most of the company retirees still live in the homes they had purchased from the sugar company. A few new houses have been built since the strike. The plantation manager's home, with an addition, is now the site of the Sea Mountain Punaluu Bake Shop and Visitors' Center. The Naalehu Coffee Shop, a short distance from the highway on Kaʻalāiki Road, is still ensconced in the original building, though newly renovated. Churches line the main street where department heads had their homes. And the rutted road that once channeled flood waters from the upper cane fields to the front of Tommy's Service Station, now called B&E Union 76, is paved with asphalt and there is a flood control drainage ditch. There are fewer residents in the town, estimated now at about 1200 and even fewer, if the 2000 U.S. Census figure of 919 residents is accepted as the count, down from about 1700 in 1954.

In 1953, Nāʻālehu celebrated Independence Day with a parade/rodeo/carnival, a three-day festive affair. It was the 13th annual observance and by far the largest according to police reports. An estimated crowd of 10,000 people traveling from all parts of the Big Island attended the event. The rodeo even attracted some cowboys from Oʻahu. Cars lined the highway early in the morning to secure vantage parking spaces. The event was annually sponsored by the Naalehu Community Association, and through the help of all of its resident-members and the support of the sugar company, derived revenues in 1953 of about $8000. Independence Day in 1954 found the community in the throes of a strike and the association cancelled that year's observance. On the 4th of July 1955, the event was resumed, although on a smaller scale. That it was continued at all the year following the strike and the ensuing years, reflects the resiliency of the residents of this community and their ability to bounce back after an adversity. The rodeo/carnival lost much of its grandeur with the merger change in 1973 which reduced the company support, and the ultimate abandonment of all sugar operations in Kaʻu in 1996. Yet, today, Nāʻālehu still observes the 4th of July and holds a rodeo two to three times a year. Nāʻālehu, the "southernmost community of the United States," remains the remote and tranquil country village it was in 1954. To its present residents, it still is the most friendly and harmonious place to live. Most residents have not heard of the Tachibana Incident, and those few who do remember, don't dwell on him or the incident.

NOTES

[1] Jack Burby, "Labor Row Splits Little Town of Naalehu in Two," *HA*, 6 June 1954.

[2] Iwao Yonemitsu, retired crop control superintendent of Kaʻu Sugar Co., in an interview at Nāʻālehu, March 2003.

[3] Jack Acojido, former factory maintenance man at Hutchinson Sugar Co., and former chairman of union membership services committee, in an interview at Nāʻālehu, March 2003.

[4] Tokuichi Nakano, retired machine shop & electrical supervisor of Kaʻu Sugar Co., in an interview at Nāʻālehu, March 2003.

[5] 442nd Regimental Combat Team Museum.

[6] *Naalehu News*, a monthly house organ publication of Hutchinson Sugar Co., May 1954.

[7] John Griffin, "Shutdown at Naalehu," *HSB*, 16 June 1954.

[8] Kazuo Ikeda, in a phone conversation, Honolulu, December 2002.

[9] Bernice Nakamura, an employee of the C&C of Honolulu Drivers Licensing Bureau, in a conversation, Honolulu, February 2003.

[10] Julie Acojido, a homemaker and wife of Jack Acojido, in an interview at Nā'ā-lehu, March 2003.

[11] Toshio 'Casey' Fujimoto, retired labor relations director of C. Brewer & Co. and former industrial relations superintendent at Hawaiian Agriculutral Co., in an interview at Honolulu, May 2003.

[12] Burby, *HA*, 6 June 1954.

[13] Burby, *HA*, 6 June 1954.

[14] Minutes, Meeting of Sugar Plantations Negotiating Committee, 2 March 1954, microfilm #7-1975, Hawaii's Employers Council, Honolulu.

[15] Kuniyoshi Arakaki, retired garage serviceman of Ka'u Sugar Co., and former unit chairman and unit secretary at Hutchinson, in an interview at Nā'ālehu, March 2003.

[16] This activity of canvassing workers for past complaints was a normal tactic for a labor union faced with a grievance that lacked substance and did not call for a strike, but which posed a threat to the union as an institution. To provide a stonger rationale and thus generate greater support for a strike, the union sought, in this instance, a pattern of company misconduct by combining past incidents with the present. But as far as the union leadership was concerned, the matter for redress was the discharge of Tachinbana.

[17] "Shutdown at Naalehu," Part 3 by Griffin, *HSB*, 18 June 1954, who after getting universal feedback from the workers about Tachibana's ill-tempered conduct, reported that Tachibana seemed a poor rallying point for a strike.

[18] Jack Acojido, interview.

[19] This number of 277 reported by the *Naalehu News* was the correct number. Press reports referred to the number of strikers at 311 or 315; the discrepancy was due to the press use of total bargaining unit, which overlooked the fact that the total included two unionized groups, including 37 men of the company who remained employed throughout the strike. They were the workers who had to tend to livestock at Kaaulualu Ranch and the Naalehu Dairy, operations covered by the labor contract.

[20] Burby, *HA*, 6 June 1954.

[21] "315 Remain Off Job in Walkout at Hutchinson," *HA*, 29 april 1954.

[22] Burby, *HA*, 6 June 1954.

[23] Letter to the stockholders of Hutchinson Sugar Co. from Alan S. Davis, president of both C. Brewer and Hutchinson, 12 May 1954.

[24] Sanford Zalburg, *A Spark is Struck! Jack Hall & the ILWU In Hawaii* (Honolulu: U of Hawai'i P, 1979) 372.

[25] Zalburg, 372.

[26] Burby, *HA*, 28 Aug. 1954.

[27] "Chronology of Strikes," Hawaii Employers Council, Honolulu. This was a running log kept of strikes.

28 However, the enforcement of such contract provision was difficult, since the punishment of those engaging in unlawful behavior could not be undertaken lightly by the plantation. Disciplinary suspension of strikers, whether it involved the entire workforce or just a few key employees, merely extended the period of work loss. A long delay in harvesting mature cane could reduce the juice content and quality, affecting the sugar yield of that crop. It also set back the scheduled harvesting of succeeding fields. By stopping irrigation (at companies where irrigation was supplied by ground water, but not at Hutchinson, which depended on natural rainfall to irrigate the cane) or fertilization, or control of weeds, growth of future crops could be severely impaired. Hence, a sugar company was troubled by the need to suspend workers from work, realizing that such punishment only increased its production loss. Such was the character of operating a business involving such a perishable product as sugar cane. At Hutchinson, however, because of its underage cane, the strike helped to offset in the long run some of the losses incurred during the long strike. By adding four months of growth to the standing cane, the yield of Hutchinson's fields rose in three years from 8–9 tons of sugar per acre to about 12 tons, establishing a yield record for a non-irrigated plantation. Agriculurists said that cane in Kaʻu did not tassel as much as in other areas. As a result, cane grown in Kaʻu could continue its growth as it aged beyond the normal two year growth cycle to as much as 36 months and even longer, adding sugar content along the way.

29 Sachiko S. Nakagawa in a phone interview in Honolulu, Dec. 3, 2002.

30 In a longshore strike at Port Allen, Kauaʻi in 1940, which had run almost 300 days, Bridges bluntly told the unit to return to work because he was concerned about the financial ability of the longshoremen to hold out longer. The strike would not only hurt the union's finances but it would erode its public support. He always felt uneasy about strikes when workers were responding to moves by management, according to Edward Beechert, *Working in Hawaii: A Labor History*, (Honolulu, U of Hawaii Press, 1985) 278–279.

31 "Sugar Workers will End Hutchinson Strike Today," *HSB*, 27 Aug. 1954.

32 Letter to employees of Hutchinson Sugar Co. from J.S. Beatty, manager, on their return to work, 30 Aug. 1954.

33 Burby, "Not Much Excitement in Naalehu as Strike Ends," *HA*, 28 Aug. 1954.

34 Burby, *HA*, 28 Aug. 1954.

35 Industrial Relations Committee Meeting Minutes, 1 Sept. 1954, Hawaiian Sugar Planters' Association.

36 Yonemitsu, interview, Mar. 2003.

37 Yonemitsu, interview, Mar. 2003.

38 Yonemitsu, interview, Mar. 2003.

Book Reviews

I Myself Have Seen It: The Myth of Hawai'i. By Susanna Moore. Washington, D.C.: National Geographic, 2003. 184 pp. Illustrated. Bibliographic references. $20 cloth

Susanna Moore's first nonfiction book is part of the National Geographic Directions series that the publisher describes as "featuring works by some of the world's most prominent and highly regarded literary figures" (among them Oliver Sacks and W. S. Merwin) and capturing "the spirit of travel and place for which National Geographic is renowned, bringing fresh perspective and renewed excitement to the art of travel writing." In a *Honolulu Advertiser* interview, the author stated she had been contracted by National Geographic to write about India, but when that project began to interfere with the writing of her fifth novel (*One Last Look,* also published in 2003 and set in 1836 Calcutta), she asked to write about Hawai'i where she had grown up and would soon thereafter be spending Christmas. The author of the controversial novel *In the Cut* (adapted for the screen by Jane Campion), Moore has published three other novels, each with a female protagonist who holds a complicated but compelling relationship to the Hawai'i in which she grew up.

I Myself Have Seen It is an uneasy mix of cultural history and memoir that centers on the multivalent notion of *myth*. As Moore writes in the first of her fifteen chapters, "If we take for myth an exaltation of the primeval reality that satisfies moral cravings as well as practical needs, my assumption of the myths of a race not my own, a race nearly annihilated by my kind, possesses a romanticism full of irony, an identification with the past, and a self-delighting pride at being a liminal participant in an authentic culture that continues, despite attempts to the contrary, to fear the ghostly night marchers and to honor the goddess of fire and her terrifying relatives." This first definition of myth is vague but points to some of the strengths of the project: the openness with which Moore positions herself as a non-Hawaiian from Hawai'i, her acknowledgement of the negative impact on Native Hawaiians of the Euro-

American presence in the islands, and her recognition of Native Hawaiian cultural resilience. At the same time, this statement also anticipates some of what, to this reviewer, are problematic aspects of the book.

Precisely because Moore positions herself as "liminal," she becomes ultimately *the* protagonist of a mythic journey, an initiation process that culminates in the final chapter with her and her daughter Lulu eating a single guava picked from "the sacred grove, Ulukukuʻi o Lanikaula" (p. 171) on Molokaʻi, which is compared to the "labyrinth in which the Minotaur [was] imprisoned" in Greek myth (p. 174). Thus, as readers, we are supposed to become more interested in her *iter* (journey) both as young girl in the 1950s and 1960s in Hawaiʻi and as an adult than in the history of the islands and the myths of the Hawaiian people. The last three chapters ("The Paradise," "The Musician," and "The Grove") center on Moore's memoirs and, in what she acknowledges to be the tradition of Western imagination, on her contribution to "the creation of new myths" (p. 77), first as a naive but sensitive child and now—in her self-representation—as a knowing and attuned writer. As a girl, she lived in that "mythic" paradise that included the highly reputed private school Punahou and the exclusive Outrigger Canoe Club, but also the mountains where she would go "to pick ginger and dig up rare ferns to grow in pots" (p. 140) and the ocean where, she longingly states, "I felt as if I were, each time and at last, the self my heart would have chosen had it been asked" (p. 151). As an adult, she calls out the "dangers of myth" (p. 155)— this "paradise" myth—by stating its reliance on "island snobbery" and "unconscious" as well as "institutionalized" racism towards "non-haoles" (p. 154). And she also elaborates her own or personal myth by making her way into the "sacred grove" of the prophet Lanikaula to eat of a somewhat "forbidden" fruit—the guava—but also metaphorically the book itself. Whatever its relation to "myth," the book is for me at its strongest in these last chapters where the "I" is not embarrassed to be protagonist and the genre is clearly that of a memoir. Black-and-white photographs illustrate the book and also become more personal as we turn the pages.

Native Hawaiians, in Moore's myth-filled world of childhood—and, I would say in her mythopoeic world of writing—are the object of "a confused (not articulated or even understood) reverence" (p. 130). Beginning with chapter two, "The Returning God," she presents a condensed version of the myth-filled interactions of Native Hawaiians and Euro-Americans since the ritual welcoming of Captain James Cook in 1778. While these chapters moving up to the twentieth century constitute the bulk of the book, they provide what I consider snapshots ("The Great King," "The Kapu," "The Islands," "The Collectors," "The Missionary," "The Kanaka Maoli") of those cultural, social and economic transformations that brought about—as Moore foregrounds—the near annihilation of Hawaiians and their dispossession in their own land. Perhaps such a sketch is all that can be achieved within the genre, but I found the narrative strategy in these chapters perplexing in that Moore relies excessively on quotations from a number of sources, ranging from *The Journal of William Ellis* (1827), R. M. Daggett and Kalākaua's *The Legends and Myths of Hawaii* (Honolulu: Mutual Pub., 1990), and Thomas G. Thrum's *Hawaiian Folk Tales: A Collection of Native Legends* (Honolulu: Mutual Pub., 1998) to Bob Krauss's *Here's Hawaii* (New York: Coward-McCann, 1960), Mary Kawena Pukui and Alfons L. Korn's *The Echo of Our Song: Chants & Poems of the Hawaiians* (Honolulu: University Press of Hawaii, 1973), John Dominis Holt's *Monarchy in Hawaii* (Honolulu: Ku Pa'a Pub., 1995), Bernard Smith's *Imagining the Pacific: In the Wake of the Cook Voyages* (Carlton, Victoria: Melbourne University Press, 1992), and David Forbes's splendid *Encounters with Paradise: Views of Hawaii and Its People, 1778–1941* (Honolulu: University of Hawaii Press, 1992). With endnotes, the book appears to be researched, but the long quotations are often not commented on or contextualized; missionary, general-public, and scholarly sources are presented indiscriminately; and the quotations are also in several cases presented to make much more authoritative or definite statements than their authors' full discussions of the topic might suggest. Furthermore, while Moore refers to how since the 1980s the "growing sense of a Hawaiian identity" resulted in "the new scholarship and the publication of many good books" (p. 158), there is scarcely a trace of revisionist history or recent indigenous scholarship to be found in *I Myself Have Seen It*. The death of Captain Cook is vividly presented as the breakdown of cultural expectations and possibly a "religious rite" (p. 18) but the ongoing polarized interpretive debate about how to read this mythic and violent encounter is missing; the Great *Māhele* takes up a sentence (p. 97); the difficult role of Hawaiian monarchs in the nineteenth century is reduced to "Monarchy in the Islands had long been a charming *tableau vivant* permitted by those men [white businessmen, ranchers, and politicians] to indulge the myth of the native nobility so long as business was not compromised" (p. 115–116); the Hawaiian Renaissance is only hinted at: "The study of Hawaiian culture, and the awareness of a specific and important history was to come in the 1980s [sic], to the point that many activists today demand the sovereignty of a Hawaiian nation" (p. 157–158).

This is not to say that Moore's narrative is unsympathetic to Hawaiians. The losses Native Hawaiians have suffered because of Euro-American colonization are not hidden in this book. In fact, this information—the fruit of Moore's declared "curiosity about Hawai'i and its culture and history" (p. 157)—is bound to have a somewhat de-mythologizing and demystifying impact on readers who seek to engage in armchair traveling with her. But the picture of Hawaiians that she sketches remains tied to what Johannes Fabian calls the "ethnographic present": Hawaiian culture, religion, myth, and literature are referred to in an essentializing manner, as if they lived on in the past. Native Hawaiians' cultural resilience and resistance take on a "primeval" note since holding on to their unchangeable myth-filled past is, within this framework, their only option. Gabby Pahinuʻi's music—the subject of the brief chapter, "The Musician"—is appreciated but not recognized as a vital contribution to the Hawaiian Renaissance. I must note that Moore bravely acknowledges her contribution to the nostalgic myth of old Hawaiʻi in her novel *Sleeping Beauties* (p. 91), but I cannot conclude that this new book escapes it.

Within the book's framework, Hawaiian culture can only be the "myth" of an "authentic culture" that is sustained by the interest of the I/eye who eventually takes center stage. Ostensibly about "the demise of the monarch" (p. 116) or its overthrow, chapter twelve, "The Queen," ends in the celebration of *kaona* (secret, multiple and self-referential meanings) in Queen Liliʻuokalani's song "Ka Wiliwiliwai" ("The Sprinkler"); when the Hawaiian monarchy exits, the playful and curious girl enters. Here is a precarious hinge of history and memoir: "Queen Liliʻuokalani composed many *mele* and chants . . . written on the *lanai* of Washington Place (the house in which, when I was fifteen, I had my first serious flirtation)" (p. 118). While the girl's "first" experience is literally in parentheses, it is the Queen's "exile" to her Honolulu residence in Washington Place as well as the larger historical drama that recedes or fades into the background as Moore's personal history and myths are developed in the ensuing chapters.

Moore's narrative strategy is announced in the opening chapter, "The Night Marchers," where she quotes extensively from Harriet Ne's *Tales of Molokai* (see Lāʻie, Hawaiʻi: Institute for Polynesian Studies, 1992). In particular, by citing Ne's experience with the Night Marchers when she was a child (p. 5–6), Moore emphasizes the conflation of myth and memorate in the storyteller's formulaic coda," I myself have seen it" (p. 6). While adopting that formula herself, Moore is clearly aware that she and Ne are not similarly positioned in relation to Hawaiian myths, but if she is striving for a "romanticism full of irony" (p. 4), this reviewer perceives much more romanticism than irony in *I Myself Have Seen It*. Perhaps the irony would gain more weight if there were less carelessness in suturing myths of very different kinds and in presenting published and oral materials. For one, narrowly focusing on the passage from Ne's story, its source in *Tales of Molokai* (p. 118–120) is much richer than Moore's excerpt would lead us to believe, and Moore does not mark all cuts she makes in the text with ellipses. A different kind of inac-

curacy is evident when Moore states that Koko Head was "once named Kohe-
lepelepe or Vagina Labia Minor" because "the fire goddess Pele was saved
from being raped there by the pig-warrior Kamapua'a when her occasionally
loyal sister, Hi'iaka [sic], displayed her vagina to distract him" (p. 151).

More broadly, as a scholar of narrative, I find it difficult to swallow how
this book exploits the multivalence of myth without exploring it and instead
allows divergent definitions to shift into one another with little acknowledg-
ment of collision or strife. Following the statement about myth quoted in the
beginning of this review, Moore accumulates others: "If we take for myth a
theatrical ritual that transforms the mystery of the heroic into the sacred and
magical, . . ." (p. 9); and then "If we take for myth the means by which the
transcendent idea of existence is both reaffirmed and protected" (p. 39);
and then "If we take for myth an explanation of the natural world and how
it came into being" (p. 61); and then "I understood that myth was a luxury"
(p. 165). None of these definitions is put into conversations with the others,
and most crucially, no line is drawn between what Moore sees as Hawaiian
old "myths," or beliefs founded in both history and religion, and the *new*
exoticizing "myths" of Hawai'i in the Euro-American imagination. This facile
conflation and lack of clarity make for rather ambiguous statements such as,
"Despite the myth that the land itself was sacred and thus could not be
owned, Kamehameha gave to Young thousands of acres on the Kona coast of
Hawai'i" (p. 35). Is Moore taking the position that land was/is not sacred to
Hawaiians? And what does "sacred" mean? I find myself unable to answer
because Moore moves from one definition to another without taking responsibility for any. "Myth" is an empty but powerful signifier in this book. Finally,
Moore's framework for conceptualizing all "myth"—including Hawaiian
mo'olelo and belief—is, as it was for N. B. Emerson and later W. D. Westervelt,
that of Greek myth. The book begins in "the *Tantalus* forest where I lived as
a child" (p. 3, my emphasis, as Punahou students renamed Pu'u'ōhi'a (see
Pukui, Mary Kawena, Samuel H. Elbert and Esther T. Mookini, *Place Names
of Hawaii*, Honolulu: University Press of Hawaii, c1966, 1974, p. 213), and
ends yes, in Lanikaula's *kukui* grove, but as it is animated by and seen
through the myth of the Minotaur and the labyrinth.

Perhaps we can talk about "irony" when such carelessness towards sources
and terminology is evident to a reader like myself; a non-Hawaiian resident
of Hawai'i, not even raised in Hawai'i, with an interest but no formal train-
ing in *nā mea Hawai'i* or Hawaiiana. This book, like the first *Hawaiian Guide
Book for Travelers* by Henry M. Whitney (see Rutland: C. E. Tuttle, c1875,
1970) and Isabella Bird's *Six Months in the Sandwich Islands* (see Honolulu:
University of Hawai'i Press, 1964), both published in 1875, is primarily for

those who wish to travel or may be traveling to Hawai'i; as I acknowledge earlier Moore does complicate that desire, but she also perpetuates misconceptions about Hawai'i.

Cristina Bacchilega
Professor, Department of English
University of Hawai'i at Mānoa

Water and the Law in Hawai'i. By Lawrence H. Miike. Honolulu: University of Hawai'i Press, 2004. xiv + 264 pp. Illustrated. Index. $45.00 cloth

Water is power in Hawai'i. Lawrence H. Miike's *Water and the Law in Hawai'i* brings us closer to understanding the details of this fact. Miike is trained as an attorney (and a physician) and has served on the Hawai'i Commission of Water Resource Management. He has also served in other Hawai'i government posts, which allows one to observe the uneasy relationship between law, culture, and politics. Perhaps this accounts for the unusual, but innovative, organization of the book.

Miike starts with a helpful treatment of hydrology and ecology of Hawaiian streams and acquifers. Similarly, there is an introductory chapter on Hawaiian mythology and social structure that is intended to put water and land use practices in a cultural context during the period before and during the *Māhele*. What follows is the unfolding of a very complex story of how the blending of traditional and customary rights and private property rights has evolved from the the 1840 Constitution up through the Hawai'i Supreme Court's *McBryde* decision in 1973. The chapter actually titled "Water Law in Hawai'i" leads us into the modern era with a discussion of riparian rights (adjacent to the stream), appurtenant rights (water attached to the land itself), and correlative rights (groundwater) as they have been modified under the *McBryde* decision, and the State Water Code of 1987. The subsequent chapter on the Waiāhole Ditch controversy attempts to bring together the history of water law, politics, and cultural conflict into one case for analysis. The book ends with a summary of water law and discussion of ten "illustrative applications" of the law to demonstrate how it works.

Miike's treatment of the pivotal legal moments in water policy history, from the *Māhele* until the Waiāhole Ditch controversy, is one of the few accounts available. Unlike Carol Wilcox's *Sugar Water: Hawaii's Plantation Ditches* (Honolulu: University of Hawai'i Press, 1996), which provides a nice overview in one chapter (prior to the Waiāhole Ditch controversy) or other useful primers on water rights (for example, "A Short Course in Water Rights," *Environment Hawai'i* 1.2 (1990), Miike jumps readily into the legal technicalities, providing an intimate portrait of all the nuances of important court and constitutional actions. Simultaneously, he attempts to make an argument about the important role of Native Hawaiian water rights in the law. Although the book is not an easy read, it provides some important material for the non-legal mind to think about.

First, Miike implicitly recognizes the difficult relationship between the Native Hawaiian concept of water use and the Western private property concept of water use as more closely linked to concepts of ownership rather than use. Although he doesn't explore this in depth, his chapters on Native Hawaiian society, land use, and water rights leads one to think about how much the maintenance of some traditional and customary rights in the legal architecture of Hawaiian water law may be crucial to future decisons about who gets the water. We see in his analysis what was kept and what was lost, and how what was kept has survived in a Western legal world of private property rights. Hawai'i's water law is unique and begs for further exploration in this regard.

Secondly, *Water and the Law in Hawai'i* provides a fascinating portrait of the Waiāhole Ditch controversy in a historial and legal context. Here is where the politics comes in and Miike gives a glimpse of the conflict from an insider's position. His goal in this case study is to determine how the Hawai'i Supreme Court refined water law in light of the Commission's ruling on the Waiāhole Ditch case. In the process, however, Miike provides great detail on legal wrangling, technical decision-making on things such as stream flow, and political drama.

Stylistically, the book could have used the smoothing hand of an editor to enable the transition from one chapter to the next as major themes emerge and are developed. *Water and the Law in Hawai'i* is packed with information, but the reader can become lost in the details at times. The summaries at the end of each chapter help somewhat, but a more organized discussion of the issues is needed. That said, Miike's effort to bring together an informative treatment of Native Hawaiian water rights and how their incorporation into law and policy affected water practice is useful *because* of the detail.

What comes through in *Water and the Law in Hawai'i* is an implicit theme that can be traced from the *Māhele* period through *McBryde* and finally to the Waiāhole Ditch controversy: the survival of Native Hawaiian water use concepts in the face of the privatization of water and the subsequent shift to a water policy based upon a "public resource" doctrine. While Miike doesn't explicitly analyze the significance of this story, he provides a foundation from which to explore the implications and an intricate, interesting account of the legal twists and turns of water law and policy in Hawai'i.

Carol MacLennan
Associate Professor of Anthropology
Michigan Technological University

Aloha Betrayed: Native Hawaiian Resistance to American Colonialism. By Noenoe K. Silva. Durham: Duke University Press, 2004. x + 260 pp. Illustrated. Appendices. Bibliography. Index. $74.95 cloth

In her brilliant work, Noenoe K. Silva writes "a history of resistance to US colonialism that has gone unrecorded in mainstream historiography" (162–63). Silva takes on one of the most operative myths of Hawaiian history—that *Kanaka Maoli* "passively accepted the erosion of their culture and the loss of their nation"—by documenting the multiple forms of indigenous resistance to political, economic, linguistic, and cultural oppression from the time of Captain Cook to the struggle over the unilateral annexation and military occupation of Hawai'i by the United States in 1898. Silva's project is a path-breaking contribution, which brings to light a body of thought only accessible through Hawaiian language sources, which she translated and interpreted to provide an alternative reading of history and a rich inspiring legacy of indigenous agency. Silva's work is an important epistemological intervention because it is not only an addition to an existing body of knowledge; it prompts a radical reshaping of what we think we know about *Kanaka Maoli,* Hawaiian history, and resistance and activism. In responding to this erasure, the book "is simultaneously a critique of colonial historiography and an insurrection of subjugated knowledge" (p. 5).

Chapter one, "Early Struggles with the Foreigners," critiques the dominant historiography of the initial encounters between *Kanaka Maoli* and *haole.* Silva analyzes texts written by nineteenth and early twentieth century *Kanaka Maoli* in the Hawaiian language and shows how the people adapted to foreign instruction and helped direct and shape the changes to Hawaiian culture through their indigenous use of foreign technology and customs in order to bolster indigenous sovereignty. Silva examines and critiques the historiography of Cook's voyages and time in Hawai'i, subsequent *haole* travelers to Hawai'i, massive depopulation of the Hawaiian people, the overthrow of the *kapu* system, the coming of the missionaries, early struggles over sovereignty, the role of colonial capitalism in the struggle over communal tenure and privatization, and the legacy of Kauikeaouli [Kamehameha III].

Chapter two, "*Ka Hoku o ka Pakipika:* Emergence of the Native Voice in Print," recounts the materialization of Hawaiian print media and the rise of nationalist consciousness and resistance. Silva addresses politics, economy, and chiefly power, the rise of the plantation economy, and missionary planters and the colonial discourse of labor and civilization. With a focus on newspapers as discursive sites of struggle, she examines two different Hawaiian language newspapers that served colonizing functions—*Ka Hae Hawaii* and *Ka Hoku Loa*—and the response of a *hui* of Hawaiian men who formed their own venue to talk back to the colonizers. In negotiating the *haole* desire for control, they created *Ka Hoku o Ka Pakipika* and fought for the right to speak and be Hawaiian by perpetuating native language and culture, even as yet another colonial paper—*Nupepa Kuokoa*—emerged to try and quiet them.

Chapter three, "The Merrie Monarch: Genealogy, Cosmology, Mele, and Performance Art as Resistance," focuses on King Kalākaua's cultural revival and commitment to ancient Hawaiian traditional, cultural and religious traditions and practices as part of that resistance. Silva critically engages the historiography, which represents him as "the most reviled and ridiculed of the monarchs" (p. 89) and shows how the Merrie Monarch's revitalization of indigenous practices strengthened the internal domain of Hawaiians' cultural sovereignty and the identity of *Kanaka Maoli* as a people. As Silva asserts, Kalākaua's legacy of national pride "armored people against the pernicious effects of the constant denigration of *Kānaka* culture by the U.S. missionaries and their descendants and allowed *Kanaka Maoli* to know themselves as a strong people with a proud history" (p. 89).

Chapter four, "The Antiannexation Struggle," provides a rich and thorough account of the resistance movement starting from Kalākaua's overthrow and extending through the U.S occupation in 1898. Silva focuses on the activist labor of the three nationalist *hui* that were central to the anticolonial struggle and who had not been written about in English before now—Hui Kālai'āina, and the men's and women's branches of Hui Aloha 'Āina. Here we learn about *Kanaka Maoli* men and women's public writings in the Hawaiian language as a major part of their organized political resistance culminating in the 1897 *Kū'ē* petitions, which successfully defeated the Treaty of Annexation before the U.S. Senate, and which continue to be utilized in today's sovereignty movement as a legal record.

In chapter five, "The Queen of Hawai'i Raises Her Solemn Note of Protest," Silva theorizes the role of Queen Lili'uokalani as the central figure in the anti-annexation organizing through both her formal protests and cultural productions including music composition. The "battle over representation" took place on two grounds: the newspapers of 1893-1898 and in the historiography based on the English language news stories. Countering racist and sexist representations in those accounts and in U.S. print media—as well as the arguments advanced by the leaders of the Republic of Hawai'i to justify the cession of Hawai'i to the U.S. government—the Queen traveled to Washington DC to advocate for Hawaiian sovereignty and put forth her own account in *Hawaii's Story by Hawaii's Queen.*

This book is a superb contribution to the ongoing process of decolonization, recovery, and overcoming the suppression of *Kanaka Maoli* knowledge. Silva's clearly written account based on her original research is a gift to all *Kanaka Maoli*, especially those currently engaged in the restoration of Hawaiian sovereignty. This book—the fruition of Silva's meticulous and beautiful intellectual labor—is sure to win awards for its value and contribution to knowledge in the fields of political science, history, American studies, and indigenous studies, just to name a few.

J. Kēhaulani Kauanui
Assistant Professor of Anthropology
and American Studies
Wesleyan University

Completing the Union: Alaska, Hawai'i, and the Battle for Statehood. By John S. Whitehead. Albuquerque: University of New Mexico Press, 2004. xvii + 438 pp. Illustrated. Index. $45.00 cloth; $24.95 paper

John Whitehead's *Completing the Union* weaves together the histories of the 20th century statehood movements in Hawai'i and Alaska, connecting them to each other and to the outside world.

The book is part of the Histories of the American Frontier series. It is easy to see why other books belong in the series—they talk about such things as Texas, Tombstone, and Billy the Kid. But with Hawai'i and Alaska, the idea of the frontier is stretched, not only for the series, but also for the way that the United States is understood as a coherent entity. It is this issue—the possibility of imagining Hawai'i and Alaska as parts of a union—that is the focus of Whitehead's work. Up until the 1940s, the United States was typically understood as a contiguous territory whose frontier had expanded westward until it reached the Pacific Ocean. All of the other places around the world that were controlled by the United States were possessions—they were not part of the United States, they were simply external territories controlled by the federal government.

Whitehead has accepted a daunting narrative task: to describe the relationship between local and national political events and debates, to connect those debates to global events, and do all of that for both Hawai'i and Alaska.

At times, the narrative offers some interesting parallels: of how both territories were affected by the Second World War, the Cold War, or the United States military, or how the national debates over statehood were deeply affected by the fears and machinations of racist politicians in the American South. At other times, however, the narrative falters under its own complexity. The problem is evidenced by the number of times that the author mentions that something has already been talked about or will be talked about later.

A chronology of the historical events, conferences, elections, deaths, and meetings would have helped the reader organize the overall narrative. Likewise, a series of tables, providing the population data, election results and so on, would have been more meaningful than listing this data in the narrative. The index is generally limited to proper names and there is an annotated guide to the key sources but no bibliography. Finally, the presentation of the data in the book is sometimes incomplete or poorly presented. For instance, the author typically gives the ratio of key votes (3-1, 8-1 and so on), but seldom provides either the percentage (which would be easier to interpret) and, more importantly, almost never provides the raw vote tallies or connects those tallies to population data. A comprehensive table would have clarified these numbers and helped the reader immensely.

At its best, the book is an interesting story of how two different territories, connected by global events as much as by a shared imperial power, were changed, and changed themselves, from territories into states. As the author notes, the history of this change is often very boring, focusing on legislation and party politics. There are a lot of meetings and a lot of names to keep track of, but Whitehead does an admirable job of keeping the reader's attention.

At its worst, however, the book is a story written for the winners—the "statehooders"—which offers little in the way of criticism or analytical reflection. For instance, Whitehead claims that Hawai'i's citizens "had voted 2-1 in favor of joining the union in a 1940 plebiscite" (p. 15) but offers little concern for the conditions under which that plebiscite was carried out. Who, for instance, counted as a citizen? and how was the voting organized? Whitehead mentions later in the book that the vote was 46,174 in favor and 22,428 opposed. The 2-1 margin translates into 67.3% in favor and 32.7% opposed, with a total of 68,602 votes. According to Schmitt's *Historical Statistics of*

Hawaii, there were 87,312 registered voters in the 1940 election, which meant that almost 79% of the registered voters cast ballots (see Robert C. Schmitt, *Historical Statistics of Hawaii,* Honolulu: University Press of Hawaii, 1977). However, only 21.8% of the civilian population was registered to vote. According to the Sixteenth U.S. Census, there were 423,330 citizens in Hawai'i in 1940, which means in effect that 10.9% of the population voted in favor of statehood and 5.3% voted against it. This should have been discussed. Whitehead, unfortunately, takes the votes as given and rarely considers why the votes turned out like they did.

The author also does not seriously discuss people who opposed statehood. For instance, while statehooders such as Joseph Farrington and Ernest Gruening are described in detail, Kamokila Campbell, who opposed statehood, is only talked about when she is presenting at a hearing held by a subcommittee of the U.S. House Committee on Territories and, years later, when she is toasting, with some ambivalence, the passage of the statehood bill. Minor statehooders are given a greater place in the narrative, and Campbell is one of the few of those who opposed statehood that are discussed at all. The implication of Whitehead's narrative is that there was very little real opposition to statehood, except by racist Southern politicians and greedy capitalists afraid of losing local political control, and that the story of statehood is really the story of legislation, political and economic maturity, and popular votes.

One field of discussion that was missing in the narrative was the way that popular culture became part of the social debate. He notes that only 48% of Americans polled in 1941 supported statehood for Hawai'i, but how did Americans understand what Hawai'i was? There is no mention, for instance, of the *Hawaii Calls* radio show, which was broadcast to the United States beginning in the 1930s. Whitehead offers an interesting discussion of the importance of the 1931 Massie-Fortescue murder trial to the desire for statehood, but makes no mention of Shirley Temple arriving in the islands four years later on a promotional tour that brought images of a happy (and safe) Hawai'i back to the United States.

The book never directly engages the question of whether statehood for Hawai'i and Alaska was inevitable. The title suggests that the process was natural and the conclusion inevitable, as if the union was waiting to be completed and as if the result, the present, is the obvious end of historical developments. The details of his narrative, on the other hand, suggest a more complex and arbitrary history, with personalities, obscure political decisions, and economic motives dominating the process. The union was not completed, but rather the legal status of some areas of the world were changed from being territories to being states, a result that few people envisioned, that not everyone wanted, and that not everyone was allowed to participate in.

The book, reflecting back on the process, seems caught by these competing accounts, but the evident arbitrariness is ultimately trumped by the legitimacy given to the current situation and those who brought that situation to pass.

As Whitehead notes at points throughout the book, many of the people involved in the statehood movements should probably be better known now than they are. This is true, and *Completing the Union* is a useful first encounter with those people and with the topic in general. However, it is also true that many of the political questions that could be raised concerning the statehood movements should be raised in better, more critical ways.

> Brian Richardson
> Instructor and Librarian
> Windward Community College

Kū'ē: Thirty Years of Land Struggles in Hawai'i. By Ed Greevy. Text and captions by Haunani-Kay Trask. Honolulu: Mutual Publishing, 2004. vi + 170 pp. Illustrated. Photographer's notes. $36.95 cloth

Ed Greevy's photographic essay represents a wonderful visual remembrance of the land struggles that occurred just as we started to walk—just as we came into the world. The voice of Haunani-Kay Trask guides us along the paths of those legacies we are a part of, both through lineal descent and political descent. Thus, while our relative youth and removal from the earlier struggles represented therein limit our understandings, this same position allows us to evaluate the effectiveness of the book to inspire future generations to carry on the works of its forbears into the 21st century.

Greevy got his start in documentary photography when he became active with Save Our Surf (SOS), a group of young surfers led by John and Marion Kelly, whose fight to protect beaches and stave off shoreline developments received national attention. After watching John Kelly snapping photographs at a 1971 rally at the State Capitol, Greevy decided to make his camera a tool for social and political action. From that point on, he showed up to as many rallies and protests as he could with lenses aimed at speaking truth to power. In 1981, Greevy collaborated with Haunani-Kay Trask, a prominent organizer, poet, and Hawaiian nationalist, on a captioned photographic exhibit put on by the Image Foundation at Ala Moana Shopping Center. Their collaboration continued in subsequent shows featuring Greevy's photos and Trask's text, the culmination of which is this book (an idea originally raised by John Dominis Holt after the 1981 exhibit).

The first 64 photographs (as well as the cover image) document the individuals, groups, events, and landscapes of anti-eviction and anti-militarization struggles on Oʻahu, Kauaʻi, and Kahoʻolawe between 1971 and 1980. These pages pay special attention to a SOS/Kōkua Hawaiʻi (in support of Kalama Valley residents) protest at the State Capitol; Waiāhole/Waikāne Community Association (WWCA) demonstrations; PACE (People Against Chinatown Evictions) organizing; Nāwiliwili/Niumalu Tenant's Association activities; Heʻeia/Heʻeia Kea occupation of City Hall; Mokauea and Sand Island communities' battles to maintain subsistence fishing lifestyles; and efforts of the Protect Kahoʻolawe ʻOhana (PKO) to end military bombing of sacred lands. We look into the eyes of experienced and newly emerging community leaders (e.g., John and Marion Kelly, Stanford Achi, Soli Niheu, George Helm, Terrilee Kekoʻolani, Alan Nakasone, Wayson Chow); the elders that serve as the "backbone of the people's struggle" (p. 42) (e.g., the Kurisus, Tūtū Kawelo, Mrs. Matayoshi, the Teruyas, Aunty Emma Defries); and countless faces of ordinary people whose humble living conditions exhibit "[t]he dignity of the poor" (p. 68). Victories are unfortunately few (WWCA and Heʻeia/Heʻeia Kea) yet nonetheless inspiring.

Photographs 65–82 cover the period of 1982–2001 (though primarily the years of 1990–1998). This section marks the shift (first signaled by PKO assertions of Aloha ʻĀina and Sand Island residents' claims to ceded lands) from class-based and multi-ethnic struggles over tenancy-rights to the Hawaiian cultural nationalist struggles over indigenous rights to land, culture, history and sovereignty, especially in opposition to federal, state, and private institutions. Aside from one photograph on Molokaʻi, all the images focus on organizing that took place on Oʻahu (though supporters from other islands were present at such events, which also impacted the entire archipelago). These pages feature protests at the Bernice Pauahi Bishop Museum and the University of Hawaiʻi at Mānoa (UHM), acts of defiance in the face of bulldozers at a women's *heiau* that lay in the path of the H-3 highway, centennial marches contesting the legality of the 1893 overthrow and 1898 annexation, and the individuals and families involved in anti-eviction and anti-military struggles at Mākua. We see the faces of community leaders and organizers such as Mililani and Haunani-Kay Trask, Kekuni Blaisdell, Puanani Burgess, Kawaipuna Prejean, Judy Napoleon, John Dominis Holt, Setsu Okubo, Sparky Rodrigues and countless others who go unnamed. The last image of the book returns us to a 1973 Niumalu/Nāwiliwili Tenant's Association meeting on Kauaʻi and imparts a final message of determination and hope with "fists raised, but smiles all around" (p. 159).

The book serves as an important complement to—and perhaps entree into—a growing body of academic, literary, artistic and filmic treatments of community organizing since the 1970s. A very partial list includes: *The Ethnic*

Studies Story: Politics and Social Movements in Hawai'i: Essays in Honor of Marion Kelly (see Ibrahim G. Aoudé, Honolulu: University of Hawai'i at Mānoa, 1999); *From a Native Daughter: Colonialism and Sovereignty in Hawai'i* (see Haunani-Kay Trask, Honolulu: University of Hawai'i Press, 1999); *Autobiography of Protest in Hawai'i* (see Robert H. Mast and Anne B. Mast, Honolulu: University of Hawai'i Press, 1996); *Hawai'i: Return to Nationhood* (see Ulla Hasager and Jonathan Friedman, eds., Copenhagen: International Work Group for Indigenous Affairs, 1994); *He Alo A He Alo: Face to Face: Hawaiian Voices on Sovereignty* (see Honolulu: American Friends Service Committee, 1993); *Mālama: Hawaiian Land and Water* (see Dana Naone Hall, Honolulu: Bamboo Ridge Press, 1985); *Ho'iho'i Hou: A Tribute to George Helm and Kimo Mitchell* (see Rodney Morales, ed., Honolulu: Bamboo Ridge Press, 1984) and numerous documentary films produced by Nā Maka o ka 'Āina. Significantly, many of the above texts utilize Greevy's photographs.

It is important to note that to *kū'ē* (resist, oppose, protest) is not a new, isolated, or singular response to survival in these islands. In *Aloha Betrayed: Native Hawaiian Resistance to American Colonialism* (2004), Noenoe Silva's analysis of discourses of resistance in Hawaiian-language newspapers since 1861 and the anti-annexation petitions of 1897–1898 is a testimony to our people's sustained ability to make our voices heard throughout the generations (see Noenoe Silva, Durham: Duke University Press, 2004). Davianna McGregor's forthcoming book (UH Press) based on her 1989 dissertation, *Kūpa'a i ka 'Āina: Persistence on the Land,* attests to the tenacity of the *kua'āina* (rural Hawaiians) to *per*sist over the years so that their future generations would be prepared to *re*sist the exploitative maneuvers of the State in the 1970s. Finally, Lynette Hi'ilani Cruz examines the multiplicity of ways that contemporary Hawaiian communities work to maintain "right relationships" between people, gods, and land in her 2003 dissertation, *From Resistance to Affirmation, We Are Who We Were: Reclaiming National Identity in the Hawaiian Sovereignty Movement 1990–2003.*

What is unique about this book is the potential for the images to portray those excesses and overflows of meaning that are frequently lost in written texts. Greevy's photographic skills are superb. The composition and tonal quality of his portraits add texture to the people and events and portray the strength of each individual represented. In many of his images, the composition is balanced for unsettling times and events. Specifically, photograph 43 of Billy Molale captures the complications of the land struggles on Mokauea in 1975. Molale's position at the boat's helm forces the viewer's eye to the houses burning in the background on Mokauea Island. The open expanse of the sky and the whiteness of the clouds are in stark contrast to the dark grey to black plumes of smoke from the fire that draws the viewer's eye down to the burning homes. While we can only see Molale's face looking forward, there is one passenger looking back. This image evokes Lilikalā Kameʻeleihiwa's explanation that "the past is referred to as *ka wā mamua,* or the time in front or before . . . as if the Hawaiian stands firmly in the present with his back to the future, and his eyes fixed upon the past, seeking historical answers for present-day dilemmas" (see Kameʻeleihiwa, *Native Land and Foreign Desires: Pehea Lā e Pono Ai?* Honolulu: Bishop Museum Press, 1992, p. 22). This particular image represents how the past is not always glorious, but remains fraught with complications. This highlights the question: Where does each of us look to understand the history of Hawaiʻi?

Such a question is never easily answered. As with *all* histories, this text is incomplete, biased, and forgetful (see Robert Borofsky, ed., *Remembrance of Pacific Pasts: An Invitation to Remake History,* Honolulu: University of Hawaiʻi Press, 2000). Though the title promises "thirty years of land struggles in Hawaiʻi," almost 80 percent of the book focuses on just one decade (1971–1980). Nearly 90 percent of the pictures were taken on Oʻahu, and Kauaʻi was the only other island that had somewhat significant representation in its eight photographs (Judy Napoleon's is the single photograph taken on Molokaʻi, and the pictures of George Helm and the PKO were taken on Oʻahu). The absence of other islands and struggles makes more sense when considering Greevy's comments, "I never go where I'm not known" (p. 162) and "Kauaʻi had the most aroused and organized anti-eviction groups of any neighbor island [during the 1970s]" (p. 165). Wayne Muromoto, who reviewed the book for *The Hawaii Herald* (1/7/05), also notes that in the 1980s "Greevy had to pull back from running off to cover each and every struggle in order to work and support a family" (p. C-6). Given these factors, one can better contextualize this book and its focus.

We must also recognize the fact that we receive the images in *Kūʻē* twice refracted—once through Greevy's camera lens and again through Trask's textual frames. Some of the captions even feature statements in quotation marks that might be interpreted as direct quotes from the individuals pictured. Such a reading, however, is called into question when one notices that Ellen Waʻalani's quote (p.25) comes with the only citation in the book (from *We the People of Niumalu-Nawiliwili: Our Lifestyle and Environment,* 1973). Thus it is more likely that the other quotes are instances of Trask taking poetic license to (albeit effectively) convey particular messages that may arise from the images. For those who come to the text with little knowledge of the histories or personalities pictured in *Kūʻē,* we recommend both reading Greevy's notes at the end of the book and looking to other sources (such as those cited above) that provide first-hand accounts from other people who were also "there" (including those places that are not equally represented in this book).

Wayne Muromoto, who was there (even if peripherally), states that for him, the book is a call to "recapture some of that spirit of idealism again," and "For younger readers, this book demonstrates the need for them to get involved in social and political activism." (p. C-8). Yet the question arises: What *kind* of social and political activism? In an era of identity politics, is a renewal of class-based Marxist politics even possible? Can or should the two (or more) modes of activism be articulated such that class-consciousness emerges without severing the bonds of indigenity, culture, ethnicity, gender, sexuality, environmental stewardship, and so forth? Although no clear answers are presented, the final image of the book seems to suggest that we may still learn much from the Niumalu/Nāwiliwili Tenants' Association of 1973.

In order for this book to truly *speak* to us, we must not only listen, but we must also *speak back*. For *Kūʻē* to transcend its fate as just another coffee table book on display at local Borders and Costcos everywhere, it must compel us to enter into new dialogues with the authors and one another. Documentary photographers from Hawaiʻi, Maui, Molokaʻi, Kahoʻolawe, Lanaʻi, and Niʻihau may want to answer Greevy's call to produce popular visual history of their own islands. Others may offer additional images from the last 30 years (as well as before and after). In lieu of their publication, we may think about alternate/internet spaces to strike up imaged discussions, such as one between Ian Lind's "Old kine pictures" (1965–1980) website <http://www .ilind.net/oldkine.html> and "Ed Greevy's Photograph Collection" on <http://ulukau .org/> (both accessed 3/31/05). At the interpersonal and intergenerational level, we could ground our politics (or at least our understanding of the historical trajectories of politics) in the experiences of those that precede us, all the while building bridges with our allies around us in hope that future generations will carry on after us. Though our future may seem uncertain, we can draw strength from the faces and stories in *Kūʻē* that remind us that we are all connected through genealogies of people and place that, if honored, will continue to instruct and inspire us.

Ty P. Kāwika Tengan
Assistant Professor
Ethnic Studies and Anthropology
University of Hawaiʻi at Mānoa

and

J. Lahela A. Perry
Ph.D. student and instructor
Department of Anthropology
University of Hawaiʻi at Mānoa

Hawai'i's Pineapple Century A History of the Crowned Fruit in the Hawaiian Islands. By Jan K. Ten Bruggencate. Honolulu: Mutual Publishing, LLC, 2004. xii + 187 pp. Illustrated. Appendix. Index. $13.95 paper

This book on the history of pineapple in Hawai'i contains a foreword, preface, and the following chapters: The Early Years, The Pioneers, The Early Pineapple Companies, The Ten Postwar Companies, The Associations, Pineapple Plantation Practices, Working Pine, Labor Organization, Exodus, Adaptation, Appendix (Cultivating Pineapples), and Index. In this reviewer's opinion, the most outstanding feature of the book is the many photographs of people and cultural practices used in the industry, some from quite early in its development. There is also an eight-page full-color center section of photographs of some of the many labels applied to cans of pineapple shipped from Hawai'i. The photographs are without attribution and the absence of a bibliography or other reference material, a serious shortcoming, makes it impossible to know where the material came from and if there is a further wealth of information available on the subject history. The index provides links to many of the people, companies, and organizations but is inconsistent in its coverage of material in chapter six and beyond.

The book begins with an almost lyrical preface, but, on the whole, is rather dry and fails to transmit much of the color and personality of the people involved in Hawai'i's pineapple century. Chapter three, The Early Years, provides only brief descriptions of the companies and their founders; without documentation, there is no way to know if the information provided reflects everything that is available or is incomplete. In addition to its brevity, the chapter is fairly complicated and could benefit from a map or maps of locations and summary tables of converging and diverging ownership.

Presumably Ten Bruggencate's many years with Libby, McNeil and Libby account for the relatively more extensive coverage of that company (six plus pages versus mostly two pages or less except for Dole Co.) than of the other nine companies reviewed in The Ten Postwar Companies of chapter four. The history of all of the companies seems overly brief, but the brevity of discussion about eight of the ten companies, and particularly the three companies that as of January 2005 are still growing pineapples in Hawai'i, results in uneven coverage of the subject. The result is disappointing.

The associations organized by the pineapple companies and the industry's research accomplishments are reviewed in chapter five. It is this reviewer's opinion that the chapter does not adequately recognize the important contributions the industry's research programs made to the long-term survival of the industry in Hawai'i. The local pineapple industry remained viable because the industry supported an outstanding research program.

I applaud the author's effort to provide an overview of the working plantation (Working Pine, chapter seven.) While much has been written about the cultural and social aspects of plantation life in Hawai'i, it is important to provide a view into the working plantation as Ten Bruggencate has done in this chapter. A table showing the ethnic breakdown on "A Molokai Plantation Village" is particularly revealing of the broad mix of cultures that intermingled on the plantations.

Most of the statistics in the book are out-of-date with tabulations mostly ending in 1990. Since such information is now readily available on the Internet, e.g. at http://www.fao.org this may not be a serious shortcoming, but it also would have been relatively easy to obtain more current information. The book is relatively free of technical problems but one, a drop cap 'W' that should be a 'D' at the beginning of chapter five and "packed" instead of "peaked in production" at the beginning of chapter nine are particularly glaring. Others include A. L. Dean, a former president of the University of Hawai'i listed as L. A. Dean (p. 90), and the failure to introduce abbreviations for associations (chapter five) with the full name sends the reader hunting for the abbreviation meaning.

In summary, this is a short, interesting, but flawed book on the history of pineapple in Hawai'i. The breadth of coverage in the book is particularly laudable but the brevity of treatment is disappointing. The photographs are wonderful and it is hoped that originals exist in the public domain.

Duane P. Bartholomew
Agronomist emeritus and pineapple researcher at the
Pineapple Research Institute of Hawai'i (1965–66)
and in the Department of Agronomy and Soil Science,
University of Hawai'i at Mānoa (1966–1997)

Hawaiiana in 2004
A Bibliography of Titles of Historical Interest

Compiled by Joan Hori, Jodie Mattos, and Dore Minatodani,
assisted by Lisa Tanikawa and Joni Watanabe

Abarca, Thora. *Archaeology of East Hawai'i Island: Hilo, Hamakua, and Puna (with selected annotations)*. S.1: s.n., 2002. 13 p.

AhChing, Peter Leiataua. *Polynesian Interconnections: Samoa to Tahiti to Hawaii.* Morrisville, NC: Lulu Press, 2004. 131 p. Also published in another edition with subtitle "Dwayne Johnson and King Kamehameha in Culture and Science," 147 p.

Allen, Robert. *Creating Hawai'i Tourism: A Memoir.* Honolulu: Bess Press, 2004. 271 p.

Alu Like, Inc. *Annotated Bibliography of Alu Like Native Hawaiian Reports, 1976–1998.* Honolulu: Research and Evaluation Unit, Alu Like, Inc., 1999. 48 p.

Ariyoshi, Jean Hayashi. *Washington Place: A First Lady's Story.* Honolulu: Japanese Cultural Center of Hawai'i, 2004. 209 p.

Ashman, Mike. *Kauai As It Was In the 1940s and '50s.* Lihue, HI: Kauai Historical Society, 2004. 276 p. "Recollections and photographs of the days when Grampa Mike was a Teenage, Coast Haole bachelor living on Kauai during the two years prior to World War II and four years following the war."

At Hamilton Library, University of Hawai'i at Mānoa, Joan Hori is curator of the Hawaiian Collection; Jodie Mattos is a librarian in the Business, Social Science and Humanities Department; Dore Minatodani is a librarian with the Hawaiian Collection; Lisa Tanikawa is a student in the College of Arts and Sciences; and Joni Watanabe is a student in the College of Business Administration.

The Hawaiian Journal of History, vol. 39 (2005)

Bergin, Billy. *Loyal to the Land: The Legendary Parker Ranch, 750–1950.* Honolulu: University of Hawai'i Press, 2004. 379 p.

Berinobis, Shari 'Iolani Floyd. *The Spirit of Hula: Photos and Stories from Around the World.* Honolulu: Bess Press, 2004. 160 p.

Bolante, Ronna and Michael Keany. *The 50 Greatest Hawai'i Albums.* Honolulu: Watermark, 2004. 160 p. Also known as *Honolulu Magazine The 50 Greatest Hawai'i Albums.*

Byrd, Jerry. *It Was a Trip: On Wings of Music.* Anaheim Hills, CA: Centerstream Publishing, 2003. 144 p. Autobiography.

Cahill, Emmett. *The Dark Decade 1829–1839; Anti-Catholic Persecutions in Hawai'i.* Honolulu: Mutual Publishing, 2004. 134 p.

Castle, Alfred L. *A Century of Philanthropy: A History of the Samuel N. and Mary Castle Foundation.* Revised ed. Honolulu: Hawaiian Historical Society, 2004. 329 p.

Chapman, Don with William Kaihe'ekai Mai'oho. *Mauna 'Ala: Hawai'i's Royal Mausoleum: Last Remnant of a Lost Kingdom.* Honolulu: Mutual Publishing, 2004. 96 p.

Chauvin, Michael. *Hōkūloa: The British 1874 Transit of Venus Expedition to Hawai'i.* Honolulu: Bishop Museum Press, 2004. 278 p.

Chiddix, Jim. *Next Stop Honolulu!: Oahu Railway & Land Company 1889–1971.* Honolulu: Sugar Cane Press, 2004. 352 p.

Ching, Carrie. *Hawai'i: A Celebration of the History, Landmarks, Flavors, Trends and Traditions that Make Hawai'i Special.* Honolulu: Mutual Publishing, 2004. 152 p.

Christ United Methodist Church, 1903–2003: A Pictorial History. Honolulu: Christ United Methodist Church, 2003. 256 p.

Danico, Mary Yu. *The 1.5 Generation: Becoming Korean American in Hawai'i.* Honolulu: University of Hawai'i Press; Los Angeles: In Association with UCLA Asian American Studies Center, 2004. 235 p.

Day Our World Changed: December 7, 1941: Punahou '52 Remembers Pearl Harbor. Edited by John B. Bowles and Eric C. Gross. North Liberty, IA: Ice Cube Press, 2004. 203 p.

DeLa Vega, Timothy T. *200 Years of Surfing Literature: An Annotated Bibliography*. Hanapepe, HI: Timothy T. DeLa Vega, 2004. 102 p.

Draft Environmental Impact Statement: Hiluhilu Development, Tax Map Key: 3-702-05:01. [Also known as *Hiluhilu Master Plan*]. Honolulu, HI: Group 70 International Inc., 2003. 1 v. (various paging). Includes appendices:

  Clark, Matthew R., *et al.* "Archaeological Inventory Survey of the Ka'ū Development Area." (Technical Appendix C); and Orr, Maria E. Ka'imipono. "Cultural Impact Study: Hiluhilu Application Process Project: Ka'ū Ahupua'a, Land of Kekaha, District of North Kona, Hawai'i Island, Hawai'i." (Technical Appendix D).

Dukas, Neil Bernard. *A Military History of Sovereign Hawai'i*. Honolulu: Mutual Publishing, 2004. 232 p.

Evidence for Native Hawaiian Knowledge of the Northwest Hawaiian Islands Prior to Western Contact: Report to the Office of Hawaiian Affairs. Honolulu: Department of Hawaiian and Pacific Studies, Bernice Pauahi Bishop Museum, 2002. 1 v. (various paging).

Goldman, Rita. *Every Grain Of Rice: Portraits of Maui's Japanese Community*. Virginia Beach, VA: Donning Co., 2002. 240 p.

Grant, John and Ray Jones. *Legendary Lighthouses. Volume II: The Companion to the All-New PBS Television Series*. Guilford, CT: Globe Pequot Press, 2002. 206 p. Includes a chapter on Hawai'i.

Harris, Jeremy. *The Renaissance of Honolulu: The Sustainable Rebirth of An American City*. Honolulu: Mayor Jeremy Harris, 2004. 225 p.

Hawai'i Remembers September 11. Edited by Thom Curtis. Hilo, HI: Hagoth Publishing, 2002. 182 p.

Henry, "Lanakila" Lehman Lloyd (Bud). *Who's Who in the 'Ohana Kauaua-Nui-a-Mahi: Līloa to Kauaua-Nui-a-Mahi to Kamehameha Genealogy*. Kāneohe, HI?: Lanakila/Hawai'i Press, 2004. 72 p.

Howe, K. R. *The Quest for Origins: Who First Discovered and Settled the Pacific Islands?* Honolulu: University of Hawai'i Press, 2003. 235 p. Includes Hawai'i.

Hula: Vintage Hawaiian Graphics. Edited by Jim Heimann. Köln; Los Angeles: Taschen, 2003. (various pagings).

Jackson, Joe. *A Furnace Afloat: The Wreck of the* Hornet *and the Harrowing 4,300-mile Voyage of Its Survivors.* New York; London: Free Press, 2003. 283 p.

Jones, Ray. *Lighthouses of California and Hawaii: Eureka to San Diego to Honolulu.* Guilford, CT: Globe Pequot Press, 2002. 94 p.

Ka'aiakamanu, David Kaluna M. *Native Hawaiian Medicine: Volume III.* Honolulu: First People's Productions, 2003. 99 p.

Kashima, Tetsuden. *Judgment without Trial: Japanese American Imprisonment During World War II.* Seattle: University of Washington Press, 2003. 327 p.

Kawananakoa Hall Oral History Project. Coordinated by Gary Francisco. Hilo, HI: Department of Parks and Recreation, County of Hawai'i, 2001. 1 v. (various paging).

Kirsten, Sven A. *The Book of Tiki: The Cult of Polynesian Pop in Fifties America.* Köln; London: Taschen, 2003. 287 p.

Krauss, Bob and William P. Alexander. *Grove Farm Plantation: The Biography of a Hawaiian Sugar Plantation.* 3rd ed. Lihue, HI: Grove Farm Museum, 2003. 452 p.

Lightner, Richard. *Hawaiian History: An Annotated Bibliography.* Westport, CT: Praeger, 2004. 302 p. (Bibliographies of the States of the United States series, no. 11).

Loos, Chris and Rick Castberg. *Murder in Paradise: A Christmas in Hawaii Turns to Tragedy.* New York: Avon Books, 2003. 382 p. On Dana Ireland case.

MacKenzie, Melody Kapilialoha. *Native Hawaiian Claims to the Lands and Natural Resources of the Northwestern Hawaiian Islands.* 2003. 80 p. "Report to the Office of Hawaiian Affairs."

Matsuo, Jean Misaki Yoshida. *Dear Okaasan . . . . . It's pick coffee time again.* Hawaii: J.M.Y. Matsuo, 2003. 130 p.

Mauna Loa Revealed: Structure, Composition, History, and Hazards. Edited by J.M. Rhodes and John P. Lockwood. Washington, DC: American Geophysical Union, 1995. 361 p. (Geophysical Monograph series, 92).

McCabe, Larry. *Pearl Harbor and the American Spirit: The World War II Generation Remembers the Tragic Event that Transformed a Nation.* Philadelphia: Xlibris, 2004. 604 p.

McPherson, Michael. *All Those Summers; Memories of Surfing's Golden Age.* Honolulu: Watermark, 2004. 109 p.

Menton, Linda K. and Eileen H. Tamura. *A History of Hawai'i: Teacher's Manual.* 2nd ed. Honolulu: Curriculum Research & Development Group, University of Hawai'i, 2001. 300 p.

Meyer, Manulani Aluli. *Ho'oulu: Our Time of Becoming: Collected Early Writings of Manulani Meyer.* Honolulu: 'Ai Pōkahu Press, 2003. 255 p.

Miike, Lawrence H. *Water and the Law in Hawai'i.* Honolulu: University of Hawai'i Press, 2004. 278 p.

Mohr, James C. *Plague and Fire: Battling Black Death and the 1900 Burning of Honolulu's Chinatown.* New York: Oxford University Press, 2005. 246 p.

Murabayashi, Duk Hee Lee. *Korean Passengers Arriving at Honolulu, 1903–1905.* Honolulu: Center for Korean Studies, University of Hawai'i, 2001. 137 p.

Murabayashi, Duk Hee Lee. *One Hundred Years of Korean Immigration in Hawaii.* Soul-si: Chungang M&B, 2003. 238 p.

Nature Conservancy and Kumu Pono Associates LLC. *Ka Hana Lawai'a a me na Ko'a o na Kai'ewalu: A History of Fishing Practices and Marine Fisheries of the Hawaiian Islands, Compiled from Native Hawaiian Traditions, Historical Accounts, Government Communications, Kama'āina Testimony and Ethnography.* Honolulu: Kamehameha Schools Land Assets Division, 2004. 1 compact disc: sd., col.; 4¾ in.

Northwestern Hawaiian Islands: A Resource Guide. Washington, DC: U.S. Department of Commerce, National Oceanic and Atmospheric Administration, 2003. 44 p.

Oaks, Robert F. *Hawai'i: A History of the Big Island.* San Francisco: Arcadia, 2003. 160 p.

Odo, Franklin. *No Sword to Bury: Japanese Americans in Hawai'i During World War II.* Philadelphia: Temple University Press, 2004. 335 p.

Oroku, Okinawa Connection: Local-Style Restaurants in Hawai'i. Honolulu: Center for Oral History, Social Science Research Institute, University of Hawai'i at Mānoa, 2004. 481 p.

Pagliaro, Emily. *Nā Pōhaku Ola Kapaemāhū a Kapuni Restoration 1997*. Kailua-Kona, HI: Fields Masonry, 1997. 42 p. Prepared for the Queen Emma Foundation; Historic Preservation Division of the Department of Land and Natural Resources.

Pearl Harbor: The Movie and the Moment. Edited by Linda Sunshine and Antonia Felix. New York: Hyperion, 2001. 176 p.

Pioneer Mill Company: A Maui Sugar Plantation Legacy. Edited by Warren S. Nishimoto. Honolulu: Center for Oral History, Social Science Research Institute, University of Hawai'i at Mānoa, 2003. 538 p.

Pryor, Alton. *Little Known Tales in Hawaii History*. Roseville, CA: Stagecoach Publishing, 2004. 177 p.

Pu'u 'Ō'ō-Kūpaianaha Eruption of Kīlauea Volcano, Hawai'i: The First 20 Years. Edited by Christina Heliker, et al. Reston, VA: U.S. Department of the Interior, U.S. Geological Survey, 2003. 213 p.

Rayson, Ann. *Modern History of Hawai'i*. Honolulu: Bess Press, 2004. 302 p.

Rizzuto, Jim. *Kona Fishing Chronicles 2003/2004*. Kamuela, HI: Jim Rizzuto, 2004. 288 p.

Rosenberg, Emily S. *A Date Which Will Live: Pearl Harbor in American Memory*. Durham, NC; London: Duke University Press, 2003. 246 p. (American encounters/global interactions series).

Royal Order of Kamehameha I. *Mauna Kea, The Temple: Protecting the Sacred Resource*. Hilo, HI: Royal Order of Kamehameha I: Mauna Kea Anaina Hou, 2001. 1 v.

Sigall, Bob. *The Companies We Keep: Amazing Stories about 450 of Hawai'i's Best Known Companies*. Honolulu: Small Business Hawaii, 2004. 408 p.

Silva, Noenoe K. *Aloha Betrayed: Native Hawaiian Resistance to American Colonialism*. Durham, NC: Duke University Press, 2004. 270 p.

Smith, Carl. *Pearl Harbor 1941: The Day of Infamy.* Westport, CT: Praeger, 2004. 96 p. (Praeger Illustrated Military History series).

Stauffer, Robert H. *Kahana: How the Land Was Lost.* Honolulu: University of Hawai'i Press, 2004. 275 p.

Surfing: He'e Nalu, Hawaiian Proverbs and Inspirational Quotes Celebrating Hawai'i's Royal Sport. Honolulu: Mutual Publishing, 2003. 78 p. Includes historical photographs.

Ten Bruggencate, Jan K. *Hawai'i's Pineapple Century: A History of the Crowned Fruit in the Hawaiian Islands.* Honolulu: Mutual Publishing, 2004. 199 p.

They Also Served: Women's Stories from the World War II Era. Edited by Jeanie Sutton Lambright. Philadelphia: Xlibris, 2003. 419 p.

Treiber, Gale E. *Hawaiian Railway Album: Volume 1 – The Oahu Railway and Land Company, Limited, in Honolulu.* WWII Photographs by Victor Norton, Jr. Hanover, PA: Railroad Press, 2003. 57 p.

Varez, Dietrich. *The Legend of Lā'ieikawai.* Honolulu: University of Hawai'i Press, 2004. 80 p. "Abridged retelling of *The Hawaiian Romance of Lā'ieikawai,* translated by Martha Warren Beckwith, which is a translation of *Ka'ao o Lā'ieikawai* by S.N. Haleole."

Whitehead, John S. *Completing the Union: Alaska, Hawai'i, and the Battle for Statehood.* Albuquerque, NM: University of New Mexico Press, 2004. xvii, 438 p.

Williford, Glen and T. McGovern. *Defenses of Pearl Harbor and Oahu 1907–50.* Oxford: Osprey, 2003. 64 p.

Williams, Waimea. *Aloha Kaua'i: A Childhood.* Honolulu: Island Heritage, 2004. 164 p. Memories of growing up in the 1950's.

THESES AND DISSERTATIONS

Antonio, Susan Kapulani. "Stolen Identity: Defining 'Aihue from a Hawaiian Perspective." M.A. thesis, University of Hawai'i at Mānoa, 2003. iii, 105. (Pacific Islands Studies) On Hawaiian perception of ownership and stealing.

Altice, Eric DeWitt. "Foreign Missions and the Politics of Evangelical Culture: Civilization, Race and Evangelism, 1810–1860." Ph. D. dissertation, University of California, Los Angeles, 2004. ix, 334. (History)

Beyer, Carl Kalani. "Manual and Industrial Education During Hawaiian Sovereignty: Curriculum in the Transculturation of Hawai'i." Ph. D. dissertation, University of Illinois at Chicago, 2004. xiii, 306. (Education)

Caldeira, Leah Pualaha'ole. "Akua Hulu Manu Through Materials." M.A. thesis, University of Hawai'i at Mānoa, 2003. x, 155. (Art) On Hawaiian feather gods.

Chester, Robert K. "In the Margins of Memory: Episodes in the Cultural Life of Admiral Husband E. Kimmel." M.A. thesis, University of Wyoming, 2003. v, 185 (American Studies) Concerns the Japanese attack on Pearl Harbor in 1941.

Coil, James Henry. "'The Beauty That Was': Archaeological Investigations of Ancient Hawaiian Agriculture and Environmental Change in Kahikinui, Maui." Ph. D. dissertation, University of California, Berkeley, 2004. xxvi, 453. (Anthropology)

Di Alto, Stephanie Joy. "Kū i Ka Pono (Stand Up For Justice): Native Hawaiian-U.S. Relations, 1993–2003." Ph. D. dissertation, University of California, Irvine, 2004. xiii, 494. (Political Science)

Donaghy, Joseph Keola. "Nā Hīmeni a John Kameaaloha Almeida: He Kālailaina Ho'ohālikelike me ke Kālele ma luna o ka 'Oko'a o ka Puana Kama-'ilio a me ka Puana Hīmeni." M.A. thesis, University of Hawai'i at Hilo, 2003. iv, 111. "This thesis presents a comparative analysis of Hawaiian language word and phrase stress as spoken with the stress of such words and phrases as composed and sung by John Kameaaloha Almeida."

Fielding, Emily J. "Feral Goats, People and Land Degradation on the South Slope of Haleakala, Maui, Hawai'i." M.A. thesis, University of Hawai'i at Mānoa, 2003. vii, 94. (Geography)

Gentry, April Dawn Evers. "'The South Sea Rose': Imagining the Pacific in 19th Century America." Ph.D. dissertation, Southern Illinois University at Carbondale, 2003. vi, 226 (English) Concerns incarnations of Hawai'i in the American literary imagination from 1778 to 1898.

Gonzalez, Vernadette Vicuña. "Touring Empire: Colonial Travel and Global Tourism in Hawai'i and the Philippines." Ph. D. dissertation, University of California, Berkeley, 2004. v, 348. (Ethnic Studies)

Haight, Pamela. "'A Trustworthy Historical Record': The LaterWriting of Abraham Fornander, 1870–1887." M.Ed. thesis, University of Hawai'i at Mānoa, 2004. iv, 91. (Educational Foundations)

Hood, Dale E. "The Waiwai of Waiāhole and Waikāne: The Construction and Operation of the Waiāhole/Waikāne Water Ditch and Tunnel System 1900 to 2000." M.A. Plan B paper, University of Hawai'i at Mānoa, 2004. xi, 119. (Pacific Island Studies)

Hyzy, Katharine I. "Waif Elements: A Natural History of Restoration in Hawai'i." M.S. thesis, University of Montana-Missoula, 2004. iii, 101 (Environmental Studies)

Iyall Smith, Keri Elaine. "Transformations: The State and Indigenous Movements." Ph.D. dissertation, University of North Carolina at Chapel Hill, 2003. xiii, 205 (Sociology) Includes Native Hawaiians.

Inglis, Kerri A. "'A Land Set Apart': Disease, Displacement, & Death at Makanalua, Moloka'i." Ph.D. dissertation, University of Hawai'i at Mānoa, 2004. xvii, 324. (History)

Johnson, Greg Bruce. "The Terms of Return: Religious Discourse and the Native American Graves Protection and Repatriation Act." Ph.D. dissertation, University of Chicago, 2003. iii, 213.

Johnston, Jeanne Branch. "Personal Accounts from Survivors of the Hilo Tsunamis of 1946 and 1960: Toward a Disaster Communication Model." M.A. thesis, University of Hawai'i at Mānoa, 2003. x, 142. (Communication)

Kimura, Larry Lindsey. "Nā Mele Kau o ka Māhele Mua o ka Mo'olelo 'O Hi'iakaikapoliopele na Joseph M. Poepoe: He Kālailaina me ke Kālele ma Luna o nā Ku'inaiwi Kaulua." M.A. thesis, University of Hawai'i at Hilo, 2002. ix, 157. (Hawaiian Language and Literature)

Kitayama, Mariko. "Hawai'i's Japanese Community in the Postwar Democratic Movement." Ph.D. dissertation, University of Hawai'i at Mānoa, 2004. xi, 304. (Sociology)

Kosasa, Eiko. "Predatory Politics: United States Imperialism, Settler Hegemony, and the Japanese in Hawai'i." Ph.D. dissertation, University of Hawai'i at Mānoa, 2004, xiii, 422. (Political Science)

Kurokawa, Yoko. "Yearning for a Distant Music: Consumption of Hawaiian Music and Dance in Japan." Ph.D. dissertation, University of Hawai'i at Mānoa, 2004. xix, 557 (Music)

Labrador, Roderick N. "Constructing 'Home' and 'Homeland': Identity-Making Among Filipinos in Hawai'i." Ph.D. dissertation, University of California, Los Angeles, 2003. xii, 2001 (Anthropology)

Lee, Sean A. "The Origins of Surfing and its Context in Polynesian (Hawaiian) Culture." M.A. thesis, San Francisco State University, 2004. vi, 50. (Anthropology)

Monobe, Hiromi. "Shaping an Ethnic Leadership: Takie Okumura and the 'Americanization' of the Nisei in Hawai'i." Ph.D. dissertation, University of Hawai'i at Mānoa, 2004. ix, 294. (American Studies)

Nogelmeier, Marvin Puakea. "Mai Pa'a i ka Leo: Historical Voice in Hawaiian Primary Materials, Looking Forward and Listening Back." Ph.D. dissertation, University of Hawai'i at Mānoa, 2003. xviii, 334. (Anthropology)

Olivieri, Cheryl N. "Song of the Islands: Picturing Paradise, Remembering Exoticism." M.A. thesis, University of Hawai'i at Mānoa, 2003. ix, 122. (History) "The focus of this study is the role of female comedic performances in the selling of Hawaii as a tourist attraction . . . during the nineteen thirties and forties."

Panek, Mark. "*Gaijin Yokozuna:* A Biography of Chad Rowan." Ph.D. dissertation, University of Hawai'i at Mānoa, 2004. viii, 479. (English)

Pang, Benton K. "In the Wake of Ruling Chiefs: Forest Use of the Island of Hawai'i During the Time of Kamehameha I." Ph.D. dissertation, University of Hawai'i at Mānoa, 2004. ix, 194. (Botany)

Powers, Janine A. "From Medicine to Art: Nils Paul Larsen (1890–1964)." Ph.D. dissertation, University of Hawai'i at Mānoa, 2004. ix, 278. (American Studies)

Richter, Sonja. "Das kulturelle Selbstverständnis der indigenen Elite Hawai'is 1819–1893 (The Cultural Identity of the Hawaiian Indigenous Elite 1819–1893)." M.A. thesis, Georg-August-Universität Göttinger, 2001. 130. (History)

Rifkin, Mark S. "Manifesting America: Imperialism and National Space, 1776–1861." Ph.D. dissertation, University of Pennsylvania, 2003. vii, 390 (English) Includes chapter "Foreign In(-)dependence: Debt, Autonomy, and the Transnationalization of Hawai'i."

Tengan, Ty P. Kāwika. "Hale Mua: (En)Gendering Hawaiian Men." Ph.D. dissertation, University of Hawai'i at Mānoa, 2003. xx, 390. (Anthropology)

Trask, Timothy John. "The Aloha Shirt: Tailored Expressive Culture." M.S. thesis, Utah State University, 2003. viii, 80. (American Studies)

Welford, Gabrielle. "Too Many Deaths: Decolonizing Western Academic Research on Indigenous Cultures." Ph.D. dissertation, University of Hawai'i at Mānoa, 2003. xvi, 343. (English)

Wilford, Timothy. "Pearl Harbor Redefined: USN Radio Intelligence in 1941." M.A. thesis, University of Ottawa, 2001. vi, 183. (History)

Selected Periodical References (Out-of-State Publications)

Articles in journals and magazines published in Hawai'i and the Pacific are selectively indexed in the Hawai'i Pacific Journal Index, at http://hpji.lib.hawaii.edu/

Allen, Melinda S. "Bet-Hedging Strategies, Agricultural Change, and Unpredictable Environments: Historical Development of Dryland Agriculture in Kona, Hawaii." *Journal of Anthropological Archaeology* 23.2 (June 2004): 196–224.

Amerasia Journal 29.3 (2003–2004). Special issue on "What Does It Mean to Be Korean Today? Part I. Across Nations, Generations and Identities." Includes: "Korean Population in the United States as Reflected in the Year 2000 U.S. Census" by Eui-Young Yu and Peter Choe, 2–21; "The Limits of Americanism and Democracy: Korean Americans, Transnational Allegiance, and the Question of Loyalty on the Homefront during World War II" by Lili M. Kim, 79–96. Includes Hawai'i.

Andrade, Gabriel. "Notes on the Sahlins-Obeyesekere Debate: Captain Cook's Death Viewed from the Point of View of Rene Girard's Anthropology." *Revista de Ciencias Sociales* 10.1 (Jan–Apr. 2004): 101–111. Text in Spanish.

Bacchilega, Cristina and Noelani Arista. "The *Arabian Nights* in a Nineteenth-century Hawaiian Newspaper." *Fabula* 45.3/4 (Sept. 2004): 189–206.

Brookes, Tim. "The Hawaiian Invasion." *American History* 39.5 (Dec. 2004): 48+. Concerns the popularization of the Hawaiian steel guitar in the United States at the beginning of the 20th century.

Cordy, Ross. "Who Made the Feather Cloaks in the Hawaiian Islands? Some Additional Information." *Journal of the Polynesian Society* 112.2 (June 2003): 157–161.

Edles, Laura Desfor. "Rethinking 'Race', 'Ethnicity' and 'Culture': Is Hawai'i the 'Model Minority' State?" *Ethnic and Racial Studies* 27.1 (Jan. 2004): 37–68.

Frank, Stuart M. "No Ke Ano Ahiahi: A 'Lost' Hawaiian Narrative Ballad." *Mains'l Haul: A Journal of Pacific Maritime* 38.3 (2002): 22–27. Concerns a Hawaiian song preserved by an American whaler who heard it from a Hawaiian whaleman between 1868 and 1870.

Hone, Trent. "The Evolution of Fleet Tactical Doctrine in the U.S. Navy, 1922–1941." *Journal of Military History* 67.4 (Oct. 2003): 1107–1148. Concerns the Japanese attack on Pearl Harbor in 1941.

Igler, David. "Diseased Goods: Global Exchanges in the Eastern Pacific Basin, 1770–1850." *American Historical Review* 109.3 (June 2004): 692–719. Includes Hawai'i.

Imada, Adria L. "Hawaiians on Tour: Hula Circuits through the American Empire." *American Quarterly* 56.1 (March 2004): 111–149.

Jacobsen, Philip. "Radio Silence and Radio Deception: Secrecy Insurance for the Pearl Harbor Strike Force." *Intelligence and National Security* 19.4 (Winter 2004): 695–718.

Kaeppler, Adrienne L. "Recycling Tradition: A Hawaiian Case Study." *Dance Chronicle* 27.3 (2004): 293–311.

Kirch, Patrick V. "Temple Sites in Kahikinui, Maui, Hawaiian Islands: Their Orientations Decoded." *Antiquity* 78.299 (March 2004): 102–114.

Labrador, Roderick N. "'We Can Laugh at Ourselves': Hawai'i Ethnic Humor, Local Identity and the Myth of Multiculturalism." *Pragmatics* 14.2/3 (June/Sept. 2004): 291–316.

"The Last of the Paniolos." *Islands* 24.1 (Jan.–Feb. 2004): 46–51.

Link, Matthew. "When Captain Cook Met Kalanikoa." *Gay & Lesbian Review Worldwide* 11.3 (May/June 2004): 28–30.

MacLennan, Carol. "The Mark of Sugar: Hawai'i's Eco-Industrial Heritage." *Historical Social Research* 29.3 (2004): 37–62.

March, Edward C. "The American Hawaiian Steamship Company." *Steamboat Bill* 61.3 (2004): 177–191.

Naval History 18.6 (Dec. 2004). Includes: "Pearl Harbor: A Midget Sub in the Picture?" by Andrew Biache, Jr., Peter Hsu, Carroll Lucas, and John Rodgaard, 18–22; "'Let Every Man Do His Duty'" by Zenji Abe and Robert E. Van Patten, 23+; "Preserving the 'Ultimate Shrine'" by Matthew A. Russell, 28+; "All Signs Pointed To Pearl Harbor" by Eugene B. Canfield, 42–46.

North American Society for Sports History. *Proceedings & Newsletter* (2003). Includes: "Hawaii: The Cultural Crossroads of Sport" by Jerry Gems, 48; "A New Hawaiian Monarchy: The Media Representation of Duke Kahanamoku 1911–1912" by Jim Nendel, 56.

Rapa Nui Journal 17.2 (October 2003). Includes: "Rethinking the Traditional Classification of Hawaiian Poi Pounders" by Windy Keala McElroy, 85–93; "A Classification of Hawaiian Artifacts Based on Morphology and Wear: Analyses of Discoidal Artifacts" by Julie S. Field, 94–105; "Laupāhoehoe Nui: Archaeology of a High-risk Landscape on Windward Hawai'i Island" by Peter R. Mills, 106–113.

Schultz, Fred L. "Kimmel Case Dubbed 'Totally Political'." *Naval History* 18.1 (Feb. 2004): 41. Concerns new evidence in support of the Pearl Harbor commanders during the Dec. 7, 1941 attack.

Scott-Smith, Giles. "From Symbol of Division to Cold War Asset: Lyndon Johnson and the Achievement of Hawaiian Statehood in 1959." *History* 89.294 (April 2004): 256–273.

Smith, Anita. "Are the Earliest Field Monuments of the Pacific Landscape Serial Sites?" *Records of the Australian Museum* Supplement 29 (May 19, 2004): 133–138. Includes coverage of Hawai'i.

Soguk, Nevzat. "Incarcerating Travels: Travel Stories, Tourist Orders, and the Politics of the 'Hawai'ian [*sic*] Paradise'." *Journal of Tourism and Cultural Change* 1.1 (Jan. 2003): 29–53.

Stewart, Doug. "Doris Duke's Islamic Art Retreat." *Smithsonian* 34.12 (March 2004): 70–79.

Strange, Carolyn. "Symbiotic Commemoration: The Stories of Kalaupapa." *History & Memory* 16.1 (Spring/Summer 2004): 86–117.

Tengan, Ty P. Kawika. "Of Colonization and *Pono* in Hawai'i." *Peace Review* 16.2 (June 2004): 157–167.

Young, Morris. "Native Claims: Cultural Citizenship, Ethnic Expressions, and the Rhetorics of 'Hawaiianness'." *College English* 67.1 (Sept. 2004): 83–101.

CHAPTERS IN BOOKS

The following is a list of book chapters on Hawaiian history, and includes chapters published 1997–2004.

Akindes, Fay Yokomizo. "Grandma's Photo Album: Clothing as Symbolic Representations of Identity." In Fong, Mary and Rueyling Chuang, eds., *Communicating Ethnic and Cultural Identity*. Lanham, MD: Rowman & Littlefield, 2004. 85–104.

Ancestors in Post-Contact Religion: Roots, Ruptures, and Modernity's Memory. Friesen, Steven J., ed., Cambridge, MA: Harvard University Press for the Center for Study of World Religions, Harvard Divinity School, 2001. Includes: "The Hawaiian 'Aumakua: Ancestors as Gods," by Rubellite Kawena Johnson, 29–47; "Rhythms from the Past Beating into the Future," by Pualani Kanahele, 157–165; "Aloha 'Aina: Love of the Land in Hawai'i," by David

Kaʻupu, 169–175; "Disconnection and Reconnection," by Puanani Burgess, 239–251.

Anderson, Carolyn, "Contested Public Memories: Hawaiian History as Hawaiian or American Experience." In Edgerton, Gary R. and Peter C. Rollins, eds., *Television Histories: Shaping Collective Memory in the Media Age.* Lexington, KY: University Press of Kentucky, 2001. 143–168.

Asian and Pacific Islander American Education: Social, Cultural, and Historical Contexts. Tamura, Eileen H., Virgie Chattergy, and Russell Endo, eds., South El Monte, CA: Pacific Asia Press, 2002. Includes: "Standards of Effective Pedagogy for Students of Culturally Diverse Backgrounds: Examples from Native Hawaiian Classrooms," by Lois A. Yamauchi, 21–40; "A Follow-Up Study on the Effects of Simulation on Student Attitudes Towards Reparations for Native Hawaiians," by Linda K. Menton, 41–58; "Toward Building Home-School Partnerships: The Case of Chinese American Families and Public Schools," by Sau-Fong Siu, 59–84; "At-Risk Asian and Pacific American Youths: Implications for Teachers, Psychologists, and Other Providers," by Patrick W. Lee and Sandra L. Wong, 85–116. Also "Asian American Teachers and Teacher Candidates," by Sandra B. Chong, 117–131; "The Overrepresentation of Filipinos in the University of Hawaiʻi Community College System: Filipinos and Social Constructivism," by Niki Libarios, 133–147; "Family and School Factors Influencing Academic Performance of Bilingual *Shin Nisei* Students in Hawaiʻi," by Kimi Kondo-Brown, 149–173; "The Role of Westernized Education in the Future of *Faʻa Samoa*," by Allen Awaya, 175–196.

Ayau, Edward Halealoha and Ty Kāwika Tengan. "*Ka Huakaʻi O Nā ʻŌiwi:* The Journey Home." In Fforde, Cressida, Jane Hubert and Paul Turnbull, eds., *The Dead and Their Possessions: Repatriation in Principle, Policy and Practice.* London: Routledge, 2002. 171–189.

Bayman, James M. "Stone Adze Economies in Post-Contact Hawaiʻi." In Cobb, Charles R., ed., *Stone Tool Traditions in the Contact Era.* Tuscaloosa: University of Alabama Press, 2003. 94–108.

Bird, Isabella. "Hawaii." In Chubbuck, Kay, ed., *Letters to Henrietta* by Isabella Bird. Boston: Northeastern University Press, 2003. 56–142.

Clarkson, Gavin. "United States: Native Hawaiians." In Watters, Lawrence, ed., *Indigenous Peoples, The Environment and Law: An Anthology.* Durham, NC: Carolina Academic Press, 2004. 335–354.

Eperjesi, John R. "Becoming Hawaiian: Jack London, Cultural Tourism, and the Myth of Hawaiian Exceptionalism." In *The Imperialist Imaginary: Visions of Asia and the Pacific in American Culture.* Hanover, NH: Dartmouth College, 2004. 105–129.

Friesen, Steven J. "The Hawaiian Lei on a Voyage Through Modernities: A Study in Post-Contact Religion." In Olupona, Jacob K., ed., *Beyond Primitivism: Indigenous Religious Traditions and Modernity.* New York: Routledge, 2004. 325–342.

Fuchs, Miriam. "Autobiography as Political Discourse: Liliʻuokalani's *Hawaii's Story by Hawaii's Queen.*" In *The Text is Myself: Women's Life Writing and Catastrophe.* Madison: University of Madison Press, 2004. 28–77.

Glenn, Evelyn Nakano. "Japanese and Haoles in Hawaii." In *Unequal Freedom: How Race and Gender Shaped American Citizenship and Labor.* Cambridge, MA: Harvard University Press, 2002. 190–235.

Halualani, Rona Tamiko. "Purifying the State: State Discourses, Blood Quantum, and the Legal Mis/Recognition of Hawaiians." In Goldberg, David Theo, Michael Musheno, and Lisa C. Bower, eds., *Between Law and Culture: Relocating Legal Studies.* Minneapolis: University of Minnesota Press, 2001. 141–173.

Kaomea, Julie. "Dilemmas of an Indigenous Academic: A Native Hawaiian Story." In Mutua, Kagendo and Beth Blue Swadener, eds., *Decolonizing Research in Cross-Cultural Contexts: Critical Personal Narratives.* Albany, NY: State University of New York Press, 2004. 27–44.

La Croix, Sumner J. "Explaining Divergence in Property Rights: Fiji and Hawaiʻi in the Nineteenth Century." In Engerman, Stanley L. and Jacob Metzer, eds., *Land Rights, Ethno-Nationality, and Sovereignty in History.* London: Routledge, 2004. 183–209.

Law & Empire in the Pacific: Fiji and Hawaiʻi. Merry, Sally Engle and Donald Brenneis, eds., Santa Fe, NM: School of American Research Press, 2003. Includes: "A Chief Does Not Rule Land; He Rules People (Luganda Proverb)," by Jane F. Collier, 35–60; "Talking Back to Law and Empire: Hula in Hawaiian-Language Literature in 1861," by Noenoe Silva, 101–121; "Law and Identity in an American Colony," by Sally Engle Merry, 123–152; "Kūʻē and Kūʻokoʻa: History, Law, and Other Faiths," by Jonathan Kamakawiwoʻole Osorio, 213–237.

Love, Eric T. L. "Hawaii Annexed." In *Race Over Empire: Racism and U.S. Imperialism, 1865–1900*." Chapel Hill, NC: University of North Carolina Press, 2004. 115–158.

Masterson, Daniel M. and Sayaka Funada-Classen. "Before Latin America: The Early Japanese Immigrant Experience in Hawaii, Canada, and the United States." In *The Japanese in Latin America*. Urbana, IL: University of Illinois Press, 2004. 4–10.

Merry, Sally Engel. "Criminalization and Gender: The Changing Governance of Sexuality and Gender Violence in Hawai'i." In Smandych, Russell Charles, ed., *Governable Places: Readings on Governmentality and Crime Control*. Aldershot, VT: Ashgate, 1999. 75–101. Comparison of Hawai'i criminal law of mid-19th century and late 20th century regarding family relationships.

Okihiro, Gary Y. *The Columbia Guide to Asian American History*. New York: Columbia University Press, 2001. Includes: "Hawai'i's Population Before European Contact," 45–55; "Hawaiians and Captain James Cook," 56–66; "America's Concentration Camps–Hawai'i," 120–127; "Resources– Hawai'i, Hawaiians, and Pacific Islanders," 280–285.

Pearce, George F. "Assessing Public Opinion: Editorial Comment and the Annexation of Hawaii–A Case Study." In Dudden, Arthur Power, ed., *American Empire in the Pacific: From Trade to Strategic Balance, 1700–1922*. Aldershot, England: Variorum, 2004. 189–206.

Pfeffer, Michael T. "The Engineering and Evolution of Hawaiian Fishhooks." In Hunt, Terry L., Carl P. Lipo, and Sarah L. Sterling, eds., *Posing Questions for a Scientific Archaeology*. Westport, CT: Bergin & Garvey, 2001. 73–95.

Pierce, Lori Anne. "The Whites Have Created Modern Honolulu: Hawaiian Ethnicity and Racial Stratification." In Spickard, Paul R. and G. Reginald Daniel, eds., *Racial Thinking in the United States: Uncompleted Independence*. Notre Dame, IN: University of Notre Dame Press, 2004. 124–156.

Takaki, Ronald. "The Sugar Kingdom: The Making of Plantation Hawai'i." In Wu, Jean Yu-wen Shen and Min Song, eds., *Asian American Studies: A Reader*. New Brunswick, NJ: Rutgers University Press, 2000. 21–34.

Takagi-Kitayama, Mariko. "Attempt at Sovereignty in Multi-Ethnic Hawaii: The Displacement of Hawaiians by Non-Hawaiians and the Push for Sovereignty." In Otsuru, Chieko Kitagawa, ed., *Diversified Migration Patterns of North America: Their Challenges and Opportunities.* Osaka: Japan Center for Area Studies, National Museum of Ethnology, 1997. 167–182.

Women's Suffrage in Asia: Gender, Nationalism and Democracy. Edwards, Louise P. and Mina Roces, eds., London: RoutledgeCurzon, 2004. Includes: "Settler Anxieties, Indigenous Peoples and Women's Suffrage in the Colonies of Australia, New Zealand and Hawai'i, 1888 to 1902," by Patricia Grimshaw, 407–411; " Women's Suffrage and Racial Hierarchies in Hawai'i," 425–430.

AUDIO-VISUALS

First Light. Written and produced by Roland Yamamoto. Honolulu: PBS Hawai'i, 2004. 57 min. Videocassette. Examines Hawaiian cultural, scientific and environmental values attributed to Mauna Kea, and competition for access to its peak.

Haleakalā: A Sense of Place. Directed by Jay April. Makawao, HI: Artifact Studios, 2004. 49 min. DVD. Describes the Hawaiian cultural, spiritual and environmental aspects of Haleakalā.

Hawaii's Chinatown. Written and directed by Doug Ross. s.l.: Doug Ross Communications, 2004. 57 min. Videocassette. Traces the history of Chinese immigrants to Hawai'i.

He Inoa no Kalakaua. Redondo Beach, CA: JAG Productions, 2004. DVD. Hula performances of historic and contemporary compositions honoring King David Kalākaua.

History Undercover: The Other Tragedy at Pearl Harbor. Produced by Julie Moline. New York: A&E Television Networks, 2001. 50 min. Videocassette and DVD. Recounts events leading up to the 1944 explosion at Pearl Harbor, as the U.S. military prepared to invade Saipan.

Nā Iwi Kūpuna. Honolulu: Historic Preservation Division, Hawai'i State Dept. of Land and Natural Resources, 2003. 32 min. Videocassette and DVD. Describes Hawaiian cultural traditions related to human remains and burial.

Kau Lā'au & Ma'ama'a: Traditional Hawaiian Ulua Fishing. Written and directed by Kate Emma Sample. Hawai'i: Pili Productions, 2003. 28 min.

Videocassette, DVD and streaming video on the web. http://stream
.hawaiirdp.org/library

Kaumuali'i: A Treasured Ruler of Kaua'i. Written and directed by Blaine Kama-
lani Kia. Līhu'e, Kaua'i, HI: Kaua'i Historical Society, 2004. 22 min.
Videocassette.

*Lance Larsen vs The Hawaiian Kingdom, Permanent Court of Arbitration, The
Hague, Netherlands.* Honolulu: Acting Council of Regency of the Hawaiian
Kingdom, 2003. DVD. Materials documenting and supporting Hawaiian
national Lance Larsen's charges against the Hawaiian Kingdom for failing
to protect him against laws imposed on him by the United States.

Mauna Kea: Temple Under Siege. Nā'ālehu, HI: Nā Maka o ka 'Āina, 2004. Videocassette and DVD. Documents five years of the struggle over access to
Mauna Kea.

A Most Unlikely Hero. Produced by Stephen Okino. s.l.: Custom Flix, 2003. 57
min. Videocassette. Depicts Bruce Yamashita's fight against the United
States Marine Corps for racial discrimination.

Perilous Fight: America's World War II in Color. Produced by Greg Palmer and
Scott Pearson. Alexandria, VA: PBS Home Video, 2003. 220 min. Videocassette and DVD. Includes section "The Pacific, 1943–1945."

Skin Stories: The Art and Culture of Polynesian Tattoo. Produced by Emiko Omori
and Lisa Altieri. Honolulu: Pacific Islanders in Communication, 2003.
60 min. Videocassette.

Unsolved History: Myths of Pearl Harbor. Silver Spring, MD: Discovery Commu-
nications, Inc., 2003. 40 min. Videocassette and DVD. Examines the role
Japanese midget submarines might have played in the bombing of Pearl
Harbor.

USS Arizona *to* USS Missouri: *From Tragedy to Victory.* Written and directed by
Mannie T. Silva. Sherman Oaks, CA: OnDeck Home Entertainment, 2002.
45 min. Videocassette and DVD.

*An Untold Triumph: The Story of the 1st and 2nd Filipino Infantry Regiments, U.S.
Army.* Produced by Noel M. Izon. Hyattsville, MD: Interactive Communication Technology, 2002. 85 min. Videocassette.

New Limited Edition Book
from the Hawaiian Historical Society

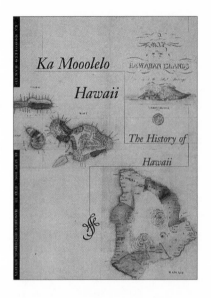

Ka Mooolelo
Hawaii

The History of
Hawaii

THIS 116 PAGE HISTORY OF HAWAI'I is called by David Forbes in his *Hawaiian National Bibliography* (2000), "one of the most important books on Hawaii. This is the first Hawaiian history written and published in Hawaii, and the first from a Hawaiian viewpoint. Sometimes cataloged as the work of David Malo, it is rather the cooperative effort of a select group of Lahainaluna students and their instructor, Sheldon Dibble."

This reprint of the 1838 Lahainaluna publication is the third in the Society's Hawaiian Language Reprint Series, *Ke Kupu Hou*. An introduction in Hawaiian and English is provided by M. Puakea Nogelmeier, Ph.D. The book is available in softcover and clothbound editions (xxviii, 116 pages).

Softcover edition ISBN 0-945048-16-5 $30 retail/$24 HHS members' special price.
Cloth edition ISBN 0-945048-15-7 $60 retail/$48 HHS members' special price.

Distributed for the Hawaiian Historical Society by the University of Hawai'i Press. Publication date: November 2005.

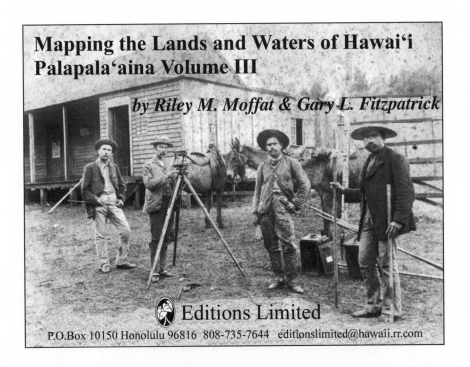
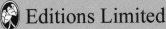

A Monarchy Transformed

The Hawaiian Monarchy tells the extraordinary story of the Hawaiian Kingdom, from its foundations in its ali'i past to its overthrow in 1898. Deeply researched and richly illustrated, it paints a colorful and multidimensional picture of life in the nineteenth century, weaving together biography, history and culture to bring Hawai'i's royal past to life. A chronology of events, full index and list of major personages is included for easy reference.

9 x 12 in. vertical, hardcover, 152 pp, $29.95

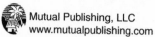

Mutual Publishing, LLC
www.mutualpublishing.com

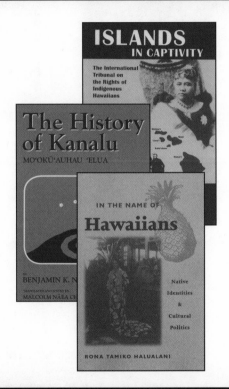

Hawai'i's History...

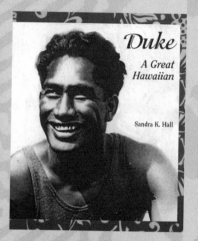

"Enlightening and invigorating"

"A small but well-designed piece."

"This keeper ought to be translated into several languages."

"This is the kind of book that visitors will want to take home and locals will want to keep."

3565 Harding A~~~~~~~~~~~~~~~~~808.734.7159

Avai~~~~~~~~~~~~~~s

Hawaiian Volcanoes
CLARENCE EDWARD DUTTON
Foreword and Appendixes by WILLIAM R. HALLIDAY

HAWAIIAN VOLCANOES, written by Clarence Edward Dutton as part of the 1883 Annual Report of the U.S. Geological Survey, is the first comprehensive study of volcanism in Hawai'i. In addition to being of both scientific and historical interest today, it is a fine example of natural history writing. It takes the form of an entrancing nineteenth-century "roadside geology" of

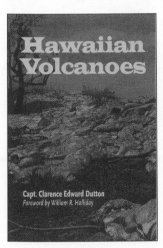

Capt. Clarence Edward Dutton
Foreword by William R. Halliday

the Big Island and much of Maui, combining Dutton's clear, elegant writing style with his eye for color and line and meticulously accurate observations of Hawai'i's people and landscape, as well as its geological phenomena.

A new foreword to this reprint discusses the importance of Dutton's ground-breaking report and its influence on subsequent research on Hawai'i's volcanoes. Also included is a colorful biographical sketch of Dutton, a discussion of his assignment to Hawai'i, and a list of his principal writings.

CLARENCE EDWARD DUTTON (1841–1912) was selected to join a U.S. Geological Survey team in the Rocky Mountains after serving in the Union Army. He spent several seasons in and around the Grand Canyon before being assigned to Hawai'i in 1882.

WILLIAM R. HALLIDAY, M.D., has long had major interests in history and geology in addition to his work in surgery and rehabilitation medicine. His fifty years of field research in Hawai'i have centered on the caldera and 'Ailaau flow field of Kīlauea volcano, Moloka'i's Kalaupapa Peninsula, the pits and pit craters of Kona's Hualālai volcano, and O'ahu's much-overlooked karstlands. He remains active in groups ranging from the Geological Society of America to the Kona Historical Society to the Washington Group of the Explorers Club, which meets at the famous Cosmos Club, founded by Clarence Dutton.

A Latitude 20 Book, August 2005, 198 pages, 25 illus.
ISBN 0-8248-2960-3, paperback, $22.00

 UNIVERSITY OF HAWAI'I PRESS
www.uhpress.hawaii.edu ▪ call toll free 1-888-UHPRESS

The Hawaiian Historical Society

ORGANIZED 1892

THE HAWAIIAN HISTORICAL SOCIETY is dedicated to preserving historical material relating to Hawai'i and the Pacific and publishing scholarly research on the history of Hawai'i and the Pacific. The Society
maintains a research library, publishes *The Hawaiian Journal of History* and limited-edition books, and holds regular lecture meetings.
The Society is a not-for-profit membership organization funded by
dues, contributions, book sales, an endowment, and grants for special
projects.

Membership in the Society is open to both individuals and institutions and includes *The Hawaiian Journal of History, Na Mea Kahiko*
newsletter, membership meetings, and discounts on publications.

_____

NAME AS YOU WANT IT TO APPEAR ON MEMBERSHIP LIST

_____

MAILING ADDRESS

_____

CITY   STATE   ZIP

ANNUAL MEMBERSHIPS

LIFE MEMBERS

☐ Founder $10,000
☐ Patron $5,000
☐ Benefactor $2,500
☐ Partner $1,000

HERITAGE CLUB

☐ Friend* $500
☐ Associate* $250
☐ Sponsor $100+
☐ Corporate $250+

☐ Contributing $50
☐ Regular (individuals) $40
☐ Senior citizen (65+) $30
☐ Student (full-time) $20
☐ Educational institution $40

Memberships at the $50 level and above are available for couples.
*Consecutive annual donations in these categories are credited toward a Life
Membership

ENCLOSED _____   DATE _____

Hawaiian Historical Society
560 Kawaiaha'o Street
Honolulu, Hawai'i 96813
Telephone (808) 537-6271
Web site: http://www.hawaiianhistory.org